Hotel House keeping Necessary Features

Hotel Housekeeping Necessary Features

K.S.Gusain

CYBER TECH PUBLICATIONS
4264/3, Ansari Road, Daryaganj New Delhi - 110002
Phone : 011-43559448, Fax : 011-23280028
Email : cybertechpublications@gmail.com

Hotel Housekeeping Necessary Features

CYBER TECH PUBLICATIONS
4264/3, Ansari Road, Daryaganj
New Delhi - 110002 (India)
Phone : 011-23244078, 011-43559448,
Fax : 011-23280028
E-mail : cybertechpublications@gmail.com
Website : www.cybertechpublications.com

First Published : 2008

ISBN 978-81-7884-367-4

Price, 1200.00

Printed at :

New Green Print Solutions, New Delhi 110078

Preface

Nutrition is the science of the exchange of matter and energy between the organism and its environment. Nutrition considers the nutritional need, which provides the basis for the exchange, the conditions determined by the need, and the feeding process through which the exchange occurs. Its perspective is not confi ned to the biology of the human organism, but includes the cultural characteristics of the group, because individuals are usually immersed in the cultural framework of a given group. All of these fi elds are in fact compatible, because they basically focus on the same issue: the exchange of matter and energy between the human organism and its environment. This exchange is dictated by the need to feed oneself (i.e. the nutritional need), a vital biological need, and is satisfi ed by the feeding process, that is the process by which man tries to meet his nutritional needs. Need is a phenomenon that arises from biological determinism.

It concerns the organism and the physiology of its exchanges. The process, on the other hand, involves a sequence of activities deployed by the human being to satisfy a need. This sequence begins with the securing of food early in the process, and ends with the excretion of material and energy waste. The effi ciency of the process is shown by the nutritional and health status of the individual. The exchange of matter and energy between the human organism and its environment (as discussed above) originally results from biological determinism; however, the process leading to the exchange is not only determined on a biological level by the organism, but also on a cultural level by the group in which the organism lives. It must thus satisfy a number of necessary and suffi cient conditions in order for the organism and the group to survive in their relationship to the natural environment.

The method used in nutrition consists in taking a multidisciplinary approach which allows the exchange to be understood as a whole: the phenomena dictating the exchange, the completion of the exchange, and the performance of the exchange. The scope of investigation covers human behaviour, both biological and social, from the search for nutrients that constitute feeding, to their digestion, absorption and utilization, in addition to the excretion of their by-products and what amounts to inevitable losses. The observation of the completion of the exchange within its environment should therefore facilitate the prediction of the survival probability of the organism and the group it belongs to.

Nutrition arises from the desire to understand – and, if possible, resolve – the problems that may appear at the different stages of the exchange. Nutrition thus intends to identify threats to health in its broadest sense, and to offer relevant interventions accordingly. This approach rests on a moral value: it is universally recognized that poverty is accidental, that the malnutrition that can result from it causes suffering, and that it is necessary to protect and care for its victims.

—*Author*

CONTENTS

1
Nutrition

INTRODUCTION

Nutrition is frequently ill-defined, probably because it is a developing contemporary fi eld in search of its own identity (Rivers, 1979; Waterlow, 1981; Pacey & Payne, 1985).

Modern nutrition has evolved from very different approaches.

- Man recognized early that growth and development are the main characteristics of childhood, and that these processes depend directly on feeding. Thus, nutrition has always been closely associated with paediatrics. As of 1550 B.C., Egyptian medical treatises recommended feeding practices for the young child in particular.
- Plato's *The Republic* (4th Century B.C.) states that a society grows around its food production and consumption. This statement is relayed by Malinowski in his functional approach to anthropology that links biology to culture (Malinowski, 1968).
- Driven by a scientifi c curiosity to clarify and understand, and so to fi nd the underlying laws that govern phenomena, Lavoisier (1743–1794) demonstrated that breathing is no less than an organic combustion made possible by the inspiration of oxygen and involving hydrogen and carbon. He opened the way for biological chemistry and the study of metabolism and digestion.
- Military organization, the industrial revolution and its management, the emergence of the welfare State, as well as the crises of recent decades and the importance of excess

pathologies, have given rise to thoughts on minimum requirements in nutritional elements. This notion is still highly controversial.

- The problem of feeding a rapidly growing world population has prompted interest in nutrition among development and agronomy specialists.

Today, nutrition remains dispersed among different fields related to specialized disciplines, and these may seem difficult to reconcile.

- Socio-economics, whose fundamental importance is increasingly recognized. Sen, among others, has contributed decisively to the understanding of the famine process, as being essentially economic and social (Sen, 1981).
- The field of excess, imbalance and deficiency pathology, studied by many in a bid to confront the gigantic public health problems resulting from nutritional deficiency, overeating and imbalance disorders.
- Ecology, because human food production methods are devastating. This is particularly true of developed countries, owing to the use of fossil energy, the exhaustion of soils and pollution, caused by the accumulation of both inputs and agricultural by-products. But ecological concerns are just as strong in developing countries, because of the frequently desperate over-exploitation of natural resources.
- Agronomy: this area is recovering with difficulty from the massive controversy caused by the agricultural development policy referred to as the "green revolution". Nonetheless, it is recognized as a key factor in approaching the increasingly grave food crises that threaten the planet.
- So-called emergency situations: this area has expanded the scope of malnutrition from dispensaries and hospitals by promoting it to the rank of epidemic. Concepts related to this area remain tentative. The most common approach is still too often restricted to assessing the nutritional status of children from a tedious epidemiological angle and through controversial techniques.

All of these fi elds are in fact compatible, because they basically focus on the same issue: the exchange of matter and energy between the human organism and its environment. This exchange is dictated by the need to feed oneself (i.e. the nutritional need), a vital biological need, and is satisfi ed by the feeding process, that is the process by which man tries to meet his nutritional needs. Need is a phenomenon that arises from biological determinism. It concerns the organism and the physiology of its exchanges. The process, on the other hand, involves a sequence of activities deployed by the human being to satisfy a need. This sequence begins with the securing of food early in the process, and ends with the excretion of material and energy waste. The effi ciency of the process is shown by the nutritional and health status of the individual. The exchange of matter and energy between the human organism and its environment (as discussed above) originally results from biological determinism; however, the process leading to the exchange is not only determined on a biological level by the organism, but also on a cultural level by the group in which the organism lives. It must thus satisfy a number of necessary and suffi cient conditions in order for the organism and the group to survive in their relationship to the natural environment.

Seen from this perspective, nutrition becomes the science whose objects of scrutiny, Rivers believes, range from the ribosome to harvesting machines (Rivers, 1979), and whose responsibility according to Waterlow is to combine and join biological and social sciences, and to reduce their fragmentation (Waterlow, 1981).

This is the very broad angle from which this Manual discusses human nutrition, considered as a science in itself. Its identifi cation is as follows.

DEFINITION OF NUTRITION

The subject

Nutrition is the science of the exchange of matter and energy between the organism and its environment.

The object

Nutrition considers the nutritional need, which provides the basis for the exchange, the conditions determined by the need, and the feeding process through which the exchange occurs. Its perspective is not confi ned to the biology of the human organism, but includes the cultural characteristics of the group, because individuals are usually immersed in the cultural framework of a given group.

The method

The method used in nutrition consists in taking a multidisciplinary approach which allows the exchange to be understood as a whole: the phenomena dictating the exchange, the completion of the exchange, and the performance of the exchange.

The scope of investigation

The scope of investigation covers human behaviour, both biological and social, from the search for nutrients that constitute feeding, to their digestion, absorption and utilization, in addition to the excretion of their by-products and what amounts to inevitable losses.

The prediction capacity

The observation of the completion of the exchange within its environment should therefore facilitate the prediction of the survival probability of the organism and the group it belongs to.

Ethics

Nutrition arises from the desire to understand – and, if possible, resolve – the problems that may appear at the different stages of the exchange. Nutrition thus intends to identify threats to health in its broadest sense, and to offer relevant interventions accordingly. This approach rests on a moral value: it is universally recognized that poverty is accidental, that the malnutrition that can result from it causes suffering, and that it is necessary to protect and care for its victims.

2

Introduction to the Nutritional Need

INTRODUCTION

Feeding is a need shared by all living beings. The nature of this need is the same for all, and obeys the same mechanisms. Moreover, life has developed in such a way that nutritional interdependencies appear between and within the three kingdoms (vegetable, bacterial and animal). To understand the position of man in the living world according to his nutritional need, and before specifi cally considering human nutrition, that which is common to the entire biosphere must be considered.

THE ORIGIN OF NUTRITIONAL NEEDS

Interactions of the Origins

The nutritional need originates in the chemical reactions that obey the principles of thermodynamics, and arose during the billion years following the formation of the earth. The different energy sources that existed at the time enabled chemical compounds such as water and water vapour (H_2O), methane (CH_4) and ammonia (NH_3) to interact and combine, thus generating the basic components of living matter. Laboratory simulations of the chemical and energy conditions assumed to have prevailed at the beginning of the earth have permitted the recreation of practically all these basic components from these three simple gases. The interaction then continued through the condensation of the basic components in long chains that generated the molecules (polymers) typical of the living world, and later the assembly of polymers in organelles – these in turn formed living cells. It took a billion years for the fi rst single-celled forms of life (or unicellulars) that compose the bacterial kingdom to come into being. It took a further three billion years for unicellulars to develop, and later assemble in, multi-cellular organisms, with the differentiation of organs, and so give rise to the vegetable and animal kingdoms. Finally, the three kingdoms continued to develop during the next 800 million years or so, by fashioning the earth and its atmosphere to bring them approximately to their contemporary form. *Homo sapiens* (or, rather, *Homo economicus,* an expression that better refl ects his exploitation of the environment) appeared only one hundred thousand years ago.

During this evolution, the principles of thermodynamics remained a denominator common to the original energy reactions and the nutritional need.

The universal principles that govern the exchanges of energy.

Thermodynamic Determinism

The evolution from the original simple gases to superior animals occurred in successive stages of association between compatible elements. Each level of association brought a new structure, but also new forms of organization, because interaction takes different forms that are specifi c to each level: atoms do not interact like particles do, nor molecules like atoms, nor polymers like basic molecules, any more than societies interact like their components do. However, the same forces always govern these different forms of interaction that occur when the conditions for exchange of energy are met. In other words, where a receptor can capture a source of energy in compliance with the principle of stability, the result is an energy fl ow. Conditions of interaction obey the principle referred to as thermodynamic determinism that governs everything that can be observed in the universe.

Thermodynamic determinism represents what is common to the original energy interactions and the nutritional need that is under scrutiny here. This nutritional need appeared at the same time as the living cell, the fi rst form of terrestrial life.

The Appearance of the Living Cell

One crucial stage of association was the combination of

constitutive elements to form a structure which became a specifi c entity: the living cell. Indeed, the living cell incorporates and specifi cally organizes energy interactions complying with thermodynamic determinism within a material structure limited by a semi-permeable membrane.

This entails several consequences, three of which are of particular interest here.

1. Thermodynamic reactions imply the presence of both a source and a receptor of energy. An organism is alive only through the thermodynamic reactions that characterize its existence; it must therefore have access to a source that can satisfy the need for energy of its material receptors. This source is initially internal, but runs out because the structure of the organism is fi nite in space. Therefore, the source must imperatively be renewed – and permanently so to avoid death – from the environment.
2. Between the original simple entities whose energy exchanges were chaotic, and animals whose energy exchanges occur within the organism, the energy fl ow was captured in increasingly complex material structures. The latter must reproduce and ensure their continued existence from materials found in the environment.
3. As complex structures developed and living matter diversifi ed into different organisms and evolved towards superior animals, they lost their capacity to create everything from simple entities (a capacity the fi rst cells had, and some unicellulars still have). Some species thus developed a dependency towards the living beings that retained that capacity, of which they must henceforth absorb all or part to extract the nutrients that they cannot create themselves.

This provides the three components of the nutritional need.

1. The renewal of the source of energy that governs reactions.
2. The provision of this source of energy with material support, and an envelope to manage its dissipation.
3. The obtaining of all or part of these material elements from other living species, if the capacity to create them is inadequate or lost.

The vital dependency towards these three components is the essence of the nutritional need. The nutritional need is one of the consequences of the appearance of the cell and the living organism, and it must be viewed in its conceptual framework.

THE PHENOMENON OF ORGANIZED ASSOCIATION

The nutritional need is the effective and direct consequence of the confi nement of molecular interactions to a specifi c spatial structure - that is, the cell or living organism. More generally, from a conceptual perspective, it results from the phenomenon of organized association.

Its principles are as follows.

1. The association occurs within a defi ned structure in which the elements of the association perform activities.
2. This structure makes sense only because activities are organized within it; for this, they must meet four conditions:
   - anchorage on a material support that provides them with a hold; q compliance with a norm;
   - subjection to a system of control that ensures the maintenance of, and respect for, the norm; q ability to be replicated, through the transmission to successors of the elements of the group of everything required to perform the activities according to the norms specifi c to the organization. These four conditions represent the basis of organized behaviour.
3. Organized association and behaviour imply specifi c demands that arise from the four conditions discussed above. These demands are as follows: q provision of the material support required to implement the activitie'] provision of a norm; q provision of a control system, q capability to replicate the association.
4. Organized association thus entails obligations that manifest themselves on two separate levels: q on the algorithmic level of any organized behaviour, activities must meet the four conditions stated under point 2 above, which constitute the determinism of the activities; q on the level specifi c to the association under consideration, the demands stated

under point 3 above must be satisfi ed – these demands defi ne its needs, which in turn represent the determinism of the association.

5. The conditions of organized behaviour, together with the needs that result from it, constitute the determinism imposed upon any organized group when it implements its activities. It is also worth noting that the determinism specifi c to the association includes the needs of the elements that compose it, and each new level of needs is related to the previous level. Generally, the global determinism (i.e. algorithmic and specifi c) of an association is defi ned according to the level of organization under consideration: thermodynamic in the case of particles, atoms or molecules, biological in the case of living organisms, cultural in the case of humans in a group. The effect of the biological and cultural determinisms on the completion of the feeding process that addresses the nutritional need is discussed in Chapter VI.

The nutritional need is a direct result of determinism insofar as the cell or living organism constitutes organized associations.

Indeed, if the living organism is an entity whose behaviour is organized, then it follows that the activities that occur within it rest on a specifi c basis, that they obey the laws of thermodynamics, and that they are subjected to the balance between substrate and product or by a neuro-endocrine system. It also follows that the organism produces replacements for its elements by using a genetic code that permits the duplication of all the elements in such a way as to function like their predecessors. For the living organism, the same demands exist, related to the following:

- the material support of the structure – the three components of nutritional need;
- the application of the norm – the laws of metabolism;
- the control of the application – among others, the necessary neuro-endocrine system among animals;
- the specifi c replication of the constituents – the genetic code, present in any living cell.

The fi nal behaviour (i.e. thermodynamic interactions and compliance with the conditions for existence) will result from the biological determinism of the organism under consideration.

To sum up, the assembly of simple elements into more complex structures that generate living things provides the transition between thermodynamic and biological determinisms. Biological determinism is characterized by the appearance of needs, among which the nutritional need according to its three components is discussed below.

THE COMPONENTS OF NUTRITIONAL NEED

Dependency on Energy

The fi rst level of nutritional dependency concerns the provision of energy, because life developed from the interaction of energies available at the beginning of earth. Without entering into excessive detail in the fi elds of physics and biology, it is important to improve understanding of the energy conversions of living things by recalling some basic principles.

General principles relating to energy

1. Matter and energy make up the universe, and they are inter-related.
2. Energy can take many forms: mechanical, electrical, thermal, and radiant (such as solar energy radiated to the earth). Energy can be converted from one form to the next while conserving the total amount of energy involved, as expressed by the fi rst principle of thermodynamics: the total energy of the universe remains constant.
3. Conversion from one form of energy into another always results in an increase of thermal energy through friction. Thermal energy is thus the ultimate or degraded form (for our purposes) of energy. For example, an engine powered electrically to perform mechanical work necessarily overheats; its energy input cannot be entirely converted into kinetic energy, as part of it is lost in thermal form. Likewise, chemical energy used in muscular contraction converts not only into mechanical energy, but also into thermal energy. This is why physical exercise heats the

organism, and shivering (i.e. rapid muscle contractions) is a mechanism that tends to maintain body temperature in a cold environment. Therefore, if conversion into thermal energy is excluded, energy conversions result in a less than 100% yield, as expressed by the second principle of thermodynamics:

universal entropy increases.

Einstein's $E = mc^2$.

Entropy is the ultimate, degraded and – for our purposes – unusable form of energy. Entropy is also said to represent the degree of universal disorder or chaos. Chaos or disorder is understood here as meaning energy dissipated at random. Indeed, thermal energy dissipates spontaneously in a chaotic manner. For example, a hot body spontaneously transfers its heat to its cooler environment until thermal balance is achieved, thus defi ning the principle of stability. On the other hand, a body will never become cooler than its environment. To achieve the latter, as in the case of a refrigerator, it is necessary to provide an input of energy superior to that algebraically required to attain a given difference in temperature, because part of the energy used to cool the refrigerator is inevitably lost in the form of thermal energy. The example of the hot body spontaneously conveying its heat to its cooler environment shows that, in the universe, energy fl ows in a specifi c direction.

4. Energy conversion from one form into another requires a material support.
5. Energy events (such as chemical reactions, mechanical work, and exchanges of heat) fall into two categories: q those that require the input of energy, as is the case for the refrigerator or the formation of glucose and oxygen gas, from carbonic acid gas and water; q those that occur spontaneously in compliance with the law of entropy, such as the transfer of heat from a hot body to its cooler environment, or the reaction between hydrogen gas and oxygen gas that produces water with the release of heat; for a spontaneous reaction to occur between two bodies, the energy content of one of the bodies must be higher than the other's, and both must interact to permit the transfer

of energy from the body with the higher content to that with the lower, until energy balance is achieved.

6. Energy is a measurable entity. Scientists have given it different units depending on its type (e.g. electrical, mechanical, radiant or thermal), and each unit follows its own logic. For example, in chemistry and biochemistry (where the exchange of heat of reactions is the main parameter), the unit in use is the calorie (cal): one calorie is the amount of heat necessary to increase the temperature of 1 g of water from 14.5°C to 15.5°C at a pressure of one standard atmosphere. This amount is small in comparison to reaction heats expressed in standard conditions; generally, therefore, the kilocalorie (kcal) is preferred, as it amounts to 1,000 calories. In mechanics, the energy unit is the joule (J), being the amount of energy required to move a mass of 1 kg over a distance of 1 m in the sense of the force applied, with an acceleration of 1 m per second per second.

The transformation of energy preserves the total amount of energy, and conversion factors therefore exist between the different units of energy measure. For simplicity's sake, one single unit - the joule - was agreed upon to express all forms of energy. Unfortunately, this unit no longer translates into something tangible, other than for the form of energy it initially applied to. The conversion factor between joules and calories is as follows:

1 calorie (cal) = 4.18 joules (J) or 1 J = 0.239 cal

as a result:

1 kilocalorie (kcal) = 4.18 kilojoules (kJ)

The advantage of using different units to express different forms of energy is clarity: what the unit refers to is known. Standardization is therefore not always an asset. This Manual uses both units, kcal and kJ, the former taking precedence, the latter indicated between brackets.

Energy and life

Beyond philosophical debates on the topic, it is now scientifi cally established that the laws of physics govern the entire universe, including biological mechanisms. Life in all its forms complies with the two types of reaction described above: its environment provides it with the energy to create highly reactive chemical bodies, the main being adenosine triphosphate (ATP);

- ATP can then enter into spontaneous reaction with its chemical environment, enabling the tasks required for life to develop and preserve its characteristics, thanks to the information contained in the genetic code.

During this process, life uses two main forms of energy: radiant and chemical. It performs three different types of work: chemical, mechanical and osmotic. In its simplest expression, Life thus depends on the conversion of forms of energy into others, of energy providing work, and of energy derived from work. As indicated above (Section 2.1.1, point 3), the yield of these operations is less than 100% in practice because, as is the case for all phenomena occurring in the universe, their friction increases the thermal energy (heat) of the system in which they occur. This heat represents a loss for any transformation whose purpose is not to generate heat. As a result, the energy transformations on which life depends occur in a single sense. They are irreversible unless they receive an energy input that compensates their losses. This implies that energy does not complete a cycle in the biosphere, but passes through it like a fl ux, not only owing to the permanent need to compensate for losses, but more importantly because after its passage through the organism in one way or another, energy is dissipated in a biologically unusable form. In the biosphere, it converts from radiation (usable energy) to heat (energy that is unusable directly and therefore amounts to an increase of entropy). This means that living organisms, that are no more than energy transformers, must continually draw from their environment the form of energy that they dissipate in work and heat. This is the essence of the nutritional need for energy.

The energy fl ux in the biosphere

It is important to examine the fl ow of energy in the biosphere more closely to gain a comprehensive understanding of the nutritional need. The notion of energy fl ux implies a beginning (i.e. an initial state) one or several intermediate stages, and an ending (fi nal state). The primary source of energy is solar radiation, and it undergoes two intermediate stages in the biosphere:

- in the fi rst stage, the radiant energy is converted into chemical energy by means of an energy-bearing molecule;
- in the second stage, the chemical energy of the bearer molecule enables reactions that perform biological work (and also generate heat).

Heat is the fi nal form of energy as it leaves the biosphere.

Only organisms that are capable of photosynthesis can carry out the fi rst stage. The obvious example that springs to mind is green plants that do so by means of their characteristic pigment, chlorophyll. However, phytoplankton in the oceans accounts for more than half of the earth's entire photosynthesis. Photosynthesis transfers radiant energy to adenosine as follows:

water (H_2O) + $NADP^+$ [4] + inorganic phosphate (Pi) + adenosine diphosphate (ADP) + energy 1 triphosphate adenosine (ATP) + oxygen (O_2) + NADPH + H^+

To simplify, this Manual will only refer to ATP.

NADP is a hydrogen exchanging molecule, just like ATP is an energy exchanging molecule.

The chemical energy carried by ATP then enables the second stage, for example glucose synthesis: carbonic acid gas (CO_2) + NADPH + H^+ + ATP 1 glucose + $NADP^+$ + ADP + Pi

This second reaction enables the production of a reduced compound (rich in available chemical energy),[5] thanks to the chemical energy of the ATP acting on oxidized molecules (i.e. poor in available chemical energy).

It is now possible to consider the entire equation for photosynthesis, as usually provided:

$6\ CO_2 + 6\ H_2O\ 1\ C_6H_{12}O_6$ (glucose) $+ 6\ O_2$

The glucose then provides the intermediary to produce the other organic compounds of plants (glucides, lipids and proteins) during reactions that also require energy provided by ATP. For proteins, nitrogenous molecules are also required, they are taken from the soil but come from the atmosphere through nitrogen fi xing bacteria.

The animal kingdom is not capable of photosynthesis. It nevertheless needs ATP to perform its biological work. Animals obtain it by consuming reduced organic compounds that all derive directly or indirectly from photosynthesis. These components are oxidized during fermentation and breathing, and the energy released by oxidation is retrieved in the form of ATP. For example, the complete oxidation of glucose will produce 38 ATP molecules.

Finally, the three kingdoms function in their environment by means of ATP that enables the completion of these biological reactions. The latter can be broken down into the three following main forms:

- chemical, essentially related to synthesis in producing the constituents of the organism itself;
- osmotic, related to the transfer and concentration of substances within the organism by means of osmosis;
- mechanical, in the form of traction forces relayed by contractile fi bres: the most spectacular example, but by far not the only one, is the muscular contraction of superior animals.

In short, two stages can be distinguished in the energy fl ux in the biosphere: the stage where radiant energy is converted into chemical energy in organic compounds, and the stage where the chemical energy contained in organic compounds is converted into work and heat. The ATP molecule plays a central role in this fl ux. Initially, it is regenerated during photosynthesis and provides the link between the two stages by controlling the formation of the precursors of all organic compounds used later in the biosphere. Then, regenerated by fermentation and breathing, it controls the reactions that perform biological work. ATP is thus not consumed but recycled, in a shuttle between the conversions for which it provides the intermediary. Biological work, together with the dissipation of heat that inevitably accompanies it, is the fi nal stage reached by the energy fl ux in the biological world. The different types of organism require more or less sustained biological work in order to survive in their medium; biological work therefore defi nes the rhythm of the adenosine cycle and, thus, the needs for energy input.

DEPENDENCY ON MATTER

The fl ow of energy through the living organism implies energy conversions, and these require a material intermediary. Furthermore, they must occur in the material structure of the organism.

The energy fl ow and the existence of the organism generate a twofold material requirement.

1. The requirement related to the energy fl ow implies adenosine recycling through the oxidation of a material intermediary, during fermentation and breathing;
2. The requirement related to the development and renewal of the material, architectural and functional structure that accommodates the energy fl ow. That is, the cell, organism, or multi-cellular living being.

It is useless here to dwell on the fi rst element: it is excessively variable according to species, and will be discussed specifi cally in relation to the human being in the following chapter. On the other hand, the second element (that deals with the material structure of living organisms) deserves specifi c attention because it is common to almost all organisms and explains their interdependency. The architectural and functional structure of living beings does not evolve from just any matter. Moreover, the universality of the energy mechanisms of the biosphere suggests that all living beings share identical material supports according to their specifi c role. Indeed, in spite of the great diversity of living species, a group of elements, essentially in molecular form, are common to the material composition of all organisms. The molecular logic of living organisms is extremely simple, and uses only very few different molecules to constitute a terrestrial biomass that is nevertheless of respectable dimensions. Despite this simplicity, the chemical characteristics of these molecules are such as to play very different roles and to combine in multiple ways. They are to be found in all living cells, and include: water, amino acids, purine and pyrimidine bases, sugars, lipids, vitamins and coenzymes, and some minerals.

Water (H_2O)

Water is the support and the liquid medium of life. It is also the most abundant component of any living organism, accounting for 70 to 90% of its mass. The molecule is highly reactive, and its ionization products (H_3O^+ and OH^-) largely determine the structural characteristics and biological properties of most cellular components. Water ionization promotes the exchange of protons (H^+), and its role is thus fundamental in the biological acid-base reactions. Owing to its polarization, the molecule is also an excellent solvent. Finally, water provides the oxygen generated during photosynthesis, and this oxygen is vital to all forms of life whose energy fl ow results from breathing.

Amino acids

There are 20 basic amino acids. All have an acid group (COOH) and a nitrogen atom (N) on the fi rst carbon atom (i.e. alpha carbon) in their carbon chain. The name "amino acids" thus comes from the combination of the acid group with "amine" (the name of the nitrogen group in the organic compounds). They differ in the rest of the chain (R).

The bases

The purine (2 molecules) and pyrimidine (3 molecules) bases are the fi ve basic components of nucleotides, of which there are eight. Four provide the infrastructure of desoxyribonucleic acid (DNA), which is the support of the genetic code. The other four provide the infrastructure for ribonucleic acid (RNA), which translates the genetic code into amino-acid sequences for protein synthesis. DNA and RNA are therefore nucleotide chains, just as proteins are chains of amino acids. Moreover, as amino acids do, these bases lead to the production of other biologically important molecules, such as some vitamins and the above-mentioned adenosine.

Glucides

Glucides, erroneously also referred to as carbohydrates because of their general formula $(CH_2O)_n$, practically all originate from glucose ($C_6H_{12}O_6$). Glucose is the main fuel of most organisms, and the infrastructure for starch and the cellulose of plants. Starch is the prime form of energy storage, whereas cellulose is the rigid external component of the cell wall, and is fi brous, ligneous tissue. Glucides are also associated with, or precursors of, very important molecules in terms of biology. The analogy with amino acids and nucleotides reappears here: simple construction units and multiple functions.

Lipids

Lipids are defi ned as molecules that are insoluble in water. There are several lipid groups, but all share the characteristic that a signifi cant part of the molecule is in reality a hydrocarbon. Lipids too perform various functions: they contribute to the structure of the cell membrane, they are elements of energy storage and transport, they provide a protective layer, and determine the identity and biological activity marker as hormones or vitamins.

Vitamins

Vitamins and coenzymes are small organic substances (carbon structures) that are indispensable to the functioning of living cells, owing to their vital contribution to many physiological processes, in particular enzyme catalysis, an indispensable process for practically all the chemical reactions of the cell.

Their importance has been recognized because many species cannot synthesize them all independently and must, therefore, obtain them from their environment. Vitamins and coenzymes are only necessary in very small quantities and only constitute a very limited part of cellular composition, unlike proteins, nucleic acids, carbohydrates and lipids that, apart from water, account for most of its mass.

Minerals

Minerals are likewise indispensable to the functioning of the organism, and their functions vary considerably depending on their specifi c chemical properties. As they cannot be created, they must be found either directly or indirectly in the mineral environment shaped by the nature of the soil and the effects of groundwater.

To exist, living beings must obtain all these molecules. This is the essence of material nutritional need. Apart from water and minerals, they all originate in simple precursors that are found in the soil, water and the atmosphere. However, many species have become partly or wholly incapable of such operations, and survive to the direct or indirect detriment of those that maintain this capability, by consuming all or part of organisms or their decomposition and excretion products. This constitutes the third level of nutritional dependency.

DEPENDENCY ON LIVING SPECIES

The third level of nutritional dependency developed in parallel with the evolution of species. Specialization, differentiation and adaptation to the environment entailed nutritional specifi cities that implied unilateral dependencies and, more importantly, symbiotic interdependencies with major consequences for the survival of the living world in general. The interdependency of species can take many different forms that fall into two main categories: dependency on a source of energy or fuel, and dependency on structural or functional matter.

Dependency on energy flow

The fi rst stage of energy fl ow in the biological world belongs to the realm of photosynthesis that uses solar radiation to create organic compounds, and the latter are the primary source of energy of organisms that are incapable of photosynthesis. The realm of photosynthesis is thus at the basis of all the energy used by the rest of the biosphere. In a way, there exists a form of "energy parasitism" in stages: the world of photosynthesis is a parasite (or predator) of sunlight, and the world of fermentation and breathing is a parasite of photosynthesis. This energy dependency can be illustrated by the chain linking carnivores to herbivores, herbivores to green plants, and green plants to sunlight. In this specifi c case, later links (carnivores) depend on earlier ones (ultimately, sunlight). Species are thus connected by the nature of their nutritional energy need in a sequence of levels or stages (referred to as trophic levels). Plants represent the fi rst trophic level, herbivores the second, and so on. Each level is a consumer of the previous, and a producer for the following level.

Dependency on matter

As discussed above, energy fl ows in an organism cause fl uxes of matter. The latter fl ows from one type of organism to another, not necessarily through trophic dependency (downstream-upstream), but according to a cyclical rhythm – in other words, an interdependency. In these cycles, organisms exchange the nutrients required for their survival. Without entering into detail as to the sometimes highly complex nutritional interdependencies that govern the biosphere, this discussion will focus on the three cycles involving practically the entire biosphere: carbon, oxygen and nitrogen. These three elements are found in the atmosphere in the form of simple gases; they can be dissolved in water or combined with solids. Their movement throughout the biosphere is thus not accidental. Furthermore, their physical and chemical features lead to the production of highly diverse molecules, on the one hand, and huge combinations of such molecules, on the other.

The carbon and oxygen cycle

Organisms capable of photosynthesis combine carbonic acid gas with water to generate organic compounds, giving off oxygen in the process. On the other hand, organisms that are incapable of photosynthesis consume organic compounds and oxygen, and give off carbonic acid gas and water in the process of breathing and fermentation. This introduces a carbon and oxygen cycle into the biosphere.

The nitrogen cycle

Nitrogen contributes to the formation of the genetic code, proteins, and other molecules essential to life. It accounts for 80% of the composition of the atmosphere, in the form of molecular nitrogen gas (N_2). In this form, it can only be absorbed by a few specifi c organisms, while others must obtain it in a combined form, such as ammonia, nitrites and nitrates, or from complex compounds such as amino acids or urea. Its cyclical exchanges are more complex than those of carbon and oxygen. The cycle of matter is just as important as the energy fl ow: both show the interdependency of living organisms on a planetary scale. All these elements and material compounds interact in many ways in exchanges between the different organisms; what is to be remembered here is the concept of their interdependency. Evolving together, all species are necessary to one another, and any imbalance, global or local, must be avoided. If one of the three kingdoms disappears, the other two cannot survive. Likewise, on less elementary dependency levels, if one species disappears, an entire biotope and an entire ecosystem can be changed or destroyed. This is the essence of interdependency.

Seen from this perspective, the object of nutrition is indeed the exchange of matter between a given organism and its environment, in addition to its related balance or imbalance. In this sense, nutrition is a branch of ecology, and the expression "feeding" (alimentation) covers more than the simple provision of food. This is particularly true of human nutrition whose process today implies massive disruptions to the environment, owing to the number of humans on the one hand, and the agricultural and industrial economy on the other.

In short, the nutritional need is based on four phenomena.

1. Molecules interact with and change one another, depending on their respective energy characteristics and the available energy sources.
2. These changes occur in a specifi c sense, dictated by the principles of thermodynamics; this implies matter and energy fl ows.
3. Living organisms provide an organized answer to the principles of thermodynamics – this answer includes the intermediary metabolism governing the interaction between matter and energy on the one hand, and the living cell, being the material structure accommodating the metabolism, on the other. This material structure (be it single-celled or multi-cellular) is an entity that is fi nite in space. A clear boundary exists between it and the external medium; in other words, it contains a fi nite amount of matter and energy that evolve from an initial to a fi nal stage in the course of transformations imposed by the principles of thermodynamics and controlled by metabolism. As a result, the organism must interact with its environment by obtaining matter and energy in it in the initial required state, according to the depletion rate of internal reserves due to metabolism.
4. The organism is a material structure based on specifi c elements found in its biological and mineral environment.

The need for a living organism to draw regularly on its environment – according to its precise characteristics – for matter and energy in a specifi c state, and the fact that its existence itself depends on this process is the essence of nutritional need. Obtaining matter and energy from the environment, transforming them and returning them in the form of waste therefore does represent an exchange between the organism and its environment. This is the very subject of nutrition.

3

The Nutritional Energy Need of Humans

INTRODUCTION

The human organism is an open biological system that interacts with its environment. The notion of system implies a group of interacting phenomena. Practically all components of the living organism are interdependent: a change in one will affect all others. The analysis of the nutritional need thus inevitably leads to a systemic approach because the use of energy governs all the activities of the organism, with respect both to its internal chemistry and to its behaviour toward the exterior. This use is extended to the search for energy itself. Fully comprehending the nutritional need, its overall manifestation and its far-reaching ramifi cations, is a challenge verging on philosophy; on the other hand, understanding human behaviour demands specifi c, pragmatic knowledge. Hence, phenomena and their inter-relations cannot be envisaged as an integrated whole, but rather factorially, that is, broken down into separate entities, even though such treatment produces fi xed images that are useful only for teaching purposes. The human nutrition need is discussed here according to the approach used in the previous chapter: need arises from a threefold dependency on energy, on matter, and on other species.

DEPENDENCY ON ENERGY

Like all living things, man needs energy to recycle ATP [1] in order to perform the biological work that is necessary for his survival. Two methods are used to assess energy needs as follows:

- the balance method, i.e. the observation of what an individual must eat to maintain a constant weight;

- the factorial method, i.e. the assessment of energy use specifi c to the organism's energy phenomena (that is, according to each use factor): the corresponding overall requirement can be deduced from the sum of energy uses considered individually.

The balance method does not clarify the manner in which energy is used, nor does it explain the amount required for different activities, or what is required at rest. The factorial method on the other hand analyses energy use factors separately, and may therefore be preferable in some circumstances. Factors of use are classifi ed as follows:

- basal use;
- the thermal effect of food consumption, or specifi c dynamic action;
- use associated with muscular effort;
- use associated with the generation of heat (thermo-genesis);
- use associated with growth, recovery and production.

The fi rst four factors are assessed by measuring overall energy use, observed per unit of time, in the relevant experimental conditions. Specifi c cost can then be derived, and is generally expressed as a multiple of the basal metabolism. Growth, recovery and production can be appraised through a combination of the balance and factorial methods, or by calculating the energy content of synthesized tissue, subject to a synthesis yield factor to deduce the synthesis cost.

The energy need and its different factors are expressed in energy units, that is, kcal (kJ).

FACTORIAL ANALYSIS OF THE ENERGY NEED

Basal energy expenditure

Warm-blooded animals (i.e. mammals and birds) in particular tend to maintain a constant temperature; the idling (i.e. the minimum functioning) rate of their biological machine is therefore rather stable. It is referred to as basal metabolic rate or, more simply, basal metabolism. The basal metabolism thus implies a consumption of energy, to be likened to the fuel consumption of a stationary car whose engine is idling. The basal metabolism represents the energy and chemical transformations required for the survival of the organism in a state of rest and thermal comfort. It includes the following:

- osmotic work to maintain chemical gradients and the electro-chemical work of the nervous system;
- mechanical work performed in rest conditions by the heart, the lungs, the digestive tube, and muscular tension;
- chemical work performed by the liver and the kidneys, and for the permanent breakdown and synthesis of the cell and tissue compounds.

The standard average basal metabolism of adult mammals and birds measured over 24 hours and expressed in kcal amounts to: seventy times their body weight elevated to the power of three-quarters

or

daily basal metabolism (kcal) = 70 × body weight$^{3/4}$ (kg)

Weight to the power of three-quarters is also expressed as weight to the power 0.75 (i.e. weight$^{0.75}$).

This general rule expresses the direct proportional relation between the energy fl ow in the organism of warm-blooded animal and their mass. Mass is understood here as active – in other words excluding the obese with a signifi cant inert adipose mass. Indeed, the basal metabolism relates to the active cells in the organism that produce work (lean mass), and not adipocytes, that are energy storage cells (fatty tissue), and whose energy use is negligible. The fi ve most active organs in the organism (i.e. the brain, the liver, the kidneys, the heart and striated muscle) account for more than 90% of the basal energy expenditure.

Human basal metabolism is measured in the following standard conventional conditions: the subject is at rest, in a reclining position, awake, emotionally calm, has not ingested food for the previous twelve to fourteen hours, and is lightly clad in an ambient temperature of 18 to 20°C. This provides a convenient measure of the inevitable energy use of the organism. However, the basal metabolism measured conventionally is not in fact the minimum metabolism. It would be better described as standard metabolism, because the individual real basal metabolism depends signifi cantly on climate, eating habits, vital physical activity, the intake of stimulants (such as tobacco or coffee), and the cultural and emotional level of the social group under consideration.

Within the species in general, basal metabolism depends mainly on the mass of the organism, but also on age and sex.

Age

The basal metabolism per kilogram of body weight increases during the fi rst year, then slowly decreases until sexual maturity. The fast basal metabolism of the young child is partly explained by its faster cell renewal rate. Among adults, it remains constant until approximately 40 to 50 years, then slowly diminishes; among the elderly (over 60 years), it is 15 to 20% lower by unit of body weight than among young adults.

Sex

Per unit of body weight, the adult male basal metabolism is 15 to 20% higher than the female rate. This is partly due to the fact that the proportion of fatty tissue is greater in women than in men. In fact, the more individuals are included, the more relevant the standard measure of the basal metabolism; it is then a statistical measure to extrapolate (with a 10% uncertainty margin) the basal metabclism of the average individual, representative of his age group and sex. Basal metabolism has been measured quantitatively on numerous occasions.

For example, the metabolism of a 28-year-old woman weighing 55 kg is calculated as follows:

basal metabolism = (14.7 X 55) + 496 = 1,304.5 kcal

or basal metabolism = (0.0615 X 55) + 2.08 = 5.4625 MJ

In contrast, the metabolism of a 3-year-old girl weighing 14 kg is 814 kcal (3.4 MJ). From this viewpoint, one can say that the girl's basal metabolism is 60% of the woman's - but this says little about their respective energy needs. The comparison is more relevant if the energy use is expressed in kcal (kJ) per kg of body mass, that is, 58.1 kcal (243 kJ)/kg for the little girl, and 23.7 kcal (99 kJ)/kg for the woman. This shows that the latter's needs are only 40% of the little girl's.

Energy use due to food consumption

The consumption of food involves the use of energy related both to the functioning of the digestive system, and to the nature of the foods and their storage. The increase of the energy use related to the nature of the food is also referred to as "specifi c dynamic action" (SDA). Statistically, the SDA is 30% for proteins, 6% for glucides, and 4% for lipids. In other words, the consumption of proteins providing 100 kcal, for example, increases the metabolic rate by 30 kcal. However, the nature of SDA remains unclear, and signifi cant variations persist depending on intake and nutritional status. As a general indication, the act of eating increases basal energy use by 20 to 30% (Trémolière, 1977).

Energy use due to muscular work

Mechanical muscular work, also called physical activity, can account for much of an individual's daily energy use. The use related to physical activity depends on the type of effort, but also on the manner in which it is made (movement effi ciency, emotional tension), the food intake and adaptation to the environment (e.g. ambient oxygen pressure, that diminishes with increasing altitude). Therefore, major variations exist between individuals and societies, and so a statistical approach is necessary to assess muscular energy use. Furthermore, measurement methods do not distinguish between the specifi c components of energy use during work, but focus instead on the fi nal overall total. Principally for these reasons, the assessment of muscular use involves the drafting of statistical tables refl ecting the cost of specifi c activities (expressed as multiples of the standard basal metabolism), based upon the overall energy use registered during effort. These tables show that activities involving the greatest energy use amount to approximately eight times the basal metabolism.

Energy expenditure due to thermo-genesis

The heat produced through entropic loss in the course of biological work is not directly usable from a physiological perspective. It nevertheless plays a vital role among mammals and birds because their biological system must maintain a temperature of 35 to 42°C to operate normally. Temperature maintenance requires a very reliable supply of energy – this is indeed a dependency, but allows the organism to adapt to extreme climatic conditions. On earth, some mammals and birds survive in temperatures ranging from -50 to +50°C. To survive in these conditions, they have physiological heating and cooling mechanisms, and protective insulation methods such as are provided by fur and feathers, subcutaneous fat and the use of shelter.

Man attempts to maintain his temperature around 37°C. He can fi nd himself in colder or warmer environments, just like any mammal or bird and, as discussed above, will transfer his heat spontaneously to his colder environment. Moreover, the organism can "overheat" during effort or owing to infection, thus requiring cooling. The exchange of heat occurs through the skin, by radiation (infrared radiation), conduction (transmission through contact), convection (exchange related to the movement of air) and vaporization (water evaporation through perspiration). A thermo-neutral zone exists between excessive heat and excessive cold where the entropic losses of the basal metabolism suffi ce to maintain body temperature, and where perspiration is thus unnecessary.

When the organism overheats or exists in a warmer environment, its cooling does not imply energy costs, but losses in water and mineral salts. On the other hand, the cooling of the organism in a colder environment requires a thermo-genetic energy use to maintain body temperature. Thermo-genesis, implemented by muscular exercise, shivering or the consumption of brown adipose tissue (BAT), begins when the environment reaches a "lower critical temperature". This threshold varies signifi cantly according to the availability of protection against the cold (clothing and shelter) and food. For a healthy, naked adult man with an empty stomach, the lower critical temperature is approximately 28°C. Following a rich meal, it falls to 22°C and, with light clothing, will further fall to 18°C. The body surface of newborn babies is proportionately much greater than that of adults. Therefore, they lose heat faster, and their lower critical temperature is 33°C. Very young children are also less mobile than adults, and cannot shiver before 18 to 24 months; cold thus represents a great danger for them.

From a quantitative perspective, the energy cost of thermo-genesis can be enormous, up to three or four times the basal metabolism. For example, a lightly-clad, immobile man weighing 65 kg in a 15°C environment free of draughts must spend approximately 750 kcal (3,135 kJ) per day to maintain his temperature – this amounts to a 45% increase of his basal metabolism (Rivers, 1988). The cost of thermo-genesis increases exponentially when ambient temperature drops linearly. Moreover, the cost is proportional to conduction: for instance sleeping on the bare ground or in contact with water (e.g. wet clothing, shipwreck). Generally speaking, Rivers considers that, between 28 and 20°C, the basal metabolism increases by 30 kcal (125 kJ) per day, for each ambient temperature drop of 1°C below the lower critical temperature. Between 20 and 13°C, this increase multiplies by three to fi ve per 1°C drop in ambient temperature (Rivers, 1988).

When the organism cannot warm itself, its cooling causes hypothermia that is generally deadly when body temperature falls below 25°C – this is equivalent to a one-hour immersion in icy water. This provides an idea of how fast a malnourished, poorly clad individual exposed to the elements becomes chilled, a common scenario in disasters. In famines, where malnutrition becomes general and extreme, mortality peaks among the homeless at night and in rainy weather. It is impossible to anticipate thermo-genetic energy demand, simply because man dresses, fi nds shelter and eats according to his environment when he can do so. Nevertheless, cold causes signifi cant energy loss from common climatic conditions, even in the tropics; people lacking food and shelter are particularly vulnerable to this.

Energy need due to synthesis

Biological synthesis is a permanent phenomenon, mainly related to the renewal of cell and tissue components (i.e. maintenance synthesis). From this angle, its energy cost is taken into consideration in the basal use. But the synthesis of new tissue related to individual growth, pregnancy, breastfeeding and the recovery of lost tissue must also be considered.

Growth

Growth is the development of living beings to reach their adult physical stature. The assessment of the energy need specifi c to growth poses three main problems:

- measurement,
- distinction between the energy expenditure for normal functioning and the energy used for the accumulation of tissue,
- composition of the average deposited tissue – which varies according to age and sex.

In fact, the attempt to calibrate growth accurately encounters the validity limitations of the factorial approach to needs, which becomes overly simplistic. The two reference values generally used are discussed here; they correspond to the average statistical values of existing data, and apply mainly to young children. Waterlow uses 4 kcal (17 kJ) as a reasonable estimate of the overall cost required for the elaboration of 1 g of balanced tissue (Waterlow, 1992). An FAO/WHO/UNU team of experts quotes 5 kcal/g (21 kJ/g) as a widely accepted energy cost for growth (WHO, 1985). The difference is not important: on the one hand, the two values are quite close (being statistical averages whose standard deviation is greater than 1), on the other, following the fi rst months of life during which growth is relatively fast and can account for 15 to 20% of the overall energy requirements, human growth is slow and only costs approximately 5% of energy needs on average.

Pregnancy

Pregnancy includes the growth of the foetus and the placenta, as well as the growth and change of maternal tissues, which obviously requires energy. Normal pregnancy is generally accepted to involve a weight gain of the order of 10 ± 2 kg, and an approximately 20% increase in the basal metabolism during the last quarter (Trémolière, 1977). Classic estimations set the overall cost of pregnancy at 80,000 kcal (335,000 kJ), of which 36,000 kcal (151,000 kJ) represent the deposit of approximately 4 kg of fat. It could follow that a pregnant woman must increase her daily food intake by 300 kcal (1,250 kJ); these fi gures however warrant caution. A study conducted in fi ve countries shows that reality could be quite different: the average increase of the energy supply is less than 100 kcal (420 kJ) per day among well-fed Europeans. Data indicates a lower cost than classical estimates among women in three differently developed countries (Durnin, 1987). The difference between new and former estimates does not appear to result from a reduction of physical exercise during pregnancy. The study group led by Durnin found that caution is necessary when discussing the energy cost of pregnancy, and showed the vastness of areas requiring further research. Major differences are probable owing to the multiplicity of factors involved. As a result, it is most likely impossible to defi ne an overall cost from which to issue universal intake recommendations for all women.

Breastfeeding

The production of maternal milk varies considerably from one woman to another; commonly quoted values range from 750 to 850 ml/day. The energy value of maternal milk varies signifi cantly according to the origin of the women under consideration; it also varies according to the duration of breastfeeding (Waterlow, 1992). Food composition tables provide values ranging from 67 kcal (280 kJ) to 75 kcal (313 kJ) per 100 ml. The cost of synthesis is calculated based on an 80% minimum synthesis effi ciency factor (WHO, 1985). For example, if a woman produces 800 ml of milk per day, the milk's energy value will represent at least 80% of the cost of synthesis, i.e. between 536 kcal (2,240 kJ) and 600 kcal (2,508 kJ); the maximum synthesis cost will be between 670 kcal (2,800 kJ) and 750 kcal (3,135 kJ). Beyond calculated assessment, it is common knowledge that the production of maternal milk will cost at least the energy value contained in the milk itself. This value is high, and breastfeeding thus amounts to considerably more energy stress for the mother than her pregnancy; it is equivalent to approximately half her basal metabolism prior to pregnancy.

Recovery

Recovery follows the loss by an individual of part of his body mass owing to illness, accident, or a food supply that is insuffi cient to maintain normal body weight. "Nutritional recovery" and "catch-up growth" are common terms for the recovery process that follows malnutrition. The cost of catch-up growth varies according to the composition of the synthesized tissue and the yield of the synthesis. Tissue composition varies greatly, the yield of protein synthesis is unclear, and rapid weight gain increases specifi c dynamic action (Waterlow, 1992). However, research (WHO, 1985; Ashworth and Millward, 1986) suggests that, on average, the energy cost of catch-up growth is in the vicinity of 5 kcal/g (21 kJ/g) of synthesized tissue. This cost is high, and signifi cantly increases daily energy requirements for nutritional recovery to be successful. Daily catch-up growth rates can exceed 20 g/kg of body mass, amounting to a cost of at least 100 kcal (418 kJ)/kg/day. The maintenance requirement for a 3-year-old malnourished girl weighing 11 kg is 100 kcal (418 kJ)/kg; this maintenance supply will need to be doubled for her to reach a recovery rate of 20 g/kg/day. The proportional cost is higher still for a malnourished adult: the maintenance supply must be trebled to reach this recovery rate.

Maintenance requirements

The energy cost of maintenance is a useful notion in nutrition; it includes basal use, specifi c dynamic action, and the use resulting from minimal physical activity (e.g. eating, personal hygiene, clothing, etc.). Maintenance requirements amount to the minimal need to remain alive when doing nothing special; the idle time spent between sleep and professional activities, leisure or house cleaning. Initially, the expression "maintenance requirements" was used only in relation to animal feeding, that is, to express the minimum conditions required for a breeding animal to maintain

CALCULATING DAILY ENERGY REQUIREMENTS

Energy requirements over 24 hours are determined by assessing daily energy use based on the following stages.

1. Calculation of the daily basal metabolism according to body mass, age and sex, based upon the equations provided in Section 1.1.1 above.
2. Calculation of the hourly basal metabolism, that is, the daily basal metabolism divided by 24.
3. Assessment of the number of hours spent daily on the following occupations: sleep, maintenance, professional or domestic activity, and leisure.
4. Calculation of the daily energy use related to each occupation by multiplying the hourly basal metabolism by the factor specifi c to the occupation under consideration and by the number of hours spent daily on this occupation,

based on the following conventional multiplication factors (WHO, 1985; Rivers, 1986): q sleep: 1 × basal metabolism (both sexes);

- maintenance, or residual energy requirement: 1.4 to 1.5 × basal metabolism (both sexes); q professional physical activity.
- light professional physical activity: 1.7 × basal metabolism (both sexes);
- moderate professional physical activity:
  - women: 2.2 × basal metabolism
  - men: 2.7 × basal metabolism q heavy professional physical activity:
  - women: 2.8 × basal metabolism
  - men: 3.8 × basal metabolism q leisure: the appropriate factor can be found in Annex 1; q house cleaning: the appropriate factor can be found in Annex 1.

5. Calculation of the overall daily energy use by adding the requirement related to each activity (calculated under point 4 above) and possible use related to specifi c physiological states - such as growth, pregnancy, breastfeeding, and catch-up growth - or climate. The total use defi nes the daily energy requirement.

It is convenient to express energy use on a daily basis. In reality, it varies in time and according to activity cycles. As a result, if the energy requirement of an individual or a group is to be defi ned with a view to recommending food rations, the assessment must refl ect average needs over an extended period.

LIMITATIONS OF THE FACTORIAL APPROACH

The factorial approach consists in the breaking down of energy use into factors related to understandable physical entities: temperature, work, growth. It states that the overall energy requirement can be extrapolated, provided each factor of the daily energy use is defi ned accurately.

This approach nevertheless has two weaknesses.

1. The arithmetic or algebraic sum of expenses is artifi cial, and ignores the following fundamentals:

    - the different factors of energy use are integrated into the overall functioning of the organism, which is regulated by the neuro-endocrine system – this system governs the energy metabolism according to criteria that differ from those providing the basis of the factorial approach;

    - energy use factors relate to and depend upon one another in frequently complex ways that escape factorial analysis – for instance, muscular activity reduces the need for thermo-genesis, whereas pregnancy increases needs but reduces physical activity and can result in overall metabolic adaptation;

    - emotional state, nutritional intake and adaptation are common variations in real situations – they change energy use signifi cantly, without it being possible to analyse and quantify them for prediction purposes: for example, when preparing his fi eld, a farmer's nervous and muscular tension changes according to whether conditions are normal or precarious.

    A better approach would involve the integration of all three real components of energy use as behaviours:

    - the behaviour of cells and organs;

    - the behaviour determined by the nervous system (emotional state, feeding behaviour);

    - the behaviour related to physical activity.

    These three behaviours determine the overall energy use. They regulate the metabolic level of different organs and, thus, the overall energy metabolism of the organism, via the neuro-endocrine system.

2. The factorial method relies on measurement methods. These do not permit suffi cient analysis of energy use, owing to the uncertainty resulting from the measurement of each factor, and to the diffi culties of refl ecting integrations, inter-relations and behaviours that govern energy use

globally. Measurement methods therefore condition both knowledge and the approach to energy requirements.

As a result, available data provides average statistical magnitudes of energy requirements as assessed in standard circumstances. They apply to a so-called reference subject, refl ective of a given society at a specifi c moment in time. Variability related to physiological, nervous and mechanical behaviour induces an uncertainty that is impossible to appraise globally. The uncertainty grows further when the focus is not a laboratory subject, but a social group confronted with its environment. Observation of the energy situation resulting from a defi ned calorie intake among individuals or groups shows that, in most cases, reality does not agree with theory... It is then necessary to adapt to reality through the thorough study of energy situations and by using these data for what they are, invaluable working guides in the approach to the nutritional need, but certainly not intangible laws.

4

The Nutritional Need of Humans

Factorial analysis must be applied to need in order to understand man's energy requirements properly. This analysis consists in identifying and quantifying the factors of energy use, notably:

- basal metabolism, amounting to the energy use of the organism at rest;
- specifi c dynamic action related to food consumption;
- physical activity;
- thermo-genesis;
- growth, production (pregnancy and breastfeeding) and recovery.

The measure of the basal metabolism aims to explain the energy use of the organism at rest in its functional entirety. For the sake of comparison, it is performed in standard conditions that are not universally realistic. Except for the tissue synthesis related to growth, production and recovery, the energy use of the organism is expressed in multiples of the basal metabolism.

Factorial analysis is a tool that only clarifi es the magnitudes of the different types of biological work. Expressed in multiples of the basal metabolism, they improve the accuracy of purely factorial sums. It is therefore necessary to bear in mind that this is a method for the analysis of need, and that any calculation inevitably implies a degree of uncertainty related to the following:

- the permanent interactions between all components of need;
- the changes that any single component imposes on all the others;

- the different forms of balance;
- the biological variability proper to any species;
- the impact of behaviour on consumption and energy use.

DEPENDENCY ON MATTER

Energy fl owing through the living organism implies energy conversions, and these require a material intermediary. Furthermore, they must occur in the material structure of the organism.

Energy fl ow and the existence of the organism generate a twofold material requirement.

1. The requirement related to the energy fl ow including the recycling of adenosine.
2. The requirement related to the development and renewal of the material, architectural and functional structure that accommodates the energy fl ow. That is, the development and renewal of cells, organs and tissue – that in this case constitute the human being.

The management of matter in the organism occurs through what is known as the intermediary metabolism; this is the "institution" formed by the sum of chemical reactions in the organism, as a result of thermodynamic determinism in the living being.

This management of matter fulfi lls four functions.

1. The obtaining of chemical energy from fuel molecules.
2. The conversion of nutrients into construction units or precursors of the macromolecules constituting the cell.
3. The assembly of these precursors into proteins, nucleic acids, lipids and other cell components.
4. The production and breakdown of molecules that perform a specialized function in the cell.

All reactions are catalysed by enzymes and are governed by a regulation system, resulting in a highly organized activity. The entirety of these reactions is quite complex; their analysis, however, shows that the intermediary metabolism operates in a simple manner through metabolic pathways. The latter govern two main effects on molecules:

- synthesis, through anabolic channels;
- breakdown, through catabolic channels.

NEED ARISING FROM ENERGY FLOWS

The nature of fuel

Adenosine recycling defi nes the needs of the organism for fuel or oxidizable matter and, obviously, oxidizing matter, that accept electrons.

The different forms of fuel carried in the blood for use by the organs are as follows.

Main source

- Glucose, which is found in food, glycogen reserves or is synthesized in the liver from specific amino acids and glycerol.
- Fatty acids, that make up complex lipids and, specifi cally the triglycerides present in oils and fats found in food or which are synthesized from glucose, some amino acids and the produce of the breakdown of other fatty acids.
- Amino acids that are present in food in the entirety of circulating amino acids or that are synthesized from other amino acids reacting with glycolysis and the citric acid cycle substrates.

Secondary source

- Ketone bodies formed from the oxidation products of fatty acids and some amino acids, when the available glucose is insuffi cient (for example in fasting).

Minor source

- Lactic acid, formed from the anaerobic oxidation of glucose.
- Glycerol, from the triglycerides splitting into fatty acids and glycerol.

Additional source

- Ethyl alcohol, found in food.

- Fructose and galactose, both glucides found in food.

The main electron acceptor is oxygen.

Fuel molecules transfer their energy through the oxidation of their carbon and hydrogen atoms during fermentation (i.e. anaerobic glycolysis) and breathing (the citric acid cycle combined with the respiratory chain). As suggested by its name, anaerobic glycolysis does not require oxygen, but its ATP recycling yield is low and breathing accounts for most of the work. The organism recycles a huge amount of ATP every day.

An adult man weighing 65 kg and exercising moderate activity would recycle an estimated 70 kg of ATP every day. On the other hand, the overall amount of ATP present in his body at any time would probably not exceed 100 g, an energy reserve equivalent to approximately two minutes (a few seconds for the brain). This is because the utilization and recycling of ATP is extremely rapid, and explains the speed at which an individual deprived of oxygen loses consciousness and the irreversible damage to his brain after only two minutes of deprivation.

Energy produced by combustion

The energy use of the organism can only be measured in energy units, and not in ATP molecules converted into ADP. Energy produced by combustion is therefore expressed in kcal or kJ. To this end, it is necessary to fi nd conversion factors between fuel grams and produced energy expressed in kcal (or kJ).

In line with the principles of thermodynamics, the complete combustion of a nutrient always produces the same amount of energy, whatever its course (direct combustion in a calorimetric bomb or staggered combustion through catabolic pathways). As a result, it is possible to burn different types of nutritional fuel in a calorimetric bomb to deduce their calorie value.

Reality is however complicated by different factors, some of which are discussed below:

- man does not usually eat specifi c nutrients but foodstuffs whose composition is more varied, and that he digests and absorbs only partially;
- proteins are not entirely oxidized when they serve as fuel;

- the energy yield of nutrients varies according to their storage and their metabolic path;
- biological variability affects both food itself, and its digestion, absorption, and utilization process in humans;
- the method faces the same limitations as the factorial measure of energy use: it measures a heat production capacity, as opposed to the energy transformation process itself, in the complexity of homeostasis and the interchangeability of fuels.

It then follows that the energy value of nutrients measured in a calorimetric bomb is a ceiling value; it thus requires a statistical correction factor that allows for the physiology and nature of the food under scrutiny. Scientists have long studied this subject, and it is still not resolved satisfactorily. Opinions differ on the conversion factors to be applied, as illustrated by different food composition tables.

This Manual provides the factors most commonly used, being those calculated by Atwater in the early 20th century. No difference is made between energy produced by construction units and their polymers (e.g. glucose or starch), and the approach is limited to the nutritive principles of foodstuffs, to the exclusion of intermediate metabolites such as glycerol, lactic acid or ketone bodies that are all included in the overall balance of ingests.

Along these lines, the combustion of glucides and amino acids or proteins produces 4 kcal (17 kJ)/g, that of fatty acids 9 kcal (37 kJ)/g, and that of alcohol 7 kcal (29 kJ)/g.

Expressing the energy yield of fuels in kcal or kJ in this way facilitates the linking of the energy need (as discussed in the previous point) and the amount of fuel that the organism needs to absorb (and, therefore, ultimately replace). This practical approach however does not adequately refl ect reality. It introduces the uncertainty related to conversion factors that combines with the appraisal of energy use. Nutrients are food substances that can be absorbed entirely and directly.

Calculating fuel requirements

An individual whose maintenance requirement is 2,000 kcal (8,360 kJ) can meet it by burning 500 g of amino acids or glucides

(2,000 kcal/(4 kcal/g) = 500 g) or 222.2 g of fatty acids (2,000 kcal/(9 kcal/g) = 222.2 g).

In fact, this individual burns a blend of glucides, amino acids and fatty acids for an overall consumption of between 222 and 500 g of nutrients. Man does not eat nutrients, strictly speaking, but food; therefore, fuel requirements are extrapolated from food composition tables, according to the specifi c foods consumed, in order to determine which proportion of each in combination yields 2,000 kcal (8,360 kJ) overall.

The calculation of the food quantities necessary to meet energy requirements is simple. However, it refl ects reality only insofar as the needs assessment does; this brings us back to the limitations of factorial analysis discussed above.

In calculating the maintenance requirements of an obese individual according to the method described in Section 1.2 above, one would already introduce the enormous aberration of the weight of his inert fatty mass that hardly consumes energy at all. The introduction of a correction that allows for his real lean mass (for example, by referring to the weight of an individual of same height), one would still be underestimating the following in particular:

- the preferential utilization of high-yield metabolic pathways;
- the physical activity economy specifi c to obese individuals;
- the reduced lower critical temperature that signals the starting of thermo-genesis.

These elements constitute three factors of energy use reduction that, incidentally, do not simply add up but reinforce one another.

Finally, the estimation of the fuel requirement faces three uncertainties related to the following:

- the assessment of the need;
- metabolic effi ciency in processing nutrients;
- the conversion factors of food into energy production capacity.

To address this, one can only use available data and compare it with reality.

Fuel reserves in the organism

Storage systems: Following a meal, the food absorbed by the organism is processed in part to address the immediate need, while the excess is stored for later utilization.

Excess glucose can be either assembled in glycogen chains, to be stored in the liver and muscle tissue, or converted into fatty acids to be stored in the fatty tissue in the form of triglycerides (three fatty acids bound to glycerol). The quantitative importance of the latter is proportional to the input because the glycogen reserves in the organism are limited, unlike fatty tissue reserves that are extensible to the extreme (obesity).

Fatty acids are conveyed in the form of triglycerides to the fatty tissue to be stored.

Amino acids are mainly used to produce proteins; these do not serve primarily as energy reserves, strictly speaking. However, proteins are permanently renewed, in combination with the continuous renewal of body tissues. The renewal of proteins implies that they be broken down and synthesized (i.e. turnover) at a frequency that varies according to the type of tissue and protein. From a functional perspective, protein turnover ensures the permanent availability of amino acids to respond to uneven enzyme synthesis rhythms for the renewal of degraded tissue proteins, and possibly as a source of energy. Protein turnover is quantitatively signifi cant: in a normal situation of balance, daily synthesis and degradation involve four to fi ve times more amino acids than the amount provided by food. This indicates a high turnover of the pool of circulating amino acids that are immediately available either as direct sources of energy, or as precursors of glucose, when the latter is scarce.

During fasting, the hormone management of protein turnover permits the slowing down of synthesis, and the increase of breakdown or degradation. In such a case, the skeletal muscle provides the main energy reserve since it is the most signifi cant one. When the diet provides more protein and energy than required, the unused amino acids cannot be stored as such; they then lose their nitrogen, become energy metabolism substrates and are eventually converted into fatty acids to be stored in the fatty tissue.

Available reserves

As discussed above, the energy reserves of the organism are glycogen, proteins and fatty tissue. The latter is the ultimate storage of excess food energy, since glucides and amino acids are eventually stored as fat. It is only through this storage that the organism can manage food excesses. As a result, fatty tissue has a real capacity to expand or shrink according to energy excess and defi ciency.

Cahill's study of fasting (Cahill, 1970) has shown that the potential energy reserves of an adult 70-kg man consist of approximately 15 kg of triglycerides (135,000 kcal/564,300 kJ), 6 kg of proteins (24,000 kcal/100,320 kJ), 0.225 kg of glycogen (900 kcal/3,760 kJ) and 0.023 kg of circulating fuel (100 kcal/418 kJ). The same individual is then placed in a situation of complete fasting (with the exception of water and minerals) and of basic energy use.

The glycogen and the circulating fuels are insuffi cient to meet his energy needs for one day, whereas the fats alone would allow him to survive for approximately 90 days, and the proteins would support him for another 15. In fact, compulsory glucose consumers (the main one being the brain) cause an increased protein degradation to allow for glucose synthesis. Thus, proteins are highly solicited from the onset; this solicitation then diminishes but does not disappear once the brain adapts partly to the utilization of ketone bodies, derived from lipids, as a source of fuel. Moreover, the protein losses resulting from normal operation persist. Therefore, the initial protein quantity determines survival time during complete fast.

Unlike fatty tissue, this amount is only slightly extensible (through physical exercise). A 140-kg obese individual will have about 2 kg muscular proteins more than a 70-kg man, simply to carry his fat. His survival will be longer, owing to these 2 kg of protein, not his approximately 65 kg of excess triglycerides. The example of total hunger strike (except for water) among males shows that survival - in conditions of almost basal energy use - is of the order of two months plus or minus one week.

We refer here to kilos of protein dry weight, and not kilos of muscle whose energy density is much lower.

Fuel utilization in the organism

The utilization of fuel in the organism depends on the organ under consideration, the anticipated work and diet.

Utilization by the organs

- The liver is the fi rst organ to receive nutrients after their absorption by the intestine. It is the organism's chemical plant *par excellence* and, as a result, adapts with ease to any available fuels (except ketone bodies that it produces itself). The energy consumption by the liver of an individual at rest amounts to approximately 25% of the basal expenditure.
- The activity of the skeletal muscle at rest accounts for approximately 30% of the basal expenditure. Some 85% of the energy derives from the oxidation of fatty acids, the remainder from glucose oxidation.
- The energy consumption of the brain remains constant, regardless of intellectual effort; its activity accounts for 20 to 25% of basal expenditure. Normally, the brain utilizes only glucose as fuel.
- The heart at rest mainly burns fatty acids that provide approximately 70% of the utilized fuel.

  Its activity at rest accounts for 7 to 10% of basal expenditure.
- The metabolism of the kidney is extremely fl exible; it can operate by burning amino acids or glucose, ketone bodies or fatty acids. It functions in a fairly constant way, and accounts for approximately 7% of basal expenditure.

Utilization of fuel according to work done

Mechanical work changes the energy consumption of both heart and muscle.

The heart adapts easily to effort: its predominant consumption of fatty acids at rest is simply replaced by a predominant consumption of glucose within mere seconds after the beginning of a major effort; a few minutes later, its energy again derives mainly from fatty acids. The skeletal muscle adapts to effort in the same way.

Utilization of fuel according to diet

Since this aspect is discussed in Chapter VIII, the present section only deals with utilization principles. The food input from different meals is uneven and can even be suspended for several days without serious consequences for the organism. Breathing, on the other hand, if suspended for more than three minutes entails death. The organism therefore accommodates mechanisms for the mobilization and redistribution of nutrients to ensure continuous and constant supply, particularly to the brain, once the food ration has been disseminated by the liver to the different organs. The mobilization of fuel is subjected to endocrinal control, and occurs according to the concentration of the different substrates involved in the energy metabolism, nervous stimuli, and physical effort. This mobilization capacity is moreover related to permanent protein turnover.

NEED RELATED TO THE DEVELOPMENT AND RENEWAL OF THE MATERIAL STRUCTURE

Energy fl ows in the biosphere occur in the material structure of living organisms. The mere existence of this structure implies the use of materials.

As is the case for energy expenditure, and with the same limitations, one can analyse the utilization of the materials required to develop man in a factorial way.

- Materials are required to develop the structure during growth, pregnancy and breastfeeding.
- Materials are also necessary to compensate for the inevitable losses of the organism in the course of its functioning. These losses are related on the one hand to the permanent renewal of cells and tissue, which involves an inevitable leakage; and on the other hand to the completion of biological work, which involves the utilization without recycling of specifi c molecules, bringing about their destruction and excretion.
- Finally, materials are sometimes required to rebuild or repair tissues lost by accident or infection, or consumed mainly as sources of energy owing to inadequate food intake.

To determine what is required for the development of the human body, its composition must fi rst be understood. The organism and its different components can be analysed individually, and according to different criteria: atomic, molecular, cellular, or relative to tissue.

Atomic composition: the adult human being comprises 60% oxygen, 23% carbon, 10% hydrogen, 2.6% nitrogen, 1.6% calcium, 0.7% phosphorus, 0.2% potassium and sulphur, 0.14% sodium and chlorine, 0.03% magnesium and silicon, plus some 0.3% of fi fteen or so other elements.

Molecular composition: Davidson *et al.* provide the following composition, relating to an adult man weighing between 65 and 70 kg: 17% protein, 13.8% fats, 1.5% glucides, 6.1% minerals and 61.6% water (Davidson, 1979). In fact, signifi cant variations can occur without serious functional repercussions.

Cellular composition: healthy body consists of lean cells that account for most energy expenditure (55% of overall weight), fatty cells that form the fatty tissue (15% of overall weight), and extra-cellular support tissue (30% of overall weight), itself divided into extra-cellular liquid and support fi bres and minerals (Davidson, 1979). Tissue composition: the organism consists of fatty (i.e. adipose) tissue, the skeletal muscle, bone tissue and internal organs (viscera).

In terms of nutritional needs, the logic of what must be absorbed by the organism to build its structure must be understood. Man feeds on animal and plant tissue; he cannot absorb them as such, and he must therefore fi rst degrade them into molecular components that constitute the food units that he can absorb. Anabolic synthesis pathways operate from construction units, as discussed earlier in Chapter III. The following also serves as a reminder of the nature of fuel:

- glucides are the precursors of amino acids, fatty acids and other glucides;
- amino acids are the precursors of glucides, fatty acids and other amino acids;
- fatty acids are the precursors of amino acids and other fatty acids, but not of glucides.

The construction units are therefore highly adaptable among themselves through metabolic pathways, and man can utilize some of these construction units to synthesize others. For instance, he need not absorb nucleic acids because he can synthesize them from simpler molecules derived from his diet or its recycled components. Theoretically, he should therefore only absorb synthesis precursor molecules and those that he cannot synthesize. Dependency on construction units thus occurs in two forms.

1. Quantitative: a minimum number of construction units derived from diet are required to build the infrastructure, replace losses and possibly repair the structure, whatever the adaptability of the molecules involved. Construction units also serve as fuel, to cover energy use. It is important to understand that covering energy use takes precedence over all the other components of the nutritional need except, to a certain extent, for pregnancy and breastfeeding. As a result, growth, compensation for inevitable losses and repairs imply that the diet provides construction units in addition to those that have been burned to meet energy requirements.
2. Qualitative: man must absorb enough of the molecules that he cannot synthesize, i.e. water, some amino acids, some fatty acids, vitamins and mineral salts. These molecules are qualifi ed as "essential" in nutrition, because they constitute a limiting factor in the functioning of the metabolism.

This somewhat debatable distinction between the quantitative and qualitative form, aims to underscore a fundamental aspect of the material need: whether the diet contains glucides is unimportant, as long as it includes enough amino acids to meet the need for them and for them to serve as precursors for glucides. On the other hand, if an otherwise balanced diet lacks an essential construction unit such as zinc, the organism will waste and die. This clarifi es how diet can contribute more or less proteins, glucides and fatty acids that are highly adaptable between themselves, but must provide quite accurate minimum amounts of essential molecules. Quantifying the need for construction materials is discussed and defi ned in practical terms in the following chapter in relation to recommended intakes, because:

- the quantitative nutritional need is defi ned more easily in its entirety;
- the attempt to express the phenomenon factorially is futile, because the components of the nutritional need all interact in an almost inextricable way – factorial analysis cannot refl ect these interactions quantitatively, but only highlight the factors that modify the need;
- the adaptability of construction units does not permit the expression of the need for glucides, amino acids and fatty acids for a specifi c utilization factor – quite different intakes can lead to the same conclusion, whereas set intakes will result in different outcomes according to the individual.

This discussion therefore focuses on the qualitative aspect of the nutritional need related to the material structure of the organism.

Water and oxygen

Water is just as essential to the body structure as oxygen is to the energy metabolism – to the point that it is often not mentioned. Oxygen is not yet rationed, and does not demand specifi c discussion in this study. The need for water, on the other hand, is vital particularly in view of the limitations imposed on the planet by human expansion. Nowadays, water is free in only a few privileged places. Everywhere else, its acquisition process is becoming just as costly economically and politically as the procurement of food. It is urgent to consider access to safe drinking (i.e. potable) water as an important aspect also of food economy, in a resource management perspective.

Glucides

There are no essential glucides in human nutrition. They can all be produced from glucose that can itself be synthesized from some amino acids.

Amino acids

Of all the components of the nutritional need, the requirement for amino acids is the one whose analysis and understanding are the most complex, to the point where we still lack a comprehensive model. The protein metabolism is one of the most complicated elements of the physiology of nutrition. In spite of his extensive research, Professor Waterlow chooses not to provide estimates of the required daily protein intake in grams among children, because of the uncertainties related to the components of factorial calculation. He even goes so far as to depart from the line of the WHO expert team to which he belonged, and which issued recommendations on energy and protein needs (WHO, 1985). He prefers, from a practical perspective, to scrutinize the quality of food required to maintain a child in good health, rather than investigate the child's needs. Mothers, health offi cials and foodstuff producers face the same dilemma (Waterlow, 1992). Literature on the assessment of protein need is considerable and continues to grow based on new data, but reference texts concur in recognizing the diffi culty of defi ning this need accurately (WHO, 1985; Shils *et al.*, 1994; Waterlow, 1992; Millward and Rivers, 1988; Millward *et al.*, 1989; Trémolière, 1977).

The idea here is to provide thinking tools for fi eld work to facilitate responsible decision-making, rather than to offer "reassuring" fi gures which are anyway subject to variation and caution.

Non-essential amino acids can be synthesized, provided the amine group is available from the degradation of other amino acids. The need for amino acids therefore rests on the availability of two main components:

- enough amine groups;
- enough essential amino acids.

The amine group includes a nitrogen atom; this is why one often refers to the "nitrogen need" rather than the need for proteins or amino acids. Man does not eat isolated amino acids but chains of them, that is, proteins. The nutritional value of proteins depends on two factors: their capacity to supply the organism with nitrogen (this determines their digestibility), and their capacity to supply the amino acids required by the organism (defi ned by their composition).

Protein digestibility

The most convenient way of quantifying the digestibility of proteins is to measure their nitrogen content. All proteins contain roughly the same amount, and it is thus possible to deduce protein quantity as follows:

proteins = nitrogen X 6.25

The digestibility of proteins can be calculated by measuring the nitrogen contained in food, and then the amount of nitrogen contained in the faeces after digestion (allowing for faecal nitrogen loss that exists even without eating protein). Without entering into detail as to the calculation of digestibility, one can say that animal protein (milk, eggs, meat and fi sh) have a 95% digestibility rate, meaning that 5% is lost in the faeces. The digestibility of refi ned cereal fl our proteins is likewise approximately 95%, that of unmilled cereals and legumes approximately 85%.

The digestibility of proteins is not only determined by the nature of the protein, but also by the agents present in the food ration (fi bres, tannin, phytates and digestive enzyme inhibitors), cooking and industrial treatment processes.

The concept of protein digestibility is only important in situations where a protein defi ciency is suspected, requiring specifi c measures. We will see that such situations are in fact rare.

Protein value according to amino-acid composition

The amino acids that are constantly circulated in the course of protein turnover can provide the organism with fuel. This is incidentally probably one of the reasons for protein turnover, otherwise quite costly in energy. The primary function of amino acids nevertheless remains related to synthesis (fi rstly the synthesis of renewed proteins, then pregnancy, breastfeeding, recovery and growth).

Human proteins combine different amino acids in specifi c proportions. This proportionality also applies to essential amino acids. Moreover, man cannot choose to consume separate amino acids. He eats proteins. It is therefore preferable for him to consume proteins whose proportional essential amino-acid composition is as close as possible to that of the proteins he wishes to produce. From this perspective, it could be said that human proteins are probably the most appropriate for human consumption, in terms of essential amino-acid supply. The average dietar y protein supply must of course provide all essential amino acids in the proportions required for synthesis. Clearly, the consumption of proteins leads to optimal synthesis only if their essential amino-acid composition is identical to that of the proteins to be synthesized. If, on the other hand, the proportions of essential amino acids in the food differ from those of the proteins to be synthesized, then synthesis will only occur to the point where the least available essential amino acid has all been consumed (this amino acid is the limiting factor of synthesis); the remaining essential amino acids in the food are then recycled in the energy metabolic pathways, losing their amine group in the process. For example, if the limiting essential amino acid is only 70% of what is needed, then synthesis only occurs to 70% of the ideal. Thus, in this example, at least 30% of essential and non-essential amino acids are unusable for synthesis.

This is only a problem if the diet with respect to minimum nitrogen requirements lacks essential amino acids over long periods. This type of situation is found in experimental laboratory conditions or in very specifi c famine circumstances.

In everyday life, man consumes foods containing different proteins that supply a pool of amino acids. A diet must contain more proteins than those required to meet the nitrogen need, combined with a limiting amino acid of, after absorption, at least 100% of needs, in order to enable normal protein synthesis.

As discussed above, the construction units provided by the diet are fi rst used to satisfy energy needs. Natural foods are generally tissue provided by living organisms, and they supply proteins, glucides and lipids in different proportions. They therefore serve fi rst as fuel, and then as construction units, if any remain after the energy need has been met. The most balanced diets are those supplying – in addition to energy – no more than the amount of quality proteins required to avoid protein and energy waste. Such diets administered intravenously are laboratory products. Although useful to the physiologist and the patient, they are not the foods normally consumed by man in his social and economic environment. What is, then, the protein quality of habitual diets?

Adults

Trémolière has compiled balance studies that show how the nitrogen requirements of adults can be met by proteins from different diets.

The table above shows that the nature of ingested proteins infl uences the effi ciency of retention, according to the combination of digestibility and composition in essential amino acids; but it also shows that, in all cases, nitrogen balance can be achieved. This means that these diets provide enough nitrogen and essential amino acids. Assuming that 95% of the intake of milk proteins – which have the highest yield and the best digestibility coeffi cient – are used as protein, the organism must retain 63 mg of nitrogen per kilogram to achieve nitrogen balance, i.e. 0.4 g of protein per kg. If all these elements are integrated into the global need to achieve nitrogen balance and meet energy requirements, then simple calculations demonstrate that, when they are consumed in suffi cient quantity to meet energy requirements, almost all the foods or food groups supply much more amino acids than are required to meet protein needs.

Trémolière and the WHO report therefore both conclude that most diets cover the adult need for essential amino acids, provided that energy requirements are met (Trémolière, 1977; WHO, 1985).

In the same logic, it is possible to demonstrate that the proteins required to cover protein needs account for 5 ± 3% of the amount of food required to meet energy needs for maintenance.

There are of course exceptions, as shown by the following examples.

- In some food scarcity and famine situations, it is possible for the supply to be of a single food type, whose protein content and/or quality are inadequate. Corn and sorghum are defi cient in tryptophan; this results primarily in pellagra, and is often associated with kwashiorkor as seen among populations displaced by war and prisoners. However, this is even more dramatic in cassava, which is generally poor in nitrogen, and can thus cause actual kwashiorkor epidemics especially when eaten by displaced and starving populations, or people who are unfamiliar with its preparation.
- Abnormal feeding behaviour, resulting from psychological anorexia, alcoholism, and drug consumption can all cause protein defi ciencies. This, however, is more an overall nitrogen defi cit than a shortage of essential amino acids.

Children

The needs for essential amino acids decrease from birth to adulthood. However, in the overall perspective of protein and energy needs, adults require more proteins per energy unit dissipated than children do. If the child's consumption of the foods and food groups above is suffi cient to cover its energy needs, then its requirements in nitrogen and essential amino acids are necessarily also met.

Excluding the severe shortage situations discussed above for adults, risks exist nevertheless arising from local food production, eating habits, poverty and ignorance.

- In all regions where cassava and banana constitute staple foods, the prevalence of kwashiorkor is higher than elsewhere and is directly caused by protein defi ciency. Episodes occur particularly at the end of the hunger gap, when intake is marginal (or most defi cient) before the following harvest, a period which frequently coincides with the onset of the rains that promote infection.

Weaning practices can be brutal, combining the introduction of porridges made from a single fl our, diluted and contaminated, with the simultaneous cessation of breastfeeding. Marginal protein intake, infection and psychological stress often cause severe malnutrition, and can be fatal. Moreover, a diet based on food groups does not necessarily mean that all household members enjoy the same access to these foods, owing to hierarchies, beliefs and taboos. During weaning and until the age of about 6 years, discriminatory practices can have morbid, or even fatal, consequences. However, their initial justifi cation may well have been good, and have only become dangerous because of changed living conditions. Furthermore, the perception of infantile nutritional illness varies considerably according to context; it rarely coincides with its defi nition as provided by external observers, who are trained in Cartesian thinking and are unfamiliar with cultural and social factors. Poverty often results in diets that are insuffi ciently varied to supply adequate protein quality. Poverty and ignorance are frequently quoted together; they should however be distinguished carefully. The poor usually lack the means to apply the principles of healthcare and healthy diet; as for ignorance, it cannot be addressed through education as long as poverty has not been alleviated since the poor can hardly afford to absorb the education that is so frequently imposed upon them, even if it pursues a realistic objective and is culturally understandable - this is rarely the case. Ignorance itself can be devastating in all strata of any society. Aside from ignorance, changing living conditions also cause poor practice, explaining harmful reactions in some situations. In any case, the problem reaches far beyond the lack of nutritional education: it results from an inadequate access to education in general.

Infants

It is commonly accepted that the infant's essential amino-acid needs are met by breastfeeding, provided the latter covers energy needs.

Lipids

Most lipids in the organism can be synthesized from glucose or fatty acids. Two lipids are essential - linoleic acid and á-linoleic acid - and must be absorbed to avoid various disorders. Linoleic acid is a precursor of arachidonic acid, and together they account for a signifi cant proportion of the fatty acids of the cell membrane and the white matter of the central nervous system. Linoleic acid is also a precursor of the prostaglandins, hormones whose spectrum is extremely vast. á-linoleic acid appears to play a role in vision and the regulation of some immune mechanisms. Gaps remain in the knowledge of essential fatty acids; defi ciency in these acids is however rare, owing to their prevalence in edible plants and hence the oils extracted from them.

Vitamins

Definition: Vitamins are molecules that man cannot synthesize himself. The word is derived from "vital amine". The clarifi cation of the structure of some agents indispensable to life has shown that they contain an amine group. It later became apparent that all vitamins do not contain an amine group. The expression "vitamin" applies to essential compounds that have a carbon skeleton, whose daily requirements are lower than 1/500,000th of the daily total ingests. These compounds cannot be synthesized by the organism (at least not in suffi cient quantity), and do not serve as fuel. This last point in fact sets them apart from amino acids and essential fatty acids. Vitamins do not enter metabolic pathways, but constitute tools to enable the chemical reactions of the organism. Vitamins share no chemical link and all differ in their physiological action.

History

The discovery of vitamins is due to contemporary science. In the early 20th century, essential factors were noted to provide growth accessories in addition to conventional nutrients (glucides, lipids and proteins). Some fi fty were consigned between 1915 and 1945. They were progressively identifi ed with a letter, sometimes combined with a number to distinguish them, and later a specifi c name as soon as one of these factors was isolated and its chemical structure clarifi ed. When it became obvious that many identifi ed factors were known substances that the organism could synthesize itself, they were removed from the list. This explains the different denominations and the gaps in the numbering and lettering that identifi es vitamins. Since the last discovery, that of vitamin B_{12} in 1948, 13 of these growth accessory factors have proved to be essential and constitute vitamins as we know them today. Research, facilitated by increasingly sophisticated techniques, continues into the role of vitamins. The many functions of vitamins have been demonstrated, beyond those whose defi ciency results in obvious clinical evidence and potentially deadly disease. It is becoming apparent that these functions, albeit hidden, are nevertheless very important from a biochemical perspective and certainly play an essential role in the general health status of organisms, in their resistance to infection and stress, in their recovery and detoxifi cation capacity, and in their longevity.

Classifi cation and nomenclature

Vitamins are usually distinguished according to whether they are water-soluble or fat-soluble (i.e. liposoluble). This distinction is interesting from a nutritional perspective: the organism can store fat-soluble vitamins, but not (or only little) water-soluble vitamins. Water-soluble vitamins can be further broken down into vitamins of the B group and vitamin C. The B group comprises vitamins with several molecules whose common characteristics are that they are coenzymes, that they contain nitrogen atoms, and that they are related to intermediary metabolism. In terms of nomenclature, the contemporary offi cial designation relates to the chemical name of the substance – but the alphabetical designation persists.

Unit of measurement

The main recognized unit of measurement is the weight of the active substance. For some vitamins, former international units are still in wide use and appear in this Manual with their equivalent in weight.

Water-soluble vitamins

Vitamin C or ascorbic acid

Absorption: the intestinal absorption of vitamin C is saturable, which means that it is useless to ingest more than 150 mg at a time. The excessive amounts that are sometimes ingested by vitamin C enthusiasts are mostly excreted and can result in diarrhoea and intestinal discomfort.

Metabolism, storage and excretion: the average half-life of ascorbic acid in the human body is 16 to 20 days. This time is inversely proportional to the intake and, thus, the catabolic rate is proportional to it. But the catabolism does not stop at the intake. Inevitable daily losses of several milligrams because of the irreversible degradation of ascorbic acid are observed. Hence the need to compensate for these losses to avoid fatal defi ciencies. There is no storage system specifi c to vitamin C. However, given an adequate intake of vitamin C, the cells of the organism contain enough of it to cope with a sudden drop in intake, and for clinical signs of defi ciency to appear only two or three months later.

Function: the function of vitamin C is mainly related to its reversible role as chemical reducer. It enables the reduction of metallic ions necessary to certain reactions, and plays a major role in anti-oxidizing, and in the elimination of free radicals. It contributes to the formation of collagen (conjunctive support tissue), in addition to the synthesis of carnitine (transport for fatty acids) and neuro-transmitters. It also contributes to the metabolism of hormones, medicines and drugs, and the degradation of cholesterol. The vitamin promotes the absorption of iron, and mitigates the effects of chelating agents such as the phytates and tannins that form complexes that are insoluble with iron, thus preventing its absorption. The reduction properties of ascorbic acid could improve the stability of folic acid and vitamin E.

Defi ciency: vitamin C defi ciency results in a series of symptoms characteristic of scurvy. Scurvy is deadly if it is not treated rapidly with vitamin C.

Clinical, prophylactic and therapeutic considerations: apart from its anti-scurvy activity, vitamin C is thought to play an important role in the immune system, defence against oxidation, protection against cancer and the prevention of cardio-vascular disease.

Requirements: for adults, a daily dose of 10 mg of ascorbic acid treats scurvy, without allowing the subject to build vitamin reserves. The cost of pregnancy is estimated at 3 to 4 mg/day, whereas breastfeeding costs 15 to 45 mg/day on the basis of an average daily milk production of 750 ml. The needs of an infant fed on artifi cial milk are met with 7 mg of ascorbic acid per day. As of the age of 6 months, needs gradually approach the adult's. Quantities quoted here are adequate to treat scurvy; it is however unclear whether they suffi ce in relation to the many functions of vitamin C which, when reduced, do not result in immediate clinical evidence.

Pharmacological intake: 100 to 200 mg doses are recommended to address iron defi ciency in exceptional need situations such as pregnancy, breastfeeding or antibiotic treatment. In case of injury, burns or surgical operation, vitamin C requirements could be in the vicinity of 1,000 to 2,000 mg to accelerate reparation and recovery.

Toxicity: when ingested in reasonable quantities (i.e. no more than 1 g/day), vitamin C has no toxic effect. The absorption of greater doses could/may entail negative effects, but available data remains unclear.

Thiamine or Vitamin B_{1}: Source: thiamine is found in all animal and vegetable tissues – in other words, in all natural foods. However, thiamine is not distributed equally in the tissues, and some refi nement processes can signifi cantly reduce its concentration in some foods. The most abundant sources of thiamine are cereal sprouts, oilseeds and legumes, in addition to beer and pork. Fresh foods (greens, fruits, tubers, meat, milk and milk products except butter) contain enough thiamine to preclude defi ciency if eaten regularly in suffi cient quantity.

Absorption: thiamine is absorbed actively when its concentration is inferior to 2 micromoles (ìmol) per litre, and passively when it is greater than 2 ìmol/l.

Metabolism, storage and excretion: the average half-life of thiamine in the organism is 9 to 18 days. If its concentration in the organism is excessive, it is not catabolized, but simply excreted as such. The approximate total quantity for the reference adult is 30 mg; this shows that thiamine is poorly stored in the organism, and that regular intake is indispensable.

Function: thiamine is a coenzyme that is indispensable to the energy metabolism, particularly for the junction between fermentation and breathing during the oxidation of glucides, and to the metabolism of amino acids whose carbon skeleton contains a branch. It also plays a role in nerve transmission, in terms of sodium and potassium transport.

Defi ciency: thiamine defi ciency causes a number of symptoms typical of beriberi. Beriberi is fatal if it is not treated rapidly with thiamine.

Requirements: thiamine requirements are mainly related to energy metabolism, i.e. energy use. They are therefore expressed in mg/1,000 kcal (4,180 kJ). The minimum required intake is of the order of 0.25 mg/1,000 kcal (4,180 kJ).

Pharmacological intake: thiamine-dependent patients only respond to pharmacological thiamine doses. This concerns only a few rare cases that respond to high thiamine intake, such as some forms of megaloblastic anaemia, lactic acidosis and branched chain ketoaciduria (or maple syrup urine disease, MSUD).

Toxicity: the organism is extremely effi cient in excreting thiamine excesses through urine; as a result, there is no evidence of thiamine toxicity provided it is administered orally.

Ribofl avin or Vitamin B_2: Source: ribofl avin is found in most foods. Beer yeast, liver, eggs, milk, cheese and meat are its best sources, followed by green vegetables, and then fruits, legumes and, fi nally, cereals.

Absorption: ribofl avin is absorbed through an active saturable system. Absorption is facilitated by bile salts. The oral administration of ribofl avin as a medicine must coincide with meals, because food maintains it longer on absorption sites.

Metabolism, storage and excretion: in the tissues, ribofl avin is mostly found in the form of fl avine adenine dinucleotide (FAD), and most of it is free, and the rest is related to enzymes as a coenzyme. The liver is its main storage organ, and accommodates approximately one-third of the overall ribofl avin in the organism. As a coenzyme, FAD is quite stable, and its renewal is directly connected to the renewal of the proteins to which it is bound. When proteins are saturated, the free form is degraded into free ribofl avin, which is excreted mainly in the urine. Excretion is of the order of 200 ìg per 24 hours in reference adults, and falls by approximately 75% in case of defi ciency.

Function: ribofl avin is a coenzyme that contributes to the oxidation-reduction of many metabolic pathways, particularly in energy production (ATP) in the respiratory chain.

Deficiency: ribofl avin is found in all major food categories, but in insuffi cient quantity in the essentially vegetarian diets of the poor in vast regions in the world, nor in traditional humanitarian relief food rations. As a result, moderate ribofl avin defi ciency is common, combined with other more or less serious defi ciencies typical of nutritionally poor diets. The usual clinical signs include the oro-oculo-genital syndrome, together with angular stomatitis (sores at the corners of the mouth), glossitis (tongue infl ammation), cheilitis (swelling and cracking of the lips), a magenta colouring of the tongue, photophobia, and seborrhoeic dermatitis, particularly of the scrotum and the vulva. Of all these signs, only the magenta colouring of the tongue is an absolute indication of ribofl avin defi ciency. Spotting it however requires a suffi ciently expert eye to distinguish it from other, close, colourings that indicate other defi ciencies. All the other clinical signs of ribofl avin defi ciency can also result from other group B vitamin defi ciencies. Strangely enough, ribofl avin defi ciency is not deadly, in spite of its fundamental role in the energy metabolism. This is probably because ribofl avin, once it is related to oxidation-reduction enzymes, is extremely stable, that it is found in all major food categories, and that a minimum amount is always present; in extreme food shortage situations, other defi ciencies are deadly sooner. The prescribed dose to deal with defi ciency is 5 mg oral three times daily.

Requirements: as is the case for thiamine, the minimum ribofl avin intake is expressed in mg/1,000 kcal (4,180 kJ). Unlike thiamine, however, needs do not increase signifi cantly with energy use. The resulting minimum requirements are 0.5 mg/1,000 kcal (4,180 kJ)/day for infants. Additional needs related to pregnancy are 0.3 mg/day, and 0.5 mg/day for breastfeeding.

Pharmacological intake: because ribofl avin defi ciency usually does not arise alone, it should be administered together with thiamine and, if possible, with all the other vitamins in therapeutic doses. A ribofl avin dose of 5 mg/day is suffi cient, as research has shown no additional benefi ts in higher doses.

Toxicity: ribofl avin is non-toxic, and excessive intake is rapidly excreted in the urine.

Nicotinic acid and Nicotine-Amide (Nicotinamide) or Niacin or Vitamin B_3 or PP: The vitamin activities of nicotinic acid and its amide, nicotine-amide, are identical; they share the generic name of niacin.

Source: niacin is found in practically al l foods, if only in limited amounts. The highest concentrations are provided by meat (especially offal), fi sh, beer yeast, some legumes and some cereals. In the latter, niacin is blocked and becomes available only through alkaline treatment, such as the treatment of maize with lime water as practised by American Indians. Niacin has a precursor, or provitamin, from which it can be synthesized; this precursor is the essential amino acid tryptophan. Niacin synthesis from tryptophan requires ribofl avin and vitamin B_6. Tryptophan can contribute signifi cantly to niacin intake, provided it exceeds both the protein requirements and the homeostasis of amino acids: 60 mg of tryptophan in the food are generally considered to supply 1 mg of niacin. This fi gure nevertheless calls for caution: the conversion of tryptophan into niacin probably depends just as much on the content of one as of the other in the diet. Either way, food composition tables often refer to niacin equivalent, plus one-sixtieth of the tryptophan content of the food under consideration. This is a good refl ection of reality for foods that are poor in niacin but rich in tryptophan, such as milk and eggs that are indeed effective in addressing defi ciencies. Niacin in its free form is rare in nature, where it is essentially found as nicotinamide-adenine-dinucleotide (NAD) and nicotinamide-adenine-dinucleotide-phosphate (NADP). NAD and NADP are the two complete coenzymes whose active chemical group is nicotinamide.

Absorption: NAD and NADP are hydrolysed by enzymes of the intestinal mucous membrane, resulting in the release of the coenzyme nicotinamide. The intestinal fl ora partially converts nicotinamide into nicotinic acid, and both are then absorbed without it being known exactly how. The absorption is very effi cient, even in large quantities (approximately 3 g), with or without concomitant food intake. The tissues then rapidly extract niacin from the plasma.

Metabolism, storage and excretion: after the nicotinamide and nicotinic acid have been absorbed into the cells, NAD and NADP coenzymes form. Strictly speaking, there is no niacin storage in the organism. Excessive intake is rapidly excreted through the urine, where niacin is secreted as such.

Function: nicotinamide acts as an oxidant or a reducer by the exchange of a hydrogen atom with its substrate. More than 200 enzymes use either NAD or NADP as coenzyme. NAD is more frequently involved in catabolic reactions, using fuel molecules for the production of energy, whereas NADP is used rather in synthesis processes, such as the synthesis of steroids and fatty acids. The conversion from NAD into NADP (and inversely) is easy, and the two molecules can exchange their oxidation states. Under hormonal control, this allows a balance to be maintained between synthetic reactions that consume energy and catabolic reactions that produce it. Generally, niacin's oxidation-reduction function involves it in the metabolism (synthesis and degradation) of fatty acids, glucides, and amino acids.

Defi ciency: niacin defi ciency results in a number of symptoms typical of pellagra, which is deadly if it is not treated rapidly.

Clinical, prophylactic and therapeutic considerations: nicotinic acid prevents cardio-vascular disease by reducing plasma cholesterol levels, by also reducing low-density lipoproteins, and by increasing high-density lipoproteins. Niacin also plays an important role in the treatment of dementia, depression and schizophrenia, three illnesses that modify the niacin or tryptophan metabolism, resulting in increased requirements for this vitamin. Niacin is of course indispensable in the treatment of pellagra.

Pharmacological intake: a pharmacological niacin intake (3 g/day) is prescribed in the treatment of schizophrenia and of high plasma cholesterol levels.

Toxicity: niacin is not really toxic insofar as very high doses (3–6 g/day) only cause passing side effects. These can, however, be quite unpleasant: vasodilatation and hot fl ushes, nausea, vomiting, headache, and skin irritation.

Pantothenic acid or Vitamin B_5: Source: pantothenic acid is found in all natural foods. It is particularly abundant in beer yeast, egg yolk, offal (especially liver) and is found in more moderate quantities in cereals and legumes. It is one of the constituents of coenzyme A, into which it is usually integrated. In food, it is found in both its free and integrated forms.

Absorption: the absorption of pantothenic acid appears to be passive, mainly in the small intestine, but possibly already in the stomach. The integrated form of coenzyme A must fi rst be released by enzyme action. The absorption of the vitamin is approximately 70%, the rest is excreted in the faeces.

Metabolism, storage and excretion: coenzyme A is synthesized in the cell from pantothenic acid. Following hydrolysis reactions, the latter is then released in free form and excreted as such in the urine; this means that pantothenic acid does not undergo any transformation in the organism. Pantothenic acid is not stored, excess intake is immediately excreted in the urine.

Function: coenzyme A is an indispensable vehicle of two-carbon units, both in the degradation of some amino acids, sugars, and fatty acids, and in synthesis. It is probably the most central and versatile of all coenzymes in the intermediary metabolism, while remaining just as indispensable to many more specifi c reactions, such as the synthesis of acetyl choline and porphyrines. Coenzyme A is also essential in the modifi cation of cellular proteins in terms of structure, activity, and location.

Deficiency: human pantothenic acid defi ciency is rare, although moderate forms can evolve in the case of diets made up essentially of transformed foods from the food industry. Atypical symptoms include weariness, headache, and indisposition. The burning feet syndrome only develops in experimental defi ciency conditions, or in grave forms of marasmus; its symptoms include the feeling of burning skin on the feet and ankles, that can extend up to the knee. The pain is sudden, spreads rapidly, and can be acute. Crises often occur at night and exhaust the patient by preventing him from sleeping. Cold water brings some relief. The burning feet syndrome is frequently found among malnourished prisoners whose diet is extremely monotonous and constantly unbalanced. It should be noted that the syndrome almost always appears in combination with the signs of other group B vitamin defi ciencies.

Pharmacological intake: there appears to be no indication for high doses of pantothenic acid. The burning feet syndrome is treated with an intramuscular dose of 10 mg/ day. Administered orally, the vitamin also produces fast and excellent results, as an experience with severely malnourished prisoners has shown (fortuitously, a dose of 100 mg/ day in a multivitamin preparation intended to treat beriberi was administered).

Toxicity: pantothenic acid is not toxic for humans.

Pyridoxine or Vitamin $B_{6:}$ Source: pyridoxine is found in most natural animal and vegetable foods. As is the case for most group B vitamins, it is abundant in baking yeast, liver and cereal sprouts. Avocado, banana, potato and some nuts and legumes also contain signifi cant concentrations.

Absorption: the absorption of pyridoxine is passive and non-saturable, and occurs in the small intestine.

Metabolism, storage and excretion: the liver provides the other tissues with active forms of pyridoxine (pyridoxal-5-phosphate), of which the major concentration is found in the striated muscle (80–90% of the overall pyridoxine contained in the organism). The vitamin is not specifi cally stored, and its turnover requires approximately 30 days. The pyridoxal-5-phosphate molecule is highly reactive, and excessive intake is irreversibly transformed into 4-pyridoxal acid, and eliminated in the urine.

Function: pyridoxine is primarily associated with practically all metabolic reactions of amino acids. It also contributes to gluconeogenesis, in the formation of niacin from tryptophan, in the synthesis of neuro-transmitters, in the regulation of steroid hormones, and in the compatibility between oxygen and haemoglobin. Its role in the lipid metabolism remains unclear and, generally, the function of pyridoxine is far from being comprehensively elucidated. In view of the vitamin's versatility, it is probably crucial for intake to be suffi cient and regular to ensure these multiple roles (both known and unknown), while avoiding that one function take precedence over another.

Defi ciency: human pyridoxine defi ciency is rare, because the vitamin is found in suffi cient amounts in all the major food categories. It is, however, associated with severe malnutrition or resulting from the administration of medicines that are incompatible with the vitamin, such as isoniazid, penicillamine, and oestrogen. Several illnesses related to an innate metabolic error cause a greater dependency on the vitamin.

Clinical signs among infants include convulsive crises, and anomalies in the electro-encephalogram; these are reversible through the administration of pyridoxine. Clinical signs among adults are those also associated with ribofl avin defi ciency: stomatitis, cheilitis, glossitis (less typical tongue colouring), in addition to irritability, depression and confusion. The treatment consists of a 10 mg/day dose, administered orally.

Requirements: in view of the versatility of pyridoxine, its needs are diffi cult to defi ne in terms of a dose that would eliminate clinical defi ciency signs. These signs can indicate defi ciency with respect to specifi c functions, whereas others will prove insuffi cient at sub-clinical level. In this respect, specifi c data is lacking, and it is therefore necessary to limit action to recommended intakes.

Pharmacological intake: pharmacological pyridoxine doses could be effective against nausea and vomiting during pregnancy (50 mg/day), the withdrawal symptoms in the chronic alcoholic (100 mg/day), and the treatment of illnesses resulting from radiation (25–200 mg/day). Supplements are administered simultaneously to the treatment of tuberculosis by isoniazid, and Wilson's Disease by penicillamine (10 mg/day, orally).

Toxicity: pyridoxine is considered to be hardly toxic for man, in which no side effects are noted with pharmacological doses. The "low" toxicity aspect comes from the fact that disorders have been noted following massive intake. Once again, the consumer is responsible for his excesses.

Biotin or Vitamin B_8 or H or H_1: Source: biotin is synthesized by various micro-organisms, seaweed and plants that serve as food for species that cannot produce it. The richest food sources are beer yeast, liver, soy, and egg yolk. It should be noted that the human intestinal fl ora produces biotin, but it remains unclear to what extent this production is adequate to cover human needs and avert dependency on food sources.

Absorption: the absorption of biotin probably requires a specifi c transfer system.

Metabolism, storage and excretion: the biotin metabolism among humans is not well known, but its levels in plasma and in red blood cells tends to remain constant.

Function: biotin is crucial in the intermediary energy metabolism, involved both in the fuel synthesis (glucides/lipids) and its utilization to produce ATP.

Defi ciency: human biotin defi ciency is rare. Where it arises, it is usually related to an innate metabolic problem, massive raw egg white consumption, or the scientifi c experimentation of defi ciency. Defi ciency in these cases manifests itself mainly through seborrhoeic dermatitis. It is nevertheless possible that it may be involved in sudden infant death syndrome (SIDS, or cot death) in relation to artifi cially-fed infants. In any case, biotin defi ciency is never a public health concern.

Requirements: the exact human biotin requirement is unknown. The recommended intake must therefore be deduced from the different known intakes preventing signs of defi ciency or pathology in specifi c conditions.

Pharmacological intake: doses ranging from 10 to 100 ìg/day have been administered to treat specifi c biotin defi ciencies.

Toxicity: only experimental laboratory conditions achieve toxic biotin levels for animals; the pharmacological doses usual in parenteral (i.e. intravenous) human nutrition are well tolerated.

Folic acid (pteroylglutamic acid) or Vitamin B_9: Source: folic acid is found in most natural foods; concentrated meat extracts and concentrated baking yeast are excellent sources, while offal, spinach, broccoli, asparagus, beetroot, cabbage, peanuts and avocado provide good sources. Wholemeal bread, eggs, rice, bananas and oranges provide moderate concentrations, and meat in general, grapes, apples, potatoes, and milk yield low concentrations. Losses due to cooking can be enormous, and the indications above therefore apply to the raw produce only.

Absorption: in most cases, the vitamin's natural form is tetrahydrofolic acid, which can be associated with up to six glutamate molecules. Absorption occurs mainly in the duodenum and the jejunum, following hydrolysis into monoglutamate. Absorption is active, stimulated by glucose, and saturable. However, high concentrations tend to result in passive absorption, thereby suggesting the existence of another transport system.

Metabolism, storage and excretion: the vitamin is found throughout the organism, with an overall amount of 5–10 mg, half of which is located in the liver. The folic acid metabolism is controlled by enzymes that regulate the balance between the monoglutamate (the usual form of transport) and polyglutamate forms (the active form of intra-cell storage); these proteins appear to manage a form of vitamin saving. In fact, the daily turnover rate of folic acid in the organism is less than 1%. High intakes of folic acid result in most of it remaining intact in the urine, together with 5-methyl-folic acid and 10-formyl-folic acid. However, experiments with radioactively marked vitamins show that, following major elimination of the intact form through the urine, the rest is recovered much more slowly in broken-down form. This suggests that excess folic acid is excreted rapidly, while the functional portion is fi nally broken down. Besides, some 100 ìg of active folic acid are excreted daily in the gall, most of which is absorbed again in the bowel, and the remainder is excreted in the faeces.

Function: folic acid is the acquiring and donor coenzyme of one carbon unit in the metabolism of amino acids and nucleotides, within a group of interdependent reactions where the vitamin's metabolism is cyclical, dependent on vitamin B_{12}.

Defi ciency: megaloblastic anaemia is the best known manifestation of folate defi ciency, and is common among the poor in tropical climates, particularly pregnant women, whose folic acid requirements are much higher. Defi ciency can result from cooking habits that are deleterious to the vitamin, or from a reduced absorption due to gastro-intestinal disease or to alcohol consumption. However, it can also be associated with vitamin C, niacin and vitamin B_{12} defi ciencies. As always, real defi ciency comes before – in this case, several months before – the clinical signs of anaemia, without obvious actual scope. It is nevertheless known that irritability, memory loss, hostility, and paranoid behaviour are also signs of folic acid defi ciency.

Requirements: the folic acid provided by food is only available at approximately 50%: it is therefore necessary to specify whether the needs are expressed in folic acid from food, or synthetic folic acid. This Manual discusses folic acid from food. Adults require approximately 100 ìg per day to maintain a normal level of folic acid; pregnant women require approximately 675 ìg/day, and breastfeeding women between 200 and 300 ìg. Infants require approximately 10 ìg/kg/day.

Toxicity: folic acid is non-toxic for humans.

Cobalamin or Vitamin B_{12}: Source: vitamin B_{12} is found in food as different forms of cobalamin. The long-held view that cobalamin is absent from vegetables is questioned today: some legumes may contain small amounts, although it is believed that these plants host micro-organisms that can synthesize them. The greatest concentrations of vitamin are found in offal (kidneys, liver and brain), less in egg yolk, oysters, crab and salmon. Other animal tissues and fi sh contain slighter concentrations. It should also be noted that the animal intestinal fl ora produces the vitamin, as this is the only means by which herbivores can obtain it. Human intestinal cobalamin production is insuffi cient, and diet must therefore supplement it.

Absorption: cobalamin is absorbed in the ileum, at fi rst actively through the connection of cobalamin to the intrinsic factor, which is a glycoprotein molecule synthesized by the parietal cells of the gastric mucous membrane. This process is indispensable to the absorption of the vitamin at the levels usually found in food. There also exists a dissemination process that does not involve the intrinsic factor, whereby the vitamin is administered orally, as a medicine, in doses that are higher than those found in food. Metabolism, storage and excretion: the organism does not break down cobalamin, which is found intact in the faeces and urine. Excess intake is stored in the liver, which contains more than 50% of the 2 to 5 mg of vitamin usually found in the organism. This amounts to quite a high storage in comparison to other vitamins, because its excretion is low: slightly more than 1 ìg/day through urine, whereas approximately 70% of the vitamin reaching the digestive tube through gall is absorbed again. The resulting daily excretion is estimated at between 2 and 5 ìg: this is equivalent to an autonomy of almost three years, not to mention the synthesis through the intestinal fl ora.

Function: vitamin B_{12} is essential in the regeneration of 5-methyl-folic acid into folic acid, combined with the formation of methionine amino acid. Without this regeneration, the metabolic journey of 5-methyl-folic acid inevitably ends in excretion through urine. This causes a defi ciency in another intermediary of the metabolic cycle of folic acid; this intermediary contributes to the synthesis reaction of a nucleic acid itself indispensable for the synthesis of desoxyribonucleic acid (DNA). This metabolic trap of folic acid, in the case of vitamin B_{12} defi ciency, explains why anaemia related to this defi ciency is impossible to distinguish from anaemia related to folate defi ciency. Vitamin B_{12} furthermore contributes to the transport and storage of folic acid in the cells. It plays a signifi cant, albeit still unclear, role in myelin synthesis; it also contributes to the metabolism of glucides, lipids and proteins as a reducing agent.

Deficiency: cobalamin defi ciency is caused either by insuffi cient absorption due most frequently to the incapacity to produce the intrinsic factor (but also, sometimes, to other ailments of the digestive tube), or by insuffi cient vitamin intake.

Incapacity to produce the intrinsic factor causes pernicious anaemia, which is deadly if it is not treated; it also presents impairments typical of nutritional anaemia, in addition to neuropathy (most frequently, fi rst in the peripheral nerves, followed by the spinal cord and the brain). The clinical signs of nervous impairment include tingling and a feeling of cold and numbness in the extremities, followed by muscular weakness and lack of movement coordination as the spinal cord is affected. Mental symptoms can also appear: intellectual slowness, memory lapses, confusion, depression and paranoid psychoses. The diagnosis of nutritional anaemia should include the verifi cation that it is a cobalamin and/or folate defi ciency: on the one hand, the two vitamins are not interchangeable in the treatment of nutritional anaemia and, on the other, the administration of folic acid can improve pernicious anaemia momentarily, while the neurological damage increases, sometimes irreversibly. The treatment of pernicious anaemia leads to total remission, provided there is no irreversible neurological damage yet; it consists of a monthly subcutaneous or intramuscular injection of 100 ìg of vitamin B_{12}, for life.

Insuffi cient vitamin B_{12} intake is rare and only concerns those too poor to secure animal products, or those confi ned to a strict vegetarian diet by their religion or their personal principles. Defi ciency develops slowly, since the intestinal fl ora produces the vitamin, but in amounts that are insuffi cient to satisfy the need. When the dietary insuffi ciency results from poverty, anaemia and neuropathy develop equally, because the diet is poor in cobalamin and folic acid alike. When the insuffi ciency is caused by cultural restrictions, anaemia is slight, even absent, while neuropathy can be severe, because a deliberately vegetarian diet is usually rich in folic acid, and this compensates the metabolic trap effect affecting 5-methyl-folic acid. This phenomenon also appears in pernicious anaemia in richer wealth groups that develop neuropathy primarily, and in poorer strata that develop both neuropathy and anaemia: the diet of the former tends to be richer in folic acid than the latter's. The treatment of defi ciency caused by insuffi cient intake consists of the introduction of animal produces in the diet, or the administration of vitamin preparations that supply orally 1 ìg of vitamin B_{12} per day. Another solution is the treatment of pernicious anaemia.

Requirements: a daily 1 ìg dose has been observed to contain anaemia and neuropathy entirely among adult patients suffering from anaemia due to dietary vitamin B_{12} defi ciency. The need is proportionately greater among growing children, particularly among infants.

Retinol, axerophtol or Vitamin A: Source: vitamin A is found in food, mainly bound to fatty acids, the most common of which is palmitic acid. In order of decreasing concentration, it is found in sea fi sh and sea mammal liver oils (in large quantity), in the liver of animals for slaughter and poultry, butter, cheese, wheat germ, eggs and oily fi sh, fi nally in offal other than liver, milk, lean fi sh, red and white meat. Retinol (vitamin A alcohcl) has some precursors or provitamins, mainly â-carotene, which is the main representative of the large carotenoid family. â-carotene is a retinol dimer that releases two retinol molecules per central splitting of the â-carotene molecule. It appears that â-carotene can also break down into retinaldehyde through eccentric splitting, without in this case producing two retinol molecules, but one only. Retinaldehyde is easily reduced into retinol in the presence of NADH.

â-carotene is found in vegetables and coloured fruits, among others: spinach, parsley, the leaves of cassava, amaranth and lettuce, carrots, turnips, cabbage, tomatoes, mandarins/tangerines, melons, oranges, dates, papayas, mangoes; in butter, palm oil (the richest source), wheat sprouts and fl our, yellow maize, lentils and yellow sweet potatoes. According to the ingested amounts, the biological activity of the different provitamins is inferior to that observed for retinol, because food carotenoids are less well digested and absorbed than vitamin A; furthermore, carotenoids are not entirely transformed into retinol. They are then expressed as retinol equivalents (RE): 1 RE = 1 ìg of retinol, or 6 ìg of â-carotene, or 12 ìg of other carotenoids acting as provitamins. The 1 to 6 and 6 to 12 relationships are estimated, and are used for want of a better reference. Formerly (but old habits die hard), vitamin A was also expressed in international units (IU): 1 IU amounts to the activity of 0.3 ìg of retinol, or to 0.55 ìg of retinol palmitate. Attention should nevertheless be paid to the fact that there are also IU of provitamin A, where 1 IU = 0.6 ìg of â-carotene. To clarify, retinol IU are labelled IU_a and â-carotene IU are labelled IU_c. The retinol to â-carotene ratio is 1 ìg to 6 ìg in terms of RE, and 1 ìg to 2 ìg in terms of IU. This is due to the fact that experiments that led to the defi nition of â-carotene IU were conducted in optimal conditions, neglecting many a factor that determines what ultimately remains in the form of usable retinol in the organism from a given quantity of ingested â-carotene.

Absorption: in the stomach, vitamin A and its provitamins combine with the other lipids to produce globules that pass into the small intestine. There, globules combine with bile salts to produce emulsions that permit the splitting of complex lipids into simple lipids owing to the action of digestive enzymes; these emulsions then form micelles of mixed lipids that enter into contact with the brush-shaped border of the epithelial cells of the intestinal mucous membrane. Vitamin A is transported through the intestinal wall through a specifi c system when it is in low concentrations, and by passive dissemination when its concentration is high, whereas provitamins disseminate passively. The absorption of vitamin A and its precursors is facilitated by the presence of proteins and lipids in the diet. The state of the intestinal mucous membrane is of critical importance. Bile salts are indispensable to the absorption of carotenoids, whereas vitamin A does not depend upon it (provided that it is properly soluble). Approximately 80% of the retinol contained in the diet is absorbed (this effi ciency only diminishes with very high doses of retinol), whereas only 50% of the provitamins is absorbed, and this effi ciency drops quickly with high doses.

Metabolism, storage and excretion: after its absorption, retinol is transported by chylomicrons to the liver in the form of retinol palmitate. Carotenoids are mostly broken down into two retinaldehyde molecules by central splitting, in the intestinal mucous membrane, and then transported to the liver via chylomicrons. However, a signifi cant amount of carotenoids can be incorporated as it is into chylomicrons, and then be transported and stored in other tissues than the liver (mainly adipose tissue). Retinol is either stored in the liver as retinol palmitate, or transported to other tissues by means of the retinol binding protein (RBP). Within the tissues, retinol is also bound to cellular retinol binding proteins (CRBP). Generally speaking, ingested vitamin A takes the following course: some 20% are directly excreted in the faeces in the following two days, 20% to 50% of the absorbed 80% are excreted in the faeces and urine during the week following ingestion, and the remainder is stored. Vitamin A reserves are considerable in adults: with a normal initial stock, they can live for one to three years without additional intake. Infants and children, on the other hand, only have minimal retinol reserves. Stored vitamin A is only metabolized very slowly, in two ways: by RBP-retinol degradation in the kidneys and peripheral epithelial tissues (the skin and the mucous membranes lining the internal body surfaces), or by retinol transformation in the liver and peripheral tissue, in combined or oxidized forms that are later excreted in the faeces or urine.

Function: vitamin A contributes to vision, cell differentiation, morphogenesis, in addition to complex physiological processes such as growth, reproduction, and the immune response.

Generally speaking, most tissues probably rely more or less on vitamin A, which explains the increasing recognition of its major signifi cance.

- Vision: vitamin A is one of the indispensable molecules for the transmission of information registered by the eye to the optical nerve.
- Cell differentiation: vitamin A defi ciency is observed to cause cells that produce mucus to be replaced by cells that produce keratin. The introduction of vitamin A into culture cells rapidly causes various types of cell lines to differentiate. The effect of vitamin A, or rather its defi ciency, is particularly obvious on the cells of the cornea, which keratinises and fi nally ulcerates.
- Morphogenesis: both the excess and the defi ciency of vitamin A impair embryogenesis, but the mechanism is unknown.
- Growth: vitamin A is a growth factor, through its derivative, retinoic acid. Here again, the mechanism is unknown. One of the fi rst signs of defi ciency is appetite loss, but it is not the real cause of growth problems related to vitamin A defi ciency.
- Reproduction: sperm formation (spermatogenesis) and foetal growth are affected by retinol defi ciency, probably owing to the role of vitamin A in cell differentiation.
- Immune response: vitamin A is also referred to as "anti-infection vitamin". Specifi c and non-specifi c defence mechanisms both depend on it. Its defi ciency, combined with protein-energy malnutrition has major consequences on the organism's resistance to infection.

Defi ciency: among others, vitamin A defi ciency leads to blindness and high mortality risks from infections such as measles. It should be noted, however, that any imbalance generally has a negative effect on the functions of vitamin A. Protein defi ciency reduces the â-carotene cleavage and RBP synthesis; on the other hand, protein-energy defi ciency restricts growth, and thus postpones the appearance of vision disorders caused by vitamin A defi ciency. To be absorbed, vitamin A and retinoids must be ingested together with lipids. Iron levels depend on vitamin A, whereas the utilization of retinol is related to zinc levels. The vitamin A metabolism depends to a certain extent on vitamin E. Moreover, vitamin A interacts with vitamins C, K, and D, calcium, copper, and iodine.

Chylomicrons: microscopic lipid particles common in the blood during fat digestion and assimilation, consisting of 98% lipids and 2% proteins. This defi ciency is discussed in detail in Chapter VIII.

Requirements: experimentation has defi ned minimum male adult vitamin A requirements to be approximately 400 ìg/day.

Pharmacological intake: retinoic acid and, to a lesser extent, carotenoids, are used at high dose in the treatment and prevention of a number of illnesses such as acne, skin cancer (but not melanoma), acute myeloid leukaemia (AML), and breast cancer. â-carotene intake is directly associated with low lung cancer incidence.

Toxicity: taken in high doses, vitamin A is toxic to the point of being lethal. Three different types of toxicity should be distinguished, as follows.

- Acute toxicity follows the ingestion of a single or several high doses. The threshold dose for risk of acute toxicity begins at 200 mg of retinol for adults, 100 mg for children above 5, 60 mg for small children, and 30 to 40 mg for infants. Its signs appear in the hours following absorption: nausea, vomiting, headache, dizziness, double vision, lack of coordination and muscular weakness. Fontanel swelling is possible in infants. Very high doses frequently cause vomiting, itching around the eyes, and fl aky skin, particularly around the mouth. These signs usually subside within a few days, once the ingestion of massive doses has been discontinued. By extrapolation, studies with apes (which seem to provide excellent models for vitamin A toxicity in humans) show that lethal doses would be in the vicinity of 500 mg for infants, and 11.8 g for adults (Shils, 1994).

- Chronic toxicity is quite common, because of the sometimes exaggerated popularity of vitamins, which are often imposed upon children with the best intentions. Daily intakes that can cause chronic toxicity are of the order of 10 times the recommended intake, that is, 3.75 mg for the infant, and 10 mg for adults. The most common signs of chronic intoxication include the following: skin dryness and colouring, headaches, anorexia and weight loss, alopecia (hair loss), articular stiffness and pain, and fatigue. It takes weeks, even months, for these signs to subside once normal vitamin intake has been resumed.
- Teratogenesis: vitamin A is highly teratogenic. In early pregnancy, a single dose superior to 200 mg or daily doses exceeding 30 to 90 mg for 1 week, or long-term daily intakes in the order of 7.5 mg of retinol can cause miscarriage or severe malformations of the foetus (Shils, 1994). Vitamin A supplements are therefore not recommended during pregnancy (particularly during the fi rst quarter) for healthy women whose regular diet includes fruits and greens.

Either way, intake should not exceed 3 mg of retinol per day. Carotenoids, on the other hand, are not toxic even in very high doses because their absorption is lower than retinol's, and is quickly saturated.

Cholecalciferol or Vitamin D_3. Source: vitamin D_3 is not really a vitamin, because it is synthesized by man through solar ultraviolet radiation on his skin. Ultraviolet irradiation transforms provitamin D_3 (7-dehydrocholesterol) into an intermediary, which spontaneously converts into vitamin D_3 within one or two days simply because of the organism's heat. In adults, synthesis occurs mainly in the outer layer of the skin (epidermis), whereas in infants it also occurs in the deep inner layer of the skin (dermis), because their epidermis transfers more ultraviolet radiation to the dermis. Prolonged exposure to the sun does not cause hypervitaminosis, because both the provitamin and the vitamin are rapidly broken down into inactive biological compounds. The main source of vitamin D_3 comes from endogenous synthesis. However, the vitamin is found in high concentrations in cod liver oil, and is also found

Data for other population categories is not available; readers are thus referred to recommended intakes as discussed in Chapter I V. Teratogenesis: a prenatal toxicity characterized by structural or functional defects in the developing embryo or foetus. in sea fi sh, egg yolk and dairy products. Following the rickets epidemics (vitamin D_3 defi ciency, see below) that affected the industrial cities of the northern United States and Europe mainly, vitamin D_3 or D_2 enrichment is common in milk, margarine and cereals (fortifi ed foods vary according to country). Vitamins D_3 and D_2 are analogous, and will hereafter simply be referred to as vitamin D. Vitamin D has two types of unit: micrograms (ìg) and international units (IU), 1 IU amounting to 0.025 ìg, and 1 ìg amounting to 40 IU.

Absorption: approximately 80% of the vitamin D supplied by the diet is absorbed, but absorption is highly sensitive to the state of the intestinal mucous membrane, and to its capacity to absorb fats. It is transported by chylomicrons to the liver. The endogenous vitamin travels to the dermal capillary network through a specifi c transport protein, and is then transported to the liver.

Metabolism, storage and excretion: the liver modifi es vitamin D into hydroxycholecalciferol, which is converted in turn by the kidney into dihydroxycholecalciferol, the physiologically active form of the vitamin. Vitamin D, or cholecalciferol, is stored in adipose tissue, and hydroxycholecalciferol is stored in the muscle. Blood holds the highest concentration of vitamin D and, unlike vitamin A, the liver does not store it. Little is known about the turnover and excretion process of vitamin D.

Function: vitamin D appears to function like a steroid hormone. Its most striking role is to maintain the calcium concentration within and around the cell by modulating the calcium and phosphorus metabolism in the intestine and the bones. Vitamin D does not contribute directly to ossifi cation, but promotes it by maintaining oversaturated calcium and phosphorus concentrations around the cell (i.e. extra-cellular). Apart from its action on minerals, vitamin D also contributes to cell multiplication and differentiation.

It is effective in the treatment of psoriasis, a chronic, recurrent skin disorder.

Defi ciency: vitamin D defi ciency arises from poverty, poor housing, pollution, inadequate clothing, and an over-protection against solar radiation (for fear of skin cancer). It manifests itself in children through rickets, and in adults through the softening of bony tissue (osteomalacia). In the late 19th century, up to 75% of poor children in industrial cities were rachitic (Davidson, 1979). Narrow streets, high corbelled buildings, and domestic and industrial fumes all combined to reduce ultraviolet solar radiation signifi cantly. Moreover, the poor lacked the means to purchase foods rich in vitamin D foods such as dairy products and eggs and, in the cities, had little access to fresh air.

These causes for rickets have subsided, but have by no means disappeared today; sub-clinical forms of rickets still (or again) constitute a public health problem in Western countries. Rickets is also related to protection and dressing customs for children, and the confi nement of women and small children to backyards. In parts of Ethiopia, for instance, it is customary for infants be covered from head to foot when leaving the house, up to the age of approximately 6 months, so as to be protected from negative external infl uence that could make them sick. Rickets is therefore common among very small children, but recedes rapidly as soon as the child is left to move outside uncovered.

Vitamin D defi ciency results in insuffi cient intestinal absorption, and insuffi cient re-absorption of calcium and phosphorus in the kidney. The serum protein levels of both minerals drops, resulting in the case of calcium in hyperparathyroidism (the excessive secretion of parathyroid hormone by one or several parathyroid glands). The parathyroid hormone and the remaining vitamin D then cause the demineralization and weakening of the bones. This leads to the malformations typical of rickets: bowlegs, knock-knees, a deviation of the spine, a beady appearance of the ribs (rachitic rosary), and narrowed chest and pelvis. These malformations are purely mechanical, because the bones lack the resilience to sustain normal strain. Furthermore, rachitic children are agitated, worried and irritable, are pale, perspire abnormally from the head, their muscles are soft and lack tonus, leading to a distension of the abdomen, and frequently have diarrhoea.

Hypocalcaemic tetany (spasms of the extremities caused by calcium defi ciency in the blood) can also occur. Rickets itself is not deadly, but increases the risk of mortality owing to an increased liability to respiratory infection. Its prognosis is nevertheless fairly good, because bone deformations tend to correct themselves spontaneously during growth.

Osteomalacia is the manifestation of vitamin D defi ciency in the adult. It affects mainly women of childbearing age whose calcium levels have been weakened by repeated pregnancies. Problems are aggravated if they have suffered from rickets in their childhood, if social customs require them to remain indoors, or if they come from poor backgrounds whose access to food is inadequate. The elderly are also vulnerable to this defi ciency because of their often neglected diet, their physical and psychological limitations in going out, and their reduced intestinal absorption of calcium; osteomalacia is in this case frequently combined with osteoporosis. Osteomalacia causes muscular weakness, bone pains and pelvic deformations that result in serious obstetric complications in women of childbearing age. Deformations resulting from osteomalacia are practically irreversible, or cnly through orthopaedic surgery.

The treatment of rickets and osteomalacia consists of daily doses of 25 to 125 \ig of vitamin D for 1 month, in addition to 1 to 2 g of calcium lactate per day, in order to re-mineralize the bones and avert hypocalcaemic tetany. Measures must then be taken to promote exposure to the sun and improve the diet; this is usually extremely diffi cult, as it implies addressing strong cultural values and poverty. In Western countries, the decline in school and domestic education, and the alarming increase of poverty may well cause a fresh upsurge of rickets.

Requirements: the minimum daily requirement to prevent rickets and osteomalacia is 100 IU (2.5 \ig). This does not mean much, as the proportion of endogenous synthesis is unknown. Exposure to the sun and diet vary considerably, and a daily intake in the food is therefore recommended today. It should be 400 IU (10 \ig) for children, and 100 IU (2.5 \ig) for adults.

Toxicity: vitamin D quickly becomes toxic, that is, as of doses 5 times the recommended intake. The result is hypercalcaemia in children and nephrocalcinosis in adults. In children signs of intoxication include appetite loss, often combined with nausea and vomiting. The child loses weight, is irritable and becomes depressed. Intoxication can be fatal.

Tocopherols or Vitamin E: Introduction: vitamin E is the generic reference to 8 related molecules (isomers) whose biological activities differ; the four most common are oc-tocopherol, (3-tocopherol, ytocopherol and 5-tocopherol. Little is still known about vitamin E. Various signs of defi ciency have been documented for animals, but human defi ciency appeared to be non-existent - vitamin E has only recently proven to be a real vitamin, and thus essential, for man.

Source: octocopherol and y-tocopherol are the forms most commonly found in nature, mainly in wheat germ, sunfl ower, saffl ower, rapeseed, groundnut, corn and olive oils. Other animal and vegetable foods on average only contain approximately 5% of the vegetable oil content. Some oils, such as soy oil, contain considerably more y-tocopherol than oc-tocopherol. oc-tocopherol is the isomer that contributes most to vitamin activity. (3-tocopherol, y-tocopherol and 5-tocopherol respectively contain only 40 to 50%, 10 to 30% and approximately 1% of the activity of oc-tocopherol. This once again leads to the use of international units, with the following values:

oc-tocopherol: (3-tocopherol: y-tocopherol : 5-tocopherol:

1.49 IU/mg 0.60 IU/mg 0.15 - 0.45 IU/mg1 0.015 IU/mg

1 IU = 0.67 mg 1 IU = 1.67 mg IU = 6.67 - 2.22 mg 1 IU = 66.7 mg

It is diffi cult not only to establish food composition tables but also to utilize them for any given diet because of the variable activity of the different isomers, their instability to heat, oxygen and some food preparations, and the seasonal variations of their concentration in food. The real or effective vitamin E diet content generally has little to do with values contained in tables.

Absorption: the absorption of vitamin E occurs mainly in the middle area of the small intestine. Normal dietary intake leads to the absorption of approximately 50% of vitamin E; this proportion is inversely proportional to the ingested amount. The presence of lipids in the diet promotes absorption, which also depends on bile salts and pancreatic enzymes. At this stage, no further reliable knowledge exists as to vitamin E absorption. Metabolism, storage and excretion: what is known about the vitamin E metabolism largely comes from animal research, in particular rats. The vitamin concentration in tissue rises with intake; on the other hand, different tissues and organs accommodate very different vitamin E concentrations, without it being clear why. The vitamin accumulates especially in membrane-rich cell fractions. The organs that contain most vitamin E are adipose tissue, the liver and muscle, and these are considered to be storage organs. Little is known about the vitamin E metabolism: it appears to be very slow, and the excess vitamin is excreted as such in the faeces.

Function: current knowledge suggests that vitamin E functions as an antioxidant in cell membranes. In particular, it is thought to protect polyunsaturated fatty acids from free radicals, to which the former are highly vulnerable. Some signs of vitamin E defi ciency in animals have disappeared completely following the administration of antioxidants.

Defi ciency: the only certainty regarding human vitamin E defi ciency is the increasing sensitivity of red blood cells to *in vitro* haemolysis, and their reduced *in vivo* lifespan when plasma vitamin E levels fall below 0.5 ml/dl. For want of a better threshold, plasma vitamin E levels lower than 0.5 ml/dl are considered to indicate defi ciency. Preterm (or premature) infants and most patients suffering from intestinal malabsorption (for whatever reason) fall in this category. Vitamin E defi ciency was formerly suspected of causing specifi c pathologies among preterm infants, such as retinopathy of prematurity (ROP) and haemolytic anaemia. However, recent research appears to contradict these hypotheses. In patients suffering from malabsorption, the relation between low plasma vitamin E levels and specifi c disorders, such as Duchenne's myopathy, could not be demonstrated either. On the other hand, the lifespan of erythrocytes is reduced in these patients, and this can be corrected by the daily administration of 100 to 200 IU of vitamin E. This confi rms the physiological role of vitamin E, and its inclusion among essential nutrients. Recommended daily therapeutic doses in case of malabsorption are 25 to 50 IU for infants, 50 to 100 IU for children from 1 to 10 years, 100 IU for children and teenagers from 10 to 18 years, and 200 IU for teenagers and adults above 18.

Requirements: the daily minimum adult requirement to maintain plasma tocopherol levels above 0.5 ml/dl has been shown to be 2 mg of á-tocopherol (H" 3 IU).

Pharmacological intake: there is currently no concrete evidence that pharmacological doses of vitamin E provide any benefi t whatsoever.

Toxicity: no toxicity has been observed in cases of excessive daily vitamin E intake, such as 100 to 800 mg; this may simply be due to the fact that at such levels, most of the vitamin is probably not absorbed. Vitamin E is however assumed to be toxic and, because tocopherol accumulates in tissues according to intake, caution is called for especially in case of intravenous vitamin administration.

Phylloquinone or Vitamin K: Source: vitamin K (the generic name of a range of compounds whose vitamin activity is the same as phylloquinone or vitamin K_1) is common in the vegetable, animal and bacterial kingdoms. However, only plants and bacteria can synthesize the essential part of the molecule. This is found in high concentration in green vegetables (spinach, cabbage, caulifl ower, broccoli, and lettuce), dairy and meat products, fruits and cereals. Major differences exist between foods belonging to the same category. Either way, vitamin K requirements are low, and most foods provide enough of it to prevent defi ciency; it appears that vitamin K is also produced in the intestine, which thereby also seems to contribute to a regular supply.

Absorption: vitamin K absorption requires bile salts and pancreatic juices. The vitamin is incorporated into the chylomicrons; it is absorbed in the small intestine and reappears in the lymph. Absorption effi ciency varies between 40 and 80%.

Metabolism, storage and excretion: the turnover of vitamin K is extremely fast (of the order of one day), with an overall estimated amount of approximately 100 ìg; it is therefore the vitamin whose stocks in the organism are smallest, and whose metabolism is fastest. It is however worth noting that the vitamin's metabolic cycle allows it to be stored in the liver, and without this cycle its metabolism would be faster still. Research into the radioactive vitamin has shown that, after its utilization as an enzyme cofactor, vitamin K is rapidly degraded into a range of products that are to date incorrectly identifi ed, and that these products are found in the faeces and urine.

Function: as a coenzyme, vitamin K contributes to the formation of seven proteins involved in the chain reaction that leads to blood clotting (or coagulation).

Defi ciency: vitamin K defi ciency manifests itself in bleeding and haemorrhaging. It is virtually non-existent among adults, owing to the presence of suffi cient amounts in almost all food types, but also because of the vitamin's preservation cycle and its synthesis by the intestinal fl ora. On the other hand, newborn (particularly preterm) babies are liable to develop haemorrhagic disease because their blood clotting capacity is initially very weak, their diet is low in vitamin K and their intestinal tract is sterile. The coagulation capacity usually improves spontaneously within a few days. It is nevertheless recommended to administer an intra-muscular 1 mg dose of phylloquinone to newborns.

The elderly can develop vitamin K defi ciency, particularly when their diet is poor, because the need for vitamin K increases with age, without it being known exactly why (possible explanations include less effi cient absorption, diminished hepatic function, faster turnover, and/or effectively increased requirements). Primary vitamin K defi ciency is rare, but secondary defi ciency can arise for several reasons: ineffective lipid absorption (obstruction of the bile ducts and malabsorption), intake of antibiotics deleterious to the intestinal fl ora, excessive anticoagulant doses, or the excessive intake of vitamins A and E. Secondary defi ciency appears readily, because the overall amount of vitamin K is so small and its turnover so fast that any problem has immediate repercussions - this is never so fast in the case of other vitamins.

Requirements: because normal diets contain enough vitamin K and the intestine also produces it, it is diffi cult to assess minimum vitamin K requirements. Research has nevertheless shown daily requirements to be of the order of 0.5 to 1.0 ìg of vitamin K per kilogram of body weight.

Toxicity: phylloquinone or vitamin K_1 is not toxic, even at high doses; on the other hand, menadione (or vitamin K_3) is, and should therefore not be used in the treatment of secondary defi ciency.

Minerals

Minerals are elementary chemical compounds whose atomic characteristics make them indispensable to the organism. Minerals include trace elements and are essential because they cannot be produced by the organism and therefore must be found, through food and drinking water in the mineral environment; this depends on the nature of the soil and the surface water. Minerals include major elements such as calcium and phosphorus, and trace elements of which the organism contains less than a few grams (sometimes as little as a few milligrams).

Although some minerals are present in the organism in only minute amounts, this does not mean that their defi ciency is harmless. Mineral biochemistry is a developing science, and it is far from mastered. As a result, detailed information is not available for all essential minerals.

The main minerals are the electrolytes (sodium, potassium, and chlorine), the minerals found mainly in the skeleton (calcium, phosphorus, and magnesium), and iron, zinc, iodine, copper, selenium, manganese, molybdenum, and chromium. Cobalt could also be mentioned, but it seems that it only acts as a constituent of vitamin B_{12} (see above). Trace metals exist, such as tin, bromine, lead and probably others that may well be essential to man, but research has yet to confi rm this.

Specifi c defi ciencies have not been identifi ed either. In terms of nutritional needs, electrolytes do not pose a major problem, other than in cases of dehydration. Phosphorus is so abundant in the vegetable kingdom that dietary defi ciency is virtually impossible. It is also likely that calcium defi ciency due to dietary inadequacy is rare, and problems of osteomalacia and rickets are due to vitamin D defi ciency, and osteoporosis to demineralization, whose possible connection to an inadequate dietary calcium intake remains unknown. Sulphur is supplied by proteins: its defi ciency is therefore likely to be concealed by protein defi ciency, or its effects to be confused with the latter's. Copper, manganese, magnesium, chromium, molybdenum and selenium defi ciencies do not pose public health problems, because the diet should in principle provide adequate supplies. However, in the case of severe malnutrition causing the complete loss of tissue components, or of seriously restricted access to food (as is the case in some imprisonment situations), defi ciency in these minerals and others should be taken very seriously. They must then be administered in therapeutic doses when treating severe malnutrition, and at levels equivalent to reference intakes in the case of imprisonment or any other situation where the diet is known to be defi cient. Ultimately, the minerals whose clinical defi ciency is most frequently confi rmed are iron and iodine. It is however possible that sub-clinical zinc defi ciency is more common, and plays a greater role than thought until recently in retarded growth and loss of appetite, which would corroborate zinc belonging to Type II nutrients.

Electrolytes

The three main electrolytes are sodium, potassium and chlorine. They account for the osmotic pressure of fl uids in the organism, and their repartition in the body determines their volume within (intra-cellular) and outside (extra-cellular) cells.

- Sodium is specifi cally an extra-cellular cation (or positively-charged ion), whose role is to maintain the volume of extra-cellular fl uids, the osmotic pressure of these fl uids, and the acid-base balance. It also contributes to the transmission of impulses in and between nerves and muscle, and to the transport phenomena of metabolites within cells.
- Unlike sodium, potassium is a specifi cally intra-cellular cation, together with magnesium, organic phosphates and protein anions, where its role is complementary to that played by sodium, for functions that are essentially the same as those of sodium.
- Chlorine is the electrochemical counterpart of sodium and potassium.

The chemistry of electrolytes is quite complex, as is that of hydrous and acid-base balances. These aspects do not relate to humanitarian action because when disorders arise, they require medical expertise and laboratory facilities. In crisis settings, on the other hand, victims (malnourished or not) often require rehydration salts whose composition differs according to whether there is severe malnutrition or not.

Dehydration can have two causes.

1. Water shortage that manifests itself in increased plasma chlorine and sodium levels; this occurs in case of insuffi cient ingestion of water, either because its availability is insuffi cient, or because one does not receive enough. This is typical when one depends on third parties to obtain drinking water, as is the case for small children but also, frequently, prisoners. The treatment simply consists of drinking water or, as a last resort only, the intravenous administration of a 2.5–5% dextrose solution (pure water would cause haemolysis).
2. The combined defi ciency of chlorine, sodium and water, the most frequent form of dehydration by far and whose most common – and thus best-known – causes are diarrhoea, vomiting and excessive perspiration. The preferred treatment of diarrhoea is the oral administration of rehydration salts dissolved in water; these salts are found in sachets and are based on two standard formulae:

either	*or*
3.5 g of sodium chloride	3.5 g of sodium chloride
2.5 g of sodium bicarbonate	2.9 g of trisodium citrate dihydrate
1.5 g of potassium chloride	1.5 g of potassium chloride
20 g of glucose	20 g of glucose

Both formulae are to be dissolved in 1 litre of drinking water. The dosage is 1 litre per 24 hours for infants, 1 litre per 8 to 24 hours (according to age) for children, and at will for adults. The primary purpose is rehydration, and then the compensation of losses as they occur.

Other specifi c defi ciencies, such as chlorine or potassium defi ciency, result mainly from medical problems (thus warranting medical expertise), and rarely arise in humanitarian action.

Electrolyte surges are essentially caused by the overly high intake of salt or by physiological disorders. It has long been thought that excessive sodium intake *via* salt affected high blood pressure signifi cantly. This view was later seriously challenged, but nowadays it does appear that salt intake greater than 8 g/day does indeed result in an increase in blood pressure. It is therefore recommended not to exceed this intake, which must allow for the diet's salt content. Moreover, excessive salt intake displaces calcium from the bones and could thus contribute to osteoporosis.

Bone minerals

The three minerals predominant in the bones are calcium, bound in the bones to phosphorus (in a crystal form called hydroxyapatite), and magnesium.

Calcium

Source: calcium is found (in decreasing order of concentration) in hard cheese (750 mg/100 g), oilseeds and in particular almonds, walnuts and hazelnuts (175 mg/100 g), soft cheese and milk (130 mg/100 g), and fi nally dried fruit (100 mg/100 g) (Randoin, 1982).

Absorption: calcium is absorbed in two ways. One is active, and is regulated by vitamin D, mainly in the duodenum; the other is passive and occurs throughout the intestine, but mainly in the ileum. Calcium absorption also depends largely on the other nutrients contained in the diet, hormonal levels, and physiological conditions such as pregnancy and breastfeeding. The absorption rate of calcium is only 25 to 50% of the ingested amount, and the remainder is excreted in the faeces. However, in case of need, the organism can retain much more calcium – as a result, defi ciency resulting from an inadequate diet is rare.

Metabolism, storage and excretion: bones are living tissue, undergoing changes permanently. The calcium contained in the organism therefore perpetually circulates between the bones (that contain 99% of the organism's overall calcium) and the bloodstream that contains the remaining 1%. The concentration of calcium in the bloodstream is strictly regulated because of the vital role played by calcium in many physiological processes. This regulation occurs through absorption, excretion and calcium circulation between the bloodstream and the bones, which store it. The parathyroid hormone, calcitonin (secretions of the parathyroid and thyroid gland respectively) and vitamin D all regulate the homeostasis of calcium. In the bones, the calcium metabolism is determined by age, hormonal secretion, and physical exercise. The skeleton demineralizes in postmenopausal women and men above

65; in women, the impact is far greater because of the hormonal changes associated with menopause. Physical exercise maintains the bony mass, which atrophies in case of immobility just like any unused organ. Calcium is excreted in practically equal parts in the urine and the faeces.

Function: calcium plays a fundamental structural role in bones and teeth, and is their chief mineral constituent. Calcium also performs a fundamental trigger function in a number of physiological processes such as enzyme activation, muscle contraction, vesicular secretion, the transmission of nerve impulses, the clotting of blood and cell division.

Defi ciency: calcium defi ciency caused by dietary inadequacy is rare, and is limited to specifi c circumstances (e.g. the overall defi cient diet in some prison settings). In the case of osteoporosis (the thinning of bones observed in old age), the administration of calcium supplements does not appear to impede decalcifi cation signifi cantly. As an illustration, in developing countries where calcium intake is minimal but physical exercise considerable, osteoporosis is less common in postmenopausal women than in industrialized countries, where calcium intake is greater, but physical exercise is limited. The preferred treatment of osteoporosis is the administration of oestrogen. In most cases, intake is adequate in view of the adaptability of absorption in case of low intake. Breastfeeding women secrete constant amounts of calcium in maternal milk, whatever their intake. This indicates that an intake that is inadequate in terms of breastfeeding is compensated by the calcium stored in the bones, implying a demineralization of the bones. Nevertheless, this demineralization is reversible after the cessation of breastfeeding.

Requirements: calcium requirements are determined by excretion and absorption effi ciency, but the latter itself is infl uenced by a number of factors such as diet. As a result, it is diffi cult to formulate recommendations. On the other hand, additional needs related to breastfeeding are known and should be incorporated into the diet to avert the risk of bone demineralization in the mother.

Pharmacological intake: pharmacological intakes of calcium appear to be useless, and recommended intakes are therefore suffi cient.

Toxicity: overly high calcium intake is not toxic, and does not increase the risk of kidney stone development. It does however impede iron absorption, and it is therefore preferable to adhere to recommended intakes.

Phosphorus

Source: phosphorus is abundant in animal products, oilseeds, legumes and cereals. It is therefore improbable for its defi ciency to be caused by an inadequate diet.

Absorption: man absorbs between 60 and 70% of ingested phosphorus, and the absorption of animal phosphorus is more effi cient than that of vegetable origin. Like calcium, the smaller the amount of phosphorus supplied by the diet, the more effi cient its absorption is. To date, phosphorus absorption remains ill-known; however, both an active, saturable, transport mechanism and a non-saturable mechanism (depending on the phosphorus concentration) exist. Vitamin D, which facilitates the absorption of calcium, contributes to the absorption of phosphorus likewise.

Metabolism, storage and excretion: the phosphorus homeostasis occurs in the intestine, the kidneys, bone and lean mass. Plasma phosphorus levels are mainly regulated by the kidneys that reabsorb or excrete phosphorus according to intake. The intestine, however, also plays a signifi cant role by improving its absorption effi ciency in case of low intake. Like calcium, phosphorus is mainly stored in the bones and teeth (that together contain 85% of the overall phosphorus in the organism), while 14% is found in muscle. Phosphorus excretion occurs fi rstly in the kidney, and its re-absorption is regulated by the parathyroid hormone, according to intake.

Function: phosphorus performs a number of essential functions in the organism. It combines with calcium in bone formation, it serves as a construction unit in the great molecular formations of living beings, it is indispensable to the storage and release of chemical energy, it is essential to membrane structure and permeability, and it regulates many enzyme activities.

Defi ciency: phosphorus defi ciency caused by dietary inadequacy is rare. However, in the elderly, phosphorus absorption falls, whereas its excretion in the urine increases; this can cause a defi ciency that manifests itself by anorexia, muscle weakness, debility and bone pains. Requirements: the phosphorus needs are not well known, and they are therefore assimilated on a molar basis to calcium needs.

Toxicity: infants fed on unbalanced formula supplying excessive phosphorus with respect to calcium (i.e. more than 2 parts of phosphorus for 1 part of calcium) can suffer hypocalcaemia and tetany. Recommended intakes should therefore be adhered to strictly, and the phosphorus-calcium ratio should be inferior to 2 (>2:1).

Magnesium

Source: all unprocessed foods contain magnesium, but concentrations vary greatly. Milk, wholemeal cereals, legumes, vegetables and potatoes contain particularly high concentrations of magnesium. Vegetables are generally rich in magnesium (its role to chlorophyll is analogous to that of iron to haemoglobin).

Absorption: the absorption of magnesium, as is the case for other minerals, occurs through an active mechanism for moderate intakes, and this mechanism saturates as intakes increase. Magnesium is then absorbed passively. Absorption rates vary between 20 and 70% of the intake.

Metabolism, storage and excretion: approximately two-thirds of magnesium are found in the bones and teeth, one-quarter in muscle, and practically all the rest in other cells, while less than 1% is found in extra-cellular fl uids. Magnesium's homeostasis is similar to calcium's and occurs between the reserves stored in the bones, intestinal absorption and urinary excretion. Little is yet known regarding its hormonal regulation mechanism. Its excretion through urine is as adaptable as its intestinal absorption.

Function: magnesium is a vital element and performs many, similarly important, functions. More than 300 reactions in the organism are currently attributed to magnesium. It is of particular importance to the building and development of the bone structure, the synthesis of lipids and proteins, phosphorylation and de-phosphorylation mechanisms, metabolic energy production channels and the maintenance of normal nerve signalling and muscle contraction.

Defi ciency: magnesium defi ciency caused by dietary inadequacy is improbable because all unprocessed foods, including staple foods, generally provide a good source of magnesium, and the average daily intake is usually appropriate (150 to 500 mg). However, defi ciency can result from malabsorption and during recovery from severe malnutrition. It is therefore fundamental to ensure an adequate magnesium intake during nutritional catch-up, because it is a Type II nutrient. Requirements: because dietary inadequacy can hardly account for magnesium defi ciency, it is diffi cult to determine magnesium requirements accurately – reference to a suitable intake range (150 to 500 mg/day) is therefore preferable. On the other hand, magnesium requirements during recovery from severe malnutrition are quite precise. Toxicity: overly high oral intake is not toxic because of the adaptability of magnesium excretion by the kidney. Excessive intake can nevertheless cause passing diarrhoea. On the other hand, excessive intravenous administration can cause a fatal depression of the central nervous system and muscular paralysis.

Other minerals

Iron

Source: the following, listed in order of importance, are sources of iron (Randoin, 1982):

- parsley (> 10 mg/100 g): although excellent, it is uncommon to eat parsley as a vegetable, and iron intake through parsley is therefore usually limited;
- liver, legumes and egg yolk all contain between 5 and 10 mg/100 g; egg yolk unfortunately inhibits iron absorption (that is, its own iron content, and that supplied by other foods);
- meat, oilseeds, wholemeal fl our, watercress and spinach all contain between 2 and 4 mg/100 g;
- most fresh fruits and vegetables, cheese and white fl our all contain between 1 and 0.5 mg/100 g; they are thus poor in iron, like fermented beverages, milk and fruits such as apples, pears and cherries that are poorer still, containing less than 0.4 mg/100 g;
- the iron contained in drinking water and in cooking utensils can represent a signifi cant source, but it is diffi cult to take them into account owing to their considerable variability.

Absorption: iron absorption is a phenomenon of particular importance, because it is at this level that the organism attempts to maintain a balance so as to avoid defi ciency and excess, without resorting to loss modulation. Iron absorption occurs in two ways, according to whether it is bound to the haemoglobin or myoglobin haeme group. Isolated non-haeme iron is dissolved by gastric juices, reduced into Type II iron (i.e. ferrous iron), and bound to other molecules. Where such molecules are small – such as ascorbic acid, sugars, and amino acids – they promote the absorption of iron. Some elements nevertheless impede its absorption; these are tannins, phytates, phosphates (found in wholemeal cereals and oilseeds), egg yolk, tea, and coffee. Milk and soy proteins also inhibit iron absorption. The phytates and tannins contained in tea and coffee can reduce iron absorption by approximately half. Absorption proper occurs in the small intestine, particularly in the duodenum. Organic acids, bile salts, and the peptide by-products of protein digestion all facilitate passage through the mucous membrane.

Iron binds with a specifi c protein to penetrate epithelial cells. Upon entering plasma, iron is oxidized into Type III iron (ferric iron), most is then bound to transferrin, and the rest to ferritin. Haeme iron obtained from meat/fi sh and blood is absorbed in a different way. The haeme group is absorbed directly by the cells of the intestinal mucous membrane; the iron is then separated from the haeme group and delivered into the plasma in the form of Type III iron. The absorption of haeme iron is considerably higher (approximately 25%) than that of non-haeme iron (approximately 10 to 15%); it is not affected by absorption inhibiting or promoting factors that affect non-haeme iron. Even in small amounts, haeme iron contained in the diet considerably increases the absorption of non-haeme iron. Generally speaking, this comment applies to the different promoters and inhibitors of iron absorption whose effects are cumulative. As an example, the ingestion of a small portion of fi sh or meat together with cereals greatly increases the absorption of the iron contained in the latter; this effect will be strengthened by the consumption of fruit, or weakened by the consumption of tea. Calcium, for its part, inhibits iron absorption (both haeme and non-haeme); a glass of milk containing approximately 160 mg of calcium inhibits iron absorption by more than 50%.

Iron absorption increases with food intake, but in decreasing proportions. The mechanisms regulating iron absorption boost it in case of iron defi ciency, and restrict it in case of excess – the reasons for this remain unclear. Healthy individuals absorb approximately 5 to 10% of the iron contained in their food, whereas defi cient individuals absorb between 10 and 20%. From a quantitative perspective, the maximum iron absorption among healthy adults is of the order of 1 to 2 mg/day, while it is in the vicinity of 3 to 6 mg for defi cient individuals (Shils, 1994).

Metabolism, storage and excretion: after its absorption, iron is transported to the bone marrow to be integrated into the haemoglobin during the synthesis of the red blood cells. From there, it remains in the blood together with the red cells for approximately 4 months. Following the destruction of the red blood cells by phagocytes (the lifespan of red blood cell is approximately 4 months), most of the iron returns to the plasma and extra-cellular fl uids, and a small amount is stored with ferritin and haemosiderin, which return their iron to plasma after their destruction, according to their turnover cycle. Most of the iron then resumes its cycle by returning to the bone marrow for the synthesis of red blood cells. The iron transport protein in the plasma is transferrin; it transports the iron to the bone marrow, but also to any other cell that requires it. Approximately two-thirds of the overall iron contained in the organism is located in the haemoglobin, approximately one-quarter is stored, a small proportion is found in a muscle protein (myoglobin), and the rest is found in extra-cellular fl uids and cells.

Less than 0.1% of the iron is in circulation with transferrin. The organism is remarkably effi cient in saving iron through almost complete recycling, whatever its level within its cycle between plasma and red blood cells. Defi ciency is therefore mainly caused by abnormal losses and limited absorption The excretion of iron is largely passive and related to inevitable losses or "leaks" of the organism: through the intestine, urine, bile, exfoliation (shedding of the skin) – together accounting for approximately 1 mg/day – and menstrual bleeding in women of childbearing age (in the vicinity of 25 mg per cycle). Pregnancy and breastfeeding also demand high iron levels in comparison to the absorption capacity: beyond normal losses that persist throughout pregnancy,

200 to 370 mg are transferred to the foetus, some 90 mg are utilized for the placenta and the umbilical cord, and an average 250 mg are lost in the bleeding associated with delivery; breastfeeding provides the infant with 0.5 to 1 mg of iron per day.

Function: the primary function of iron is obviously to transport oxygen and carbon dioxide in the organism, *via* red blood cells. Iron is vital for the production of anaerobic energy, being present in the active groups of most of the enzymes that contribute to this production. It also contributes to the transport of electrons by cytochromes in the respiratory chain.

Defi ciency: iron defi ciency is no doubt the most common deficiency, and mainly affects women of childbearing age. It is discussed below.

Requirements: a distinction must be made between absorbed and ingested iron, because the amount absorbed is considerably lower than that contained in the diet.

Pharmacological intake: there is no justifi cation for pharmacological iron intakes, particularly in view of its toxicity. However, supplements are often necessary to correct defi ciency.

Toxicity: the excessive intake of iron is toxic. A normal diet, however, does not lead to iron excesses, because its absorption is regulated effi ciently. Excess pathologies – haemachromatosis (where excess iron deposited in organs causes them damage) or haemosiderosis (iron overload without obvious tissue damage) – can arise only if regulation is inadequate (hereditary metabolic aberrations), in case of excessive intake resulting from specifi c circumstances, or in the case of particular ailments, such as hepatic cirrhosis, and pancreatic insuffi ciency. The circumstances leading to excessive iron intake include protracted consumption of supplements by individuals who are not anaemic, and the consumption of traditional beverages fermented in iron containers that oxidize and release large amounts of iron into the fermentation medium.

Iodine

Source: the iodine content of food is mainly determined by the iodine concentration in the soil and groundwater, and this concentration is related to geology. During the formation of the earth, iodine was quite widespread, but was subsequently leached by rain, erosion, glaciations and fl oods. As a result, most terrestrial iodine is now found in the seas and in deep terrestrial layers, in the chemical form of iodide. Solar radiation transforms marine iodine into elementary iodine, which is volatile and enters the atmosphere before returning to earth through precipitations; it fi nally returns to the sea according to rainfall and drainage. This iodine cycle nevertheless does not compensate for losses over time, as iodine returning to earth is instantly evacuated by soil drainage. This is why rugged mountains, well-irrigated and well-drained highlands, and fl ood-prone plains are most vulnerable to disorders related to iodine defi ciency. It is not useful for tables to indicate the iodine content of different food types, because of its high variability. On the other hand sea fi sh, seafood and seaweed are iodine-rich, as are coastal plants and the animals that eat them. Nowadays the most reliable source of iodine in many countries is salt, enriched in potassium iodate at between 30 to 50 mg of iodine/kg of salt (PAHO, 1986) - this is referred to as iodized salt. The iodine must be in the form of potassium iodate and not potassium iodide, which is too vulnerable to humidity and heat. One gram of potassium iodate contains 0.6 g of iodine. Thus, enrichment will consist of 50 to 83 mg of potassium iodate/kg of salt.

Function: iodine is an essential element used by the thyroid gland to produce thyroid hormones; the latter act as regulators of the metabolism, and ensure normal growth and development (both physical and mental) in children.

Defi ciency: iodine defi ciency is a serious threat to approximately one-quarter of humanity and, in some regions, constitutes a major public health problem. It is described in Chapter VIII.

Zinc

Source: zinc is found in most foods, but its concentration varies greatly. Its major sources include animal products (3–5 mg/100 g), cereals and legumes (2–3 mg/100 g). In countries where the consumption of animal products is high, the diet contains an adequate amount of zinc. In contrast, where animal products are not a major component of the diet, cereals and legumes provide most of the required zinc; this can prove inadequate if the cereals are overly processed or refi ned, because zinc is located mainly in the peripheral layers of the grain, and these are shed proportionately to the degree of processing. For example, wholemeal wheat fl our contains approximately 5.5 mg of zinc/ 100 g, whereas white fl our only contains 1.7 mg/100 g i.e. a 70% loss.

Absorption: zinc absorption is similar to that of iron insofar as it increases with its intake, but in decreasing proportions. Zinc is absorbed in the small intestine. The level of its absorption depends on the presence of promoting or inhibiting molecules; the latter are phytates, tannins and oxalates. On the other hand, zinc inhibits the absorption of copper.

Metabolism, storage and excretion: the zinc content in the organism depends on the effi ciency of its absorption, which rises in case of shortage or defi ciency, and falls in case of excess. However, as mentioned above, absorption continues to increase according to intake, even if in a smaller proportion; excesses must therefore be disposed of, because zinc can be toxic. This is done through faecal excretion, which increases in case of excessive intake. Zinc absorption increases in the fi nal stages of pregnancy; it decreases with age, but so do losses, and this facilitates the maintenance of a balance. Zinc is not stored, strictly speaking, and insuffi cient intakes rapidly lead to indications of defi ciency.

Function: zinc performs many essential functions in the organism, and is included in Type II nutrients accordingly. It is necessary to no less than 200 enzymes, it is a constituent of the cell membrane, and contributes to the stabilization of ribonucleic and desoxyribonucleic acids (RNA and DNA respectively) and ribosomes. The considerable contemporary research surrounding zinc may well lead to the discovery of further functions.

Defi ciency: acute zinc defi ciency is caused by a genetic disease – known as *acrodermatitis enteropathica* and characterized by an impaired zinc uptake from the intestine, zinc-defi cient parenteral nutrition (i.e. intravenous), different types of malabsorption, alcoholism, and kidney and metabolic disorders. In the Near East, zinc defi ciency is blamed for dwarfi sm among young teenagers and delayed sexual maturity. Moderate zinc defi ciency could be more common than assumed until recently, and results in growth retardation. Zinc defi ciency develops with the severity of acute malnutrition, and addressing this condition requires the administration of zinc in therapeutic doses, because zinc determines nutritional recovery as much as other Type II nutrients do.

Toxicity: excessive zinc intake can cause chronic or acute disorders. Acute intoxication causes gastric pain, nausea, vomiting, and diarrhoea. Intoxication can result from the ingestion of beverages contaminated by the release of zinc in galvanized containers. Doses above 200 mg always cause vomiting. Beyond this threshold, they can be fatal. Chronic intoxication begins with zinc supplementation doses no higher than 25 mg/day, which result in a secondary copper defi ciency by competition between the two elements in their intestinal absorption. Zinc supplements of the order of 150 mg/day result in low plasma levels of high-density lipoproteins (the risk of cardio-vascular disease is inversely proportional to these levels), and gastric erosion, and weaken the immune system (Shils, 1994).

Copper

Source: most foods contain copper, the richest sources (0.3–2 mg/100 g) being shellfi sh, oilseeds (including cocoa powder), legumes, and wholemeal cereals.

Absorption: like other metals, the absorption of copper increases with intake, but in decreasing proportions. Zinc inhibits the absorption of copper.

Metabolism, storage and excretion: following its absorption, copper is transported to the liver where it binds with a protein called ceruloplasmin, which transports it to the tissues. It is possible that copper could be stored in the liver, but in limited amounts. Little is known about the copper excretion mechanism, other than in the intestine by bile salts. The greater the copper intake or defi ciency, the smaller its excretion is. Copper homeostasis depends on its intake and excretion.

Function: copper contributes to a number of oxidation-reduction reactions, as an enzyme constituent. These enzymes are essential in the respiratory chain, the synthesis of collagen proteins, the synthesis and maintenance of myelin, the synthesis of neuro-transmitters, the iron metabolism, and the protection against oxidation risks. Like zinc, copper is assumed to perform many more functions and these are currently under investigation.

Defi ciency: copper defi ciency can affect preterm babies, infants fed on non-modifi ed cow milk, and children recovering from severe malnutrition. Copper defi ciency manifests itself by leucopaenia, neutropaenia, skeletal anomalies, and higher liability to infection. It is possible that inadequate intakes cause cardiovascular disease in adults.

Requirements: recommended intakes are provided in Chapter IV.

Toxicity: copper is toxic and intoxication is accidental. It is caused by the ingestion of acid beverages stored in copper containers or by winegrowers who use copper sulphate. Symptoms of copper intoxication include gastric pain, nausea, vomiting, and diarrhoea. Acute intoxication leads to coma, hepatic necrosis, vascular collapse and, ultimately, death.

Low white blood cell levels in the blood.

Low levels of white blood cells known as neutrophils in the blood.

Selenium

Source: selenium is found mainly in sea products, offal, meat, cereals, and legumes.

Absorption: selenium is usually ingested together with methionine and cysteine, and is well absorbed. Selenium homeostasis does not depend on its absorption.

Metabolism, storage and excretion: little is known about the selenium metabolism, but its excretion is mainly urinary, and its regulation determines selenium homeostasis.

Function: the main function of selenium is to act as an antioxidant agent. It probably performs other functions, such as the protection of cell immunity, and these are currently under investigation.

Defi ciency: selenium defi ciency causes Keshan disease, a fatal form of cardiomyopathy (heart muscle disease); however, the involvement of other factors appears to be required for the disease to develop. It is possible that selenium defi ciency plays a role in the aetiology (i.e. cause) of kwashiorkor.

Requirements: recommended intakes are provided in Chapter IV.

Toxicity: selenium overdose can originate in the diet in areas where the soil is selenium-rich, or by the ingestion of tablets. High doses of selenium are toxic, and cause nausea, diarrhoea, irritability, fatigue, peripheral neuropathy, balding, and brittle nails (Shils, 1994).

Chrome

Chrome is today recognized to be an essential nutrient that promotes the action of insulin and thus infl uences the mechanisms of glucides, lipids and proteins (Shils, 1994). Human defi ciency has not been demonstrated to date.

Other trace metals

Other trace metals appear to be essential and their defi ciency poses no particular problem because their intake is usually adequate. These include boron, which infl uences the mineral metabolism, manganese, an enzyme activator and a constituent of some enzymes, molybdenum, also a constituent of some enzymes, and silicon, which contributes to the synthesis of bones and cartilage. Vanadium, bromine, fl uorine, lead and tin could also be essential trace metals, but this remains to be proven. On the other hand, pharmacological doses of fl uorine provide protection against dental cavities, and possibly against fractures associated with osteoporosis.

DEPENDENCY ON OTHER SPECIES

Chapter V discusses the living species that man depends on to meet his nutritional need. This section only recalls a number of important points related to this dependency.

Beyond philosophical and religious considerations, man belongs to the biosphere like all other species. He accounts for approximately 4% of the animal biomass on earth. As such, he consumes and excretes within a vast cycle of matter exchange between the different living species, in an energy fl ow throughout the biosphere. His nutritional dependency on other living beings is total. Man's is thus a predatory position at the end of the food chain. He depends on the sun, green plants, the bacterial kingdom and, to a certain extent, the animal kingdom to meet his nutritional needs. On the other hand, other than a few parasites that are exclusively his, no living species needs man to survive. Man's main originality has been to modify his environment so as to draw as many immediate resources from it as possible. He can thus afford a high population density where an overly prolifi c and invasive organism would otherwise rapidly be restricted by the exhaustion of the resources necessary for its survival.

His overarching priority, consumption, has driven man from the need to preserve a sustainable balance with the species who determine his survival, to the point of threatening some of the biosphere's major equilibriums. A human nutrition manual must mention the key parameter that man depends on nature to survive, that he has the means to upset the biocoenose and the biotope and, as a result, the ecosystem. Man therefore has an enormous responsibility towards nature, if only to ensure his long-term survival, all the more so if pursing the noble goal of guaranteeing health for all. Man is rapidly exhausting the support capacity of the environment, and is playing dangerously with natural resources and their ecological balance. It is crucial for man to recognize his double dependency on nature and on interrelated species, this in relation to vital species and ecosystems of which he is not necessarily aware.

Humanitarian action is particularly concerned, because emergencies often obscure the need for protecting the environment; yet it is nevertheless one of the major stakes of the long-term survival of societies requiring assistance. Humanitarian assistance is often delivered to the detriment of the environment. As an illustration, food distributions to displaced people in an environment that is subjected to desertifi cation can have disastrous effects on the vegetation cover, if it is not combined with the distribution of fuel for cooking. Here again, greater responsibility and foresight are called for.

5

Nutrition Manual

INTRODUCTION

The previous chapter discusses the human nutritional need mainly from a qualitative perspective. This need must also be quantifi ed to refl ect practical daily intake recommendations in order to determine food rations and assess their appropriateness. One diffi culty arises from the fact that the nutrient requirements of seemingly similar individuals (same age group, sex, weight, height and physical activity) differ. A specifi c theoretical model is used in choosing values; although far from perfect, it nevertheless provides an idea of this biological variability. It states that the variability of the nutritional need among a group of reasonably identical individuals (i.e. a homogenous class of individuals) follows more or less a normal distribution.

This distribution illustrates the following thresholds:

- minimum intake (point a) of two standard deviations below the average value; this intake is only suffi cient for a small percentage of observed individuals;
- an average intake (point b) which is adequate for half the observed individuals;
- a safety intake (point c) of two standard deviations above average, which is adequate for almost all the observed individuals.

Evidently, the more the intake approaches point c, the greater the proportion of individuals consuming more than their requirements. The term "adequate" with reference to point b indicates that the intake allows an initially healthy individual to maintain his good health. This intake usually exceeds that required for the clinical signs of defi ciency to disappear. Research continues into the role of many nutrients whose intake, considered today as adequate, could in fact not be so and therefore result in sub-clinical defi ciencies. For lack of more accuracy, experts base their recommendations on available data. Recommendations regarding nutrient requirements make sense only for homogenous classes of individuals. In other words, they refer to groups that are homogenous from a nutritional perspective, that is, according to the specifi c needs arising from growth, pregnancy and breastfeeding, and according to sex and age group.

This study follows the European Commission's approach: within the limits of contemporary knowledge, it provides three values per nutrient and per class of individuals. These values indicate the dispersion of needs (European Commission, 1993).

The Commission moreover proposes the following nomenclature.

PRI: Population Reference Intake (illustrated by point c in Figure 4.1 above). This intake is suffi cient for most healthy members of a given homogeneous group, and can be considered as the safety intake. Generally, the PRI provides the basis for ration calculation and assessment, as it is certain to provide a security margin.

AR: Average Requirement (point b). This point should determine the PRI wherever excessive intake may be harmful, that is, when the nutrient under consideration accumulates in the organism (rather than metabolizing) because its intake exceeds requirements. This is typically the case for energy intake in wealthy Western countries.

LTI: Lowest Threshold Intake (point a). Below this intake level, most members of the group under consideration risk developing metabolic dysfunctions due to defi ciency.

A given population can refl ect several PRIs, depending on sex, age, pregnancy and breastfeeding. It is noteworthy that PRIs are not related to individuals, but to groups of individuals. If not otherwise specifi ed, this study refers to PRIs drawn from the European Commission – other reports defi ne slightly different PRIs, but these differences usually have no operational consequences in the fi eld. The PRIs mentioned in this Chapter assume that the diet covers requirements in other nutrients.

The expression "reference" is equivalent to what other reports state as "recommended" or "advised". It is drawn from the European Commission report, which confi nes itself to recommendations rather than advice.

ENERGY

Daily energy needs are expressed in Average Requirements as opposed to Population Reference Intakes. Indeed, using PRIs as the basis for the calculation of intake leads to an obesity risk for approximately 90% of the population under consideration. Obesity is a major public health problem in industrialized societies, and it is therefore preferable to base recommendations on average requirements. On the other hand, converting average requirements into actual intake removes the corresponding safety margins in humanitarian assistance, in contexts where obesity is usually not a public health problem at all. Adult requirements are provided in relation to light, moderate and heavy daily physical activity, or occupation. Data is adapted from the FAO/WHO/UNU report (WHO, 1985). The basal metabolism (BM) is provided per kilogram for different body mass and age groups, and according to sex, to facilitate calculations if intake recommendations should apply to other multiples of the basal metabolism. Values are rounded to the closest multiple of ten, and upwards if they end with 5 or more (for instance, 2,345 is rounded up to 2,350).

6

Food

INTRODUCTION

This Chapter discusses the different forms of food consumed by man; it also discusses some related notions such as food value, the effects of processing methods on their nutrient content, toxicity, and the quantitative measuring of food. In the framework of humanitarian action, nutrient supplies must be assessed within given population groups, and supplements or alternatives suggested. This Manual could confi ne itself to the description of the commonest staple foods - basically those used in relief operations - such as cereals; but fi eld work attempts to gain an understanding of crisis victims' actual access to food. Thorough assessment often reveals the wide range of food types resorted to by man, and the less obvious resources (such as hunting and gathering) that allow him to survive in spite of appearances. A comprehensive review of all food groups refl ects the diversity of available resources, even - and especially - in crises.

In terms of food, humanitarian action revolves around the following points.

1. Knowing what crisis victims eat from gathering, production, purchases, sharing, and according to their culture.

2. Defi ning normal consumption (eating preferences), the last resort in crisis, and then drawing comparisons with the current situation.

3. Discovering the traditional diet of vulnerable groups, to determine possible defi ciencies (entailing risks of malnutrition).

4. Determining food values to assess the dietary nutritional supply, allowing for the limitations of food composition tables in doing so.
5. Securing the data required for action: diet inadequacy, eating customs to be respected, major food and cooking components, state of the foods to be distributed, international import regulations, and quality specifi cations.

Man satisfi es his nutrition need thanks to the nutrients provided by edible living species. Different cultures and individuals have diverging views as to which species (or part of it) is edible or not.

Moreover, the nutrient content of foods varies. Several foods therefore must be combined to ensure a balanced and adequate intake. The foods that compose the typical meals of a given population defi ne its diet. Diets themselves vary greatly, and result from both experience and need. Generally speaking, they are determined by the following:

- the natural environment's production capacity;
- culture, according to:
- economic development;
- eating habits, which determine broad preferences, dislikes, beliefs and taboos;
- households, according to:
- food access possibilities/capacity;
- personal preferences.

Cereals

It goes without saying that food has accompanied the human race since its beginning, and has evolved with it; but this has been eventful.

Adopting a combined historical, geographical, medical, economic, agronomic, political, cultural, artistic and philosophic approach to food is a fascinating endeavour. These aspects can unfortunately not be discussed here – but the underlying statement is that the role of food is extremely important in human life, a role which goes well beyond the simple supply of nutrients.

FOOD CATEGORIES

Human food is highly varied. Many processes change the rough ingredients found in nature into actual meals; these processes include extraction, transformation, combination, preparation and cooking, and they all contribute to the diversity of food. Vast cultural diversity has resulted in a multitude of products that can be diffi cult to distinguish. A classifi cation of rough foods is therefore required. In terms of satisfying the nutritional need, what counts above all else is the nutrient content. This leads to a relatively simple classifi cation, related mainly to raw foods. Foods can be listed either in decreasing order of nutrient content, or in food categories determined by general characteristics – related to their biological origin, their appearance or their utilization. The nutrient content of specifi c foods is rarely obvious at fi rst sight. On the other hand, foods are easily grouped in categories; this is therefore by far the most commonly used classifi cation, and provides both the basis for the description of food types and the structure of food composition tables. Classifi cation based on nutrient content is especially useful to locate specifi c foods according to their vitamin and mineral content.

In nutrition, foods are usually allotted to the twelve following categories or groups.

1. Cereals
2. Starchy plants
3. Legumes
4. Oilseeds
5. Vegetables
6. Fruits
7. Mushrooms
8. Fats
9. Animal products (meat and offal, fi sh, larvae and insects, eggs, dairy products)
10. Sugars and syrups
11. Beverages
12. Herbs and spices

10. The fi rst two categories (cereals and starchy plants) alone provide the staples of most of mankind - staple foods being understood as those that cover most of the energy needs; the other categories such as legumes, vegetables, fruits and animal products provide very useful complementary foods. Exceptions exist, of course; for example, the staple foods of the middle (and upper) wealth classes of the industrialized West are increasingly diffi cult to distinguish, owing to the great variety of foods they consume. On the other hand, some traditional stock-breeders still base their diet on animal products, whereas the last remaining hunter-gatherers have a highly varied diet, based on vegetables in their broadest defi nition, fruits and animal products. These exceptions refl ect the versatility of many foods and diets.

CEREALS

Cereals are the staple food of most of mankind. As such, they contribute to covering most energy, protein and B group vitamin requirements.

Cereals belong to the grass family (*Gramineae*) whose grains are edible. These grains have certainly contributed to the diet of mankind since its origin, but they have been used massively - and later cultivated - only for the last fi fteen to twenty thousand years. Nowadays, cereals account for most of the world's staple crop production, three times that of starchy plants, and ten times that of legumes (FAO, 1993). In other words, they represent the staple food of most of the world's inhabitants, and the main income source of most. As for volume of production, cultivated cereals are listed in the following decreasing order: wheat, rice, maize, barley, sorghum, oats, rye and millet. Nowadays, oats, rye and barley only play a minor role in the staple diet, whereas the others remain crucial. The various species of cereal grains, although very different in certain respects, can be compared in terms both of food value and structure.

The structure of cereal grains

The structural description of cereal grains is important, because nutrients are not equally distributed within the grain. The processing of cereals affects grain components that are rich in some of its essential nutrients as well as fi bre, and thus destroys most of them.

Serious defi ciencies may result; some are fatal, many are of epidemic proportions. Such defi ciencies usually strike the poor, as theirs is a less diversifi ed diet and is essentially based on one cereal alone.

Wheat

Wheat is the most widely cultivated cereal, and is produced mainly for human consumption. Two types of wheat are distinguished: soft wheat (*Triticum aestivum* or *vulgare*), and hard or durum wheat (*Triticum durum*). Wheat is an excellent staple food thanks to its food value. A diet in which 75% of the energy is provided by wheat fl our (whatever its extraction), 20% from vegetables and 5% from animal products is balanced and adequate for child growth – assuming that the energy supply is suffi cient (Davidson, 1979).

Wheat is consumed in a number of ways:

- wholemeal grain is usually prepared as bulgur: it is boiled in water until soft, then dried and crushed. It is then eaten boiled or braised, together with meat and vegetables;
- milled grain ranges from coarse semolina (for example *couscous*) to pure fl our (as used in pastry);
- semolina is usually made from durum wheat; fi ne semolina is used in gruels, whereas coarse semolina is soaked in water, and then enriched with fats and braised or steamed (e.g. *couscous*);
- fl our is used to produce leavened or unleavened bread, pasta (durum wheat), fritters and pancakes (fermented or not), biscuits and pastries (soft wheat) – bread is an almost mythical food; its symbolic value has always been extremely strong, but it is waning today owing to fashion-induced cultural levelling, and constraints related to the global economy and the erosion of regional cultural values.
- wheat is also used in the production of spirits such as vodka and whisky.

Rice

Two main rice species are known to be cultivated: *Oryza sativa* (or Asian rice), predominant by far owing to the extent of its cultivation, and *Oryza glaberrima*, produced in West Africa. Originally rice was a tropical plant, but it has spread worldwide and adapted to a wide variety of climates. Rice is cultivated in four main modes: in irrigated paddies, rain-fed lowland cultivation, dry cultivation in non-fl ooded paddies (where moisture is provided by rain or fl ood recession residue), and so-called "fl oating rice", in water as deep as several metres.

Wheat is the most widespread cereal, but rice follows close behind and its role may be more important still. Firstly, it is produced almost exclusively (95%) in developing countries, unlike wheat (42% only). Moreover, most Asian countries where rice constitutes the staple food *par excellence* rely on the energy and protein it supplies far more than is the case for other staple foods elsewhere (FAO, 1993). In other words, rice is generally the predominant food in their diet, which contains only a few other nutritious foods. This situation entails a high vulnerability to any impact on the rice monoculture, and to nutritional defi ciencies related to an insuffi ciently diversifi ed diet and the consumption of overly refi ned rice.

One particularity of rice is that winnowing only removes its straw, not its husk. Winnowing produces rough or paddy rice – the expression referring to the grain still in its husk. The husk is removed manually or mechanically to produce brown or cargo rice. The bran is then polished away to produce more or less polished white rice – some mechanical equipment removes the husks and polishes the grain in one operation. To prepare artisanal rice, it must fi rst be washed, then cooked, and possibly rinsed. Enormous nutrient losses (especially B group vitamins) can occur between the husk removal to rinsing. B group vitamins are lost in the course of husk removal and polishing, but also in the washing, cooking (if the cooking water is discarded) and rinsing, owing to their great water-solubility. Table 5.2 shows that polished rice has already lost 84% of its initial thiamine content – it will lose at least 50% of the remainder during washing, cooking and rinsing. Unsurprisingly, therefore, populations who rely heavily on polished white rice can suffer actual beriberi epidemics, not to mention more vulnerable groups such as refugees, displaced persons and prisoners.

Some treatment techniques nevertheless produce a reasonably polished rice without excessive nutrient loss in the process. They are based on the parboiling or steaming and drying of the paddy rice prior to removing its husk and polishing, and are practised both at home and industrially. The parboiling process consists in soaking the rice, then boiling or steaming it, and then drying it. Parboiling or steaming splits the husk (which can then easily be removed), and hardens the grain making it more resistant to polishing, thus reducing nutrient loss. For example, steamed and highly polished rice only loses 28% of its thiamine compared to brown rice; the same rice, non-steamed but similarly polished loses 85% (FAO, 1989a). Parboiling and steaming nevertheless involve a risk: mould frequently develops during the drying phase, inducing a risk of contamination through *Aspergillus fl avus*, which produces very dangerous afl atoxins (FAO, 1989a).

The food value of rice is excellent if it has been parboiled before processing. Rice provides the most digestible and best composition protein of all cereals. Rice contains approximately 30% less protein than other cereals. However, the organism retains rice protein better than that of other cereals, resulting in a roughly equivalent outcome. Its energy, protein, B group vitamin, iron and calcium content makes it a predominant staple food that can cover most of the supply of these nutrients. It however leads to dependencies and vulnerability, as discussed above.

Rice is mainly eaten in the form of whole grains, cooked in water, and can then be prepared in different ways. Rice is also milled to produce semolina and fl our. Rice semolina is used to prepare gruels, porridges and puddings, biscuits and cakes. Rice fl our is used for biscuits and pastries, pasta (with or without added wheat fl our), fermented pancake dough, patties, fritters and turnovers. The grain or grain fragments are also used to produce beer and rice wine – the latter can later be distilled to produce rice spirits. Glutinous rice, or sticky rice, is also used in many dishes specifi c to different regions or countries.

Maize

Maize (*Zea mays*) originated in Central America and is the

third most cultivated cereal worldwide. Only one-third of this production is for human consumption, the rest is used as animal feed and in industrial starch production (FAO, 1989a). Maize is a staple food in Central America, some South American countries, and in Southern and East Africa. In Africa, it has often replaced more traditional cereals, such as sorghum and millet, because of its higher yield and the fact that its cob is better protected against predators, particularly birds. Maize is quite resistant to heat and drought (more so than wheat or rice), as long as the latter does not occur during fl owering. Owing to this, maize is less resistant than sorghum and millet, and therefore more vulnerable to drought episodes - whose frequency appears to be accelerating. Another problem associated with maize cultivation is the fungal invasion of the grains following harvest, particularly by *Aspergillus fl avus*, which produces afl atoxins. Careful handling after harvesting, during drying and storage reduces this problem.

The food value of maize is lower than that of wheat and rice, mainly because its protein is of poorer quality (its lysine and tryptophan concentrations are low), and owing to its low niacin content, which is mainly in a form that is unusable biologically. As a result, where the staple food is maize only, a serious risk of pellagra exists; this remains true in crisis situations and in prisons today, as it was in the past when maize replaced secondary cereals and became the predominant food. This risk does not exist in Central America, its place of origin, where maize is traditionally soaked in an alkaline lime solution before use and processing. This considerably increases the biological availability of niacin, improves the amino-acid balance, and reduces afl atoxin rates. However, this practice has alas not accompanied maize to other regions (nor was it perpetuated by settlers invading the South of the United States), resulting in devastating pellagra epidemics. Refi ning and processing maize increase the risk of pellagra, and even of beriberi if they result in fi nely milled white fl our. The practice of refi ning is spreading to the detriment of processes such as crushing and light milling that waste less B group vitamins in the maize. Unlike other cereals, yellow maize contains carotenoids, some of which are precursors of vitamin A.

Maize, like other cereals, is eaten in many forms including the following:

- the cob itself can be eaten unripe – its taste is sweet – or ripe, boiled or grilled and then chewed;
- particularly in Latin America, the grain is roasted, grilled or boiled and eaten with beans, spices and meat (i.e. *chili con carne*). It is also heated to bursting to produce popcorn;
- gruel is used in preparing thick (even compact in the case of the Ugandan *ugali*) porridge, patties and biscuits, weaning porridges, and beer;
- semolina is boiled (e.g. *polenta*) or used in brewing according to its coarseness;
- fl our (more or less white) is used for pancakes (*tortillas*), unleavened bread, and gruel;
- maize germ (embryo) provides an excellent quality cooking oil;
- both beer and bourbon (American whiskey) are produced from maize.

Maize eaten in combination with legumes (accounting for at least 20% of the overall energy supply) does not entail risks of pellagra, beriberi and severe malnutrition.

Sorghum

Sorghum (*Sorghum spp.*) originated in Africa, where it is most commonly eaten as a staple food, particularly in Sahelian countries, owing to its tolerance to heat and semi-arid conditions. Its food value is similar to that of maize in terms of protein: exclusive sorghum consumption – but insuffi cient to cover energy needs – can cause pellagra epidemics as has been seen in Angola, for instance. However, pellagra appears rather to arise from an amino-acid unbalance: excessive leucine seems to interfere with the utilization of tryptophan and niacin (FAO, 1995). In developing countries, particularly the poorer regions of India and Africa, sorghum is cultivated for human consumption; its yield is low, less than one tonne per hectare. In industrialized countries, sorghum is produced mainly for livestock feed, and its yield is 3 to 5 tonnes per hectare (FAO, 1997).

Different varieties exist. Light-grained varieties usually provide a staple food; dark-grained varieties contain tannins and bitter polyphenols, and are used in beer production. Sorghum is used for gruel, porridges (weaning foods), semolina (*couscous*), fl at breads, and pancakes. The grains are also eaten whole or broken after boiling, steaming or bursting (like popcorn). Malted sorghum is also largely eaten in Africa; however, the shoots and radicels of germinated sorghum contain large amounts of a precursor of hydrogen cyanide (HCN), a violent poison to which small children are particularly sensitive. Shoots and radicels (or rootlets) must therefore always be removed carefully from germinated sorghum before eating the grain (FAO, 1995). As mentioned above, sorghum plays a major role in the human diet in some regions; it also plays a culturally predominant role in the production of beer, a ritual beverage whose consumption accompanies both daily life and celebrations of all kinds.

Millet

Millet includes several, sometimes botanically distinct, plants that all produce minute seeds. Like sorghum, millet originated in Africa, and they are very similar cereals. Millet is mainly produced in low income, hot and semi-arid countries – it is the most resistant cereal to heat and erratic rainfall. It is however vulnerable to birds, which cause tremendous damage because millet cobs fan out and offer the birds an irresistible source of food. Moreover, as they ripen, the grains tend to fall out of the cob onto the ground below. The cultivation of millet is suited to marginal areas, but nevertheless poses problems of its own. Its yield is low – 250 to 500 kg per hectare. A reasonable assumption in millet-production areas is the probable absence of alternatives for survival: if irrigation were available to improve millet yields, then the local farmers would no doubt already have resorted to more profi table crops (FAO, 1997).

Little is known about the food value of millet compared to that of other staple cereals. It is assumed that its characteristics are similar to those of sorghum, but its protein quality is higher. Furthermore, millet is mainly a staple food of the poor – its processing is essentially artisanal and therefore preserves most of the grain's nutrients (Davidson, 1979). The preparation of millet for consumption is similar to that of sorghum. Different types of millet exist, but two warrant particular attention: *teff*, typical of the Ethiopian highlands, and *fonio*, common in the Sahel. The cultural importance of *teff* (*Eragrostis teff*) in Ethiopia is identical to that of bread in Western Europe until the mid-20th century. It is used in the preparation of *injera*, which is the staple food and provides the "plate" for all Ethiopian dishes: *injera* is a pancake made from fermented *teff* dough, upon which a variety of savoury foods are arranged, and is then eaten with the fi ngers. The fermentation of *injera* enriches it in B group vitamins. *Teff* adapts to diverse climates and soils but does require abundant rainfall during its sowing and the early stages of its growth; it is therefore vulnerable to drought as was tragically seen in the 1970s and 1980s.

Fonio (*Digitaria exilis*) is cultivated in the Sahel but it is also a highly popular wild cereal. It owes its popularity to the fact that it grows freely in arid and semi-arid areas and is easy to harvest – one month's labour can suffi ce for a family to cover its yearly cereal requirements. However, during droughts the competition for *fonio* can be serious and lead to confl ict. As a result, free collection areas for this wild grain tend to be strictly regulated by customary law. Enquiries into food access in Sahelian areas must assess this aspect carefully, in addition to the fact that *fonio* acts as a buffer by compensating for production shortages in millet or sorghum; surveys often overlook such gathering activities.

Barley

Barley (*Hordeum vulgare*) was a predominant staple food from the early days of agriculture. In Europe, its consumption began to decline in the Middle Ages, giving way fi rst to wheat (bread), and later to new foods such as maize and potato, whose high yields protected against scarcity and famine. The increased production of such new foods did not improve the quality of the diet, however, because their high yield caused the diet to revolve almost exclusively around them, to the detriment of diversity and nutrient richness. The introduction of maize in Italy was followed by devastating pellagra epidemics that continued until the early 20th century (Flandrin & Montanari, 1996).

Barley is unfortunately no longer a human staple food, but nevertheless remains essential in the production of beer and the best whiskies. It is also widely used in animal feeding, which is why it is the fourth most produced cereal worldwide.

Oats and rye

Oats and rye (*Avena sativa* and *Secale cereale*) were staple foods in Europe, being cheap and good-yield alternatives to wheat. They are nutritious, climate resistant and were formerly a pauper's food. However, their importance has declined since the Second World War because of increased food availability and diversity, and improved purchasing power. Nowadays, they are growing more popular again, as tasty diet foods (e.g. porridge, bread).

STARCHY PLANTS

Starches can constitute staple foods, cereal complements or reserves when the cereal production is insuffi cient. Starchy plants above all provide a source of energy, but also of protein and vitamins according to species.

Starchy plants are not necessarily related botanically, but all have edible parts such as the tuber, the fruit or the stem that all mainly contain glucides in the form of starch. By decreasing order of worldwide production, starchy plants are the following: the common potato (*Solanum tuberosum*), cassava, sweet potato (*Ipomoea batatas*), yam, plantain, taro and sago. Each species includes many varieties. Man probably identifi ed edible roots everywhere from the origins to the development of agriculture; but the main roots with starchy tubers (i.e. common potato, cassava and sweet potato) were introduced from the Americas to the rest of the world only as of the 16th century. Their easy production and their high yield allowed their use to develop rapidly. In many regions including Europe, the introduction of the cultivation of starchy plants greatly contributed to reducing the risk of famines due to the unpredictabilities of cereal production. As previously discussed nevertheless, excessive reliance on one food type alone (and its resulting near-monoculture) can lead to dependency and thus be disastrous. This was the case in Ireland in the mid-19th century, where potato had become virtually the only energy and protein source for most of the rural population; mildew attacked the crops and destroyed three successive harvests between 1845 and 1847, and the Irish endured one of the worst famines in European history.

The importance of starchy plants in human nutrition arises from the following advantages (Dunbar, 1969):

- they grow in diverse soils;
- their production is cheap and requires little labour and maintenance;
- their surface yield is enormous;
- their preparation/cooking is easy;
- they can frequently be harvested throughout the year;
- they can frequently be left in the ground after ripening to be collected later, and this entails secondary benefi ts:
- a cheap and convenient form of storage;
- a good option for reserves in anticipation of hunger gaps, and to mitigate the risks of famine;

Tuber: subterranean excrescence of the stem or root.

- they are less prone to disease, and less vulnerable to parasites and predators than cereals;
- their reproduction can be vegetative (i.e. asexual).

Starchy plants nevertheless have some drawbacks, but these remain minor in the light of their considerable advantages. They include the following:

- when fresh, their energy density is low (approximately one-third of that of cereals and legumes) – they must therefore be eaten in larger amounts to meet energy needs, and this can result in a signifi cant risk of malnutrition if they are the main weaning food;
- owing to their high water and starch content, most tubers are diffi cult to handle, store and transport once collected (cassava, sweet potato and yam can spoil within a day) – their commercial use is therefore more uncertain than that of cereals or legumes;
- with the notable exception of the common potato, most starchy plants supply foods that are unbalanced from a nutritional perspective with respect to human needs – these foods must therefore always be complemented by others that are richer in protein, vitamins, minerals, and higher in energy, particularly for small children, or risk serious defi ciencies;

- vegetative reproduction demands large volumes of stems or tubers to replant, and these are diffi cult to store.

The utilization of starchy plants

Foods derived from starchy plants are not eaten raw; they must be prepared and cooked to make them more digestible and appetizing, extend their preservation and, in the case of cassava, reduce their toxicity. Preparation methods differ, and transformation involves several stages such as peeling prior to or following cooking, washing, soaking, drying, milling, crushing, grating, and fermentation. Cooking can involve roasting, grilling, boiling, steaming, and frying. Transformation and cooking stages can be combined: for example, the peeled tuber is washed, then boiled, reduced to pulp, dried, and fi nally milled to fl our. Starchy foods are eaten whole, diced or in the form of paste, mash, patties, and their fl our is used for many dishes and mixtures with cereal and legume fl ours Starchy foods are rather tasteless, and they are therefore frequently associated with spicier foods (e.g. gravy, meat, fi sh or vegetables).

Common potato

The most extensively cultivated starchy plant is the common potato (*Solanum tuberosum*). It thrives in temperate climates where nights are cool. Its nutritional qualities have been discussed above. It can be boiled, fried, roasted, baked or braised; it is eaten whole, in chunks of all shapes and sizes, mashed, and even dried. Recipes and accompaniments for potatoes are innumerable; its fl our and starch also provide the basis for many dishes. The importance of potato is both culinary and essential to the survival of hundreds of millions of people. It also provides the main ingredient for spirits such as vodka.

P/E% refers to the protein-energy ratio; this relation is discussed in Chapter XII, in connection with the qualitative aspects of food rations.

Cassava

Cassava (*Manihot esculenta* and *M. dulcis*) tolerates drought but not freezing; it is therefore found in the tropics where it is both a staple food and a food security product. Cassava is mainly a source of energy, and must therefore be eaten in combination with foods that are rich in protein, vitamins and minerals. Alas, this is rarely feasible in times of drought or armed confl ict when it is often the only remaining source of food, resulting in defi ciency diseases such as dietary kwashiorkor. Even where food sources are varied, the excessive use of cassava as a staple and weaning food leads to serious nutritional disorders.

Cassava contains linamarin, a compound that transforms into hydrogen cyanide (HCN) under the action of a specifi c enzyme that is also present in cassava. HCN is a most toxic and violent poison. The HCN concentration in cassava can be quite high, but fl uctuates greatly according to variety. Table 5.4 below provides the HCN content of cassava plants studied in Mozambique (Ministry of Health, Mozambique, 1984).

An approximately 50 mg dose of HCN is lethal for the adult human; Table 5.4 above shows that a diet that is almost exclusively based on cassava that is little or not detoxifi ed can cause death or chronic intoxication leading to spastic paraparesia (called *mantakassa* in Mozambique) which is almost irreversible. Cassava eaters usually know perfectly well how to detoxify it. In any case, a varied diet and a normal nutritional status allow the organism to detoxify HCN at the rate of 20 mg/day.

However in conditions of drought, confi nement, involuntary displacement or forced change in eating habits, cassava is sometimes the only available food and can be prepared inadequately, leading to real epidemics of spastic paraparesia. Its symptoms appear suddenly, often after the meal or during the night, and include fever, leg pains, headache, sensitivity disorders (tingling), vomiting and dizziness. Paralysis can follow immediately or take several days – even weeks – to develop, depending probably on the HCN dose ingested. An effi cient treatment, if administered early, is the intravenous injection of thiosulphate, which converts HCN into harmless thiocyanate. The lower the protein content of the diet, the more likely this poisoning becomes. The sulphurous amino acids interact with vitamin B_{12} to detoxify HCN in the organism by transforming it into thiocyanate. A protein-poor diet reduces the number of amino acids in the blood, thus impeding detoxifi cation. A protein-poor diet also increases the likelihood of dietary kwashiorkor, which is why the epidemics of spastic paraparesia associated with cassava consumption are often combined with kwashiorkor epidemics; in these conditions, mortality is often high. The appropriate response is to vary the diet of the affected populations, teach them and provide them with the means to detoxify cassava, and to supply them with thiosulfate for injections.

Cassava transformation and preparation methods are generally adequate to transform linamarin into HCN and then remove the HCN through dissolution and evaporation (above 28°C). Pre-soaking the roots for fi ve days reduces the HCN to approximately 3% of its initial concentration (FAO, 1991).

The safest cassava detoxifi cation methods consist in peeling, soaking and fermenting (during several days), and then crushing it into a pulp that is then pressed, cooked and dried. Drying or cooking alone are inadequate methods. On the other hand, cooking the leaves in initially cold water reduces the HCN content to below its toxicity threshold.

Generally, cassava is transformed through peeling, soaking, fermenting or reducing it to pulp, paste, gruel or chips. It can also be turned into fl our after detoxifi cation through soaking and fermenting, followed by drying and pounding. Young roots contain little linamarin and can be eaten fresh and whole, after boiling. Cassava products can be boiled, steamed, braised, roasted or fried.

Sweet potato

Sweet potato (*Ipomoea batatas*) is akin to the common potato, and its cultivation spread at the same time as cassava and the common potato, with the return of the navigators of the 16th century. In Europe, its popularity was surpassed by that of the common potato, but it rapidly gained ground in Asia; its progress in Africa was slower. In Papua New Guinea, the huge yield of sweet potato per hectare eventually made it the number one energy source among cultivators. This particular monoculture showed its limits and dangers during the 1997 famine, which was caused by an unprecedented drought. Like cassava, sweet potato can be kept in the ground and is also fairly drought-tolerant. On the other hand, it spoils quickly after its harvest, and is fragile to transport.

Sweet potato does not require specifi c preparation; it is eaten boiled, roasted, fried, baked or heated on leaves spread on hot stones.

Yam

Yam (*Discoroae species*) requires considerable rainfall, and is thus found in the humid tropics and equatorial regions. It is considered to be the tastiest tuber, and is highly popular (FAO, 1989b). Common yam forms large tubers that can weigh up to 20 kg. Some varieties produce bitter and toxic molecules (they are called bitter yam), and are usually cultivated in anticipation of scarcity or to deter thieves. They are detoxifi ed by washing, fermenting and roasting. Yam is usually eaten fresh, peeled, boiled and compressed into a paste. More rarely, yam is cut up and cooked, then sun-dried and pounded or milled to produce fl our.

Plantains

Plantains are bananas picked unripe and eaten like other starchy plants: boiled, braised or baked, made into paste, roasted, fried or made into fl our. All bananas grow sweet if allowed to ripen. The plantain variety called *Musa paradisiaca* is very similar to the sweet banana *Musa sapientum* that is most commonly eaten raw; it is simply mealier than the latter, and is preferred green (i.e. unripe). In Central and East Africa, plantains are also widely cultivated to produce local beer; this production is particularly important in Rwanda, Burundi and Uganda.

Sago

The sago tree is a South-East Asian palm tree (*Metroxylon sagu*); sago is the pulp extracted from the felled tree trunk. The pulp is washed and pressed to produce a paste that contains practically only starch. The paste can be fermented or not, and is then steamed, baked, roasted, fried or dried to produce fl our whose energy content is approximately 350 kcal (1,463 kJ) per 100 g. Fermenting improves the fl avour of the paste, and simultaneously increases its nutritional quality.

LEGUMES

In terms of ingested amounts, legumes (or pulses) only seldom provide a staple food; their role in human nutrition is nevertheless central, as an indispensable complement of staple foods so as to balance the diet. This point is particularly important during weaning.

Legumes are plants that bear edible seeds in pods or shells; however some legumes such as beans can be eaten whole. Strictly speaking we eat legume grains, and not - usually - legumes, just as it would be more accurate to say that we eat cereal grains (and not cereals). The legume family is considerable (including some 18,000 species), and ranges from tiny plants to large trees. Legumes are found and cultivated throughout the world. Like cereals, legumes have always been part of the human diet, just as they have been cultivated ever since the early days of agriculture. The worldwide cultivation of legumes is one-tenth that of cereals, but the diversity of legumes is far greater, with more than one hundred cultivated species contributing to the human diet, that is not to mention wild legumes. Moreover, these species often include several botanically distinct varieties, and countless cultivars. The main edible legume families are peas, lentils and beans. The use of the word "legumes" usually refers to the dried grain, the form in which they are most commonly found. They can however be eaten fresh, straight after harvest, as is the case for green peas, green beans, snow peas (*Pisum sativum macrocarpon,* eaten with their pod) and broad beans (*Vicia faba*). The nutritional density of fresh legumes is approximately one-third that of their dried grains. A healthy way of eating legumes is to sprout them - this makes them more digestible, and causes vitamin C synthesis in signifi cant amounts (13 mg/100 g of sprouted soy bean).

The food value of legumes

The food value of legumes is excellent; thus, even if their importance is secondary in terms of ingested amounts, their role is essential in balancing cereal-based diets or enriching starch-based diets. The many edible legume varieties all share a similar chemical composition, lending them similar food characteristics. Table 5.5 below indicates typical nutrient values of legumes (peas, beans and lentils) generally.

Legumes

Dried legumes are rich in protein (twice as much as cereals, and 10 to 20 times more than starchy plants), energy (of which more than 90% is supplied by the protein and glucides) and B group vitamins. They contain no vitamin A, and little or no vitamin C. Legumes also contain greater concentrations of iron and calcium than cereals do but, as in the case of the latter, the absorption of these two elements is strongly diminished by the presence of phytates. Legumes furthermore provide a good source of fi bres that protect against bowel cancer, and their consumption helps to limit blood cholesterol levels.

In many regions, the diet of the poor is monotonous and unvaried. Legumes are then a crucial complement, particularly of cereals whose lack of protein, B group vitamin and vitamin C (after sprouting in some circumstances) are thereby compensated. In fact mankind has always and everywhere combined cereals and legumes: rice and soy in the Far East, wheat cakes and chick peas in the Middle East, wheat cakes and lentils or beans in India, maize and beans in the Americas, sorghum or millet and beans in Africa, bread and broad beans or lentils in Europe. Legumes also provide good complements for starchy plants.

Combining legumes and cereals

Protein complement

In terms of egg protein, whose human retention effi ciency is one of the best, legume protein is richer in lysine, but poorer in sulphurous amino acids (methionine/cysteine); cereal protein on the other hand is poorer in lysine and sulphurous amino acids (less so, however, than legume protein). As a result, combining cereals and legumes signifi cantly enhances the quality of the overall protein intake (but not as much as egg protein, because sulphurous amino acids remain a limiting factor). Table 5.6 below illustrates the diet improvement resulting from a 3/4 cereal – 1/4 legume combination. It compares the amount of ingested cereals (underlined) required for different age groups to meet the need for lysine and sulphurous amino acids, and the amount of the cereal-legume complement or combination (underlined) necessary to achieve the same result.

Table 5.6 clearly shows that, referring to cereals consumed alone, only half the cereal-legume combination is enough to meet the essential amino-acid needs of children. For adults, on the other hand, sulphurous amino acids remain largely limiting, and between 70 and 95% are thus required, according to the cereal under consideration. This is unimportant for adults, because (with the complement or the cereal alone) they meet 100% of their essential amino-acid need, but less than half of their energy requirements, allowing them to complete the shortfall with other foods. However, the use of a combination is essential for children, particularly infants under 1 year: for cereals alone to meet their essential amino-acid needs, babies would need to consume more than the food required to meet their energy needs, leaving no room for other foods that are rich in vitamins and minerals.

Moreover, the amount of complement/combination necessary to meet essential amino-acid requirements varies according to age and the constituents of the mix. Furthermore, these amounts also vary according to the relationship between the constituents themselves. Generally and qualitatively speaking:

- the optimal ratio allowing an adequate coverage of essential amino-acid requirements with the smallest amount of complement is not fi xed; it varies according to age group (which defi nes the nutritional need) and the constituents of the complement (which determine respective intakes of limiting amino acids);
- the smallest amount of complement required to meet the essential amino-acid need is not fi xed either, because it is determined by the age group, complement components and their relation.

The data provided in Table 5.6 leads to the following quantitative recommendations: a 60 g legume complement combined with a 180 g cereal complement (1/4 and 3/4 respectively) providing 830 kcal (3,470 kJ) and 32 g of protein represents a safety intake of essential amino acids for all age groups. On the other hand, it is suffi cient to meet overall protein requirements only up to the age of ten. Furthermore, one must allow for the need to absorb, in addition to the complement, what is required to meet the energy need, or risk the protein being utilized as a source of energy and not as protein. As a result, teenagers and adults not only require a complementary energy intake, but the latter must also consist of a protein complement so as to meet the overall nitrogen need.

The 60 g legume/180 g cereal complement only covers approximately one-third of the energy needs of teenagers and adults; the balance must be met with available cereals (and all this only makes sense if the diet is based mainly on cereal, without protein complements other than legumes).

Completing the cereal-legume complement with a cereal supplement up to the energy need also contributes to the overall nitrogen need; this can be easily illustrated as follows.

- A 16-year-old girl whose maintenance energy need is 2,150 kcal (8,990 kJ)/day, and whose safety protein need is 44 g/day must ingest 1,320 kcal (5,520 kJ) of energy supplement - approximately 380 g of cereals, that simultaneously provide 38 g of protein. Allowing for digestibility, the protein intake that is biologically available is 56 g of protein, which is amply suffi cient. The overall cereal/legume ratio thus rises to 560 g of cereal to 60 g of legumes (i.e. approximately 11% of legumes in the ration).
- A 25-year-old man whose maintenance energy need is 2,450 kcal (10,240 kJ)/day, and whose safety protein need is 52.5 g day must ingest 1,620 kcal (6,770 kJ) of energy supplement - approximately 460 g of cereals, that simultaneously provide 46 g of protein. Allowing for digestibility, the protein intake that is biologically available is 62 g of protein, which is likewise amply suffi cient. The overall cereal/ legume ratio thus rises to 640 g of cereal to 60 g of legumes (i.e. approximately 9% of legumes in the ration).

In short, a group that has access to cereals mainly can balance its protein intake by a minimal daily consumption of 60 g of legumes for all its members, completing this with cereals up to the energy requirement. This measure is crucial for infants under 1 who are highly vulnerable with respect to the coverage of their protein needs, especially if their weaning is abrupt, and if their diet is not varied and devoid of animal products.

B group vitamin supplements

Legume seeds contain slightly more thiamine and ribofl avin than cereal seeds; however, they complement the latter mainly because they usually suffer no losses during grinding, and much lower losses during preparation (especially in comparison to rice). Legumes therefore provide a good protection against pellagra and beriberi when they complete diets based primarily on maize or rice, especially if the latter is not steamed prior to husking and polishing. To mitigate the risk of beriberi in a diet mainly based on rice that has not been steamed, but polished twice, at least 20 to 25% of the energy requirement must be absorbed in the form of legumes.

Data regarding the average amount of niacin actually biologically available in maize is inconclusive. As a result, it is impossible to make fi rm recommendations regarding the amount of legumes to be added to a maize-based diet in order to mitigate the risk of pellagra. Experience with groups whose diet depends entirely on humanitarian relief nevertheless shows that a ration of 25% of legumes and 75% of maize always provides an effective protection against pellagra.

Vitamin C supplements

As mentioned above, the germination of legumes causes signifi cant vitamin C synthesis. A simple technique used in drought and famine settings, for example in India and Ethiopia, consists in soaking approximately 40 g of unshelled legumes per person for 12 to 24 hours. The grains are then removed from the water, spread in a thin layer between two wet blankets that are then kept wet by regular water sprinkling. The legumes sprout and produce ascorbic acid, and its maximum content is reached after some 30 hours of germination: 40 g of germinated legumes contain 12 to 20 mg of vitamin C – a suffi cient individual daily amount to forestall scurvy (Davidson, 1979).

The three roles of legumes as cereal complements described above are of particular relevance to food relief. The commodities that should be distributed to meet the overall nutritional need are well understood; however, many factors complicate this, and rations are therefore very often incomplete. Resorting to legumes resolves this problem to a certain extent.

A relief ration representing most of the food supply and consisting mainly of cereals and legumes (80% of the calorie intake) should contain 3 parts of cereal to 1 part of legumes – the legumes, thus account for some 20% of the overall energy intake. This meets the protein and B group vitamin requirements. Moreover, the risk of scurvy disappears if the diet includes approximately 40 g/day/person of sprouted legumes.

Such a ration however usually contains a greater proportion of legumes than are normally consumed. As a result, if the vitamin and mineral ration can be balanced by other means than legumes, the latter can be reduced down to a minimum threshold of 60 g per person per day; this ensures an adequate protein intake without involving the preparation and consumption of excessive amounts of legumes.

Combining legumes and starchy plants

In starch-based diets, legume complements offer the double advantage of varying the meals and improving their fl avour. They also increase the protein content of such diets, without however signifi cantly enhancing the quality of the ingested protein in terms of amino-acid content.

Like legumes, starchy plants are poor in sulphurous amino acids in terms of human requirements. Unlike cereals therefore, the combination of legumes and starchy plants does not result in a protein compensation.

Foods based on the common potato, yam and, to a lesser extent, sweet potato provide a satisfactory protein supply per energy unit, and the protein is of high quality. On the other hand, the energy and protein density is weak with respect to consumed amounts and thus poses a problem, especially during weaning when infants do not have the stomach capacity to absorb the amount required to meet both the energy and protein need.

As a result, legume complements are useful in providing children with an adequately concentrated diet. This role is even more important in diets based on cassava, plantain and sago, whose amino-acid composition is poor, whose protein density is weak in terms both of volume unit and energy unit, and whose energy density is likewise fairly low.

However, legume complements in poor diets based on starchy plants cannot resolve nutritional security on their own. The variety of the diet must be enhanced by all possible means, affording access to fresh fruits and vegetable, in addition to animal products and oilseeds. This also holds true for poor diets based on cereals, but special attention must be devoted to those involving starchy plants, as the latter eventually turn into the main source of food when nutritional crises become chronic.

The utilization of legumes

Legume varieties

There is a vast variety of legumes, and it is impossible to discuss them comprehensively here. Rather, fi eld investigation should determine locally used varieties in each specifi c context, together with acceptable alternatives. This Manual only discusses the most common, those whose international trade has spread widely. However, more marginal, lesser-known varieties exist; they are local specialities whose yield is often lower or that are more complicated to utilize, but they are generally well adapted to the local ecology and often suffer from the competition of imported varieties.

Problems arising from the utilization of legumes

In spite of their excellent food value, legumes are less used than would seem logical; they usually only serve as complements for staple diets, but not as staple foods themselves. Several reasons - taken in combination or in isolation - explain this.

Yield

In the subsistence economy of poor countries, the surface yield of legumes is half or one-third that of cereals, and one-tenth (or less) that of starchy plants. Where the cultivated surface matters, farmers need to optimize the overall return on their labour and make choices. Staple foods obviously take precedence. On the other hand, intercropping can result in interesting improvements for cereals, starchy plants and legumes; the former protect the legumes from heat and cold, the latter enrich the soil in nitrogen.

Flatulence

The consumption of legumes other than groundnuts causes fl atulence, which can entail considerable discomfort particularly for infants during weaning. This is one of the main reasons for legumes not being consumed in larger amounts. There is no solution to this problem, other than - to a certain extent - protracted cooking.

Preparation

Dried legumes require much time and work before they can be eaten. They also harden during drying and storage, and therefore demand lengthy cooking. This involves expenses in time and other resources to secure the required fuel, and the cooking time itself discourages a more intensive use of legumes.

Husking and preliminary soaking with or without baking soda are two methods aimed at reducing cooking times signifi cantly (by 50 to 90%). Only adding salt at the very end of the cooking process also shortens it (adding it at the beginning slows down the cooking).

Losses resulting from storage

Storage can expose legumes to rodents and insects. In the case of domestic storage, losses often reach 20%, and can exceed 50%.

Where possible, the use of insecticides during plant growth signifi cantly reduces the risk of infestation during storage. Moreover, the quality of the drying process is very important, as are fumigation and storage temperature. In subsistence agriculture, small-scale farmers can reduce storage losses by fi rmly packing clean and dry grains in airtight containers, and storing the latter away from heat.

Digestion

The protein and starch contained in legumes are more diffi cult to digest than those of cereals and starchy plants, and sometimes cause bloating and discomfort. Protracted cooking reduces these effects, as do preliminary treatments such as husking, sprouting, malting, crushing, fermenting and roasting.

Adverse factors concerning the food itself

Inhibitors of the protein digestion enzymes: These substances inhibit digestion by blocking the digestive enzymes. Boiling eliminates the inhibitors of digestive enzymes, provided it is long enough (up to several hours). Sprouting helps to some extent.

Phytohaemagglutinin (PHA)

Also called lectin, PHA agglutinates mammalian red blood cells (erythrocytes) and destroys them, causing food poisoning; it also impairs the quality of ingested protein (Aykroyd, 1982). Soaking before cooking, followed by covered boiling for several hours alters PHA and, therefore, reduces its negative effects. Sprouting also alters PHA to some extent.

Phytates

Phytates signifi cantly reduce the absorption of calcium, iron and zinc, and impair protein digestibility. Normal cooking destroys phytates, whereas sprouting only partly alters them.

Cyanogens

Legumes, particularly Lima beans, contain linamarin that produces hydrogen cyanide under the action of an enzyme. In addition to its toxic effect itself, hydrogen cyanide is transformed in the organism into thiocyanate, a substance inducing goitre. Hydrogen cyanide is a water-soluble toxin; as a result, soaking followed by rinsing and boiling eliminates the toxin almost entirely. Lima beans contain high levels of hydrogen cyanide, but also of its precursor, linamarin, which is resistant to soaking, rinsing and cooking. This bean is the most toxic in terms of hydrogen cyanide and should therefore be crushed and soaked for 24 hours at room temperature (Aykroyd, 1982).

Miscellaneous

Other factors worth mentionıng include the allergenic potential of legumes (particularly soy milk for infants), their content in anti-vitamin and anti-mineral substances, and the presence of protein digestion inhibiting tannins. In most cases, husking, soaking and boiling mitigate most of these anti-nutritional factors, allowing the organism to eliminate the remainder harmlessly.

Lathyrism

Lathyrism is an irreversible paralysis of the nervous system resulting from the excessive consumption of grass pea (*Lathyrus sativus*), which is particularly drought-tolerant. In the arid areas of India, it is planted at the same time as cereals to serve as a reserve in case of a poor cereal harvest. Normally, grass pea is consumed in far smaller amounts than the staple food, and thus presents no danger. When grass pea accounts for more than 30% of the diet, however, lathyrism develops within 3 to 6 months (Aykroyd, 1982). Lathyrism affects the lower limbs mainly. The toxin responsible for lathyrism (B-oxalyl aspartic acid) is water soluble like hydrogen cyanide. Husking, followed by soaking for 12 hours, thorough rinsing and boiling for approximately 1 hour reduce toxins to levels that are harmless for the organism. Despite the simplicity of this detoxifi cation method, lathyrism remains a serious public health problem in India, Bangladesh, and Ethiopia, because grass pea is usually crushed dry, and the resulting meal is then mixed with wheat fl our to produce patties. The toxin is therefore not eliminated. On the other hand, rinsing the peas, boiling them and leaving them in the water to cool for 2 hours, then decanting the water and allowing the grains to dry in the sun provides well detoxifi ed peas that are safe to use to produce patty fl our (Dwivedi, 1975).

Favism

Favism is associated with the excessive consumption of broad beans (*Vicia faba*) and the inhalation of the plant's pollen. The condition only affects individuals suffering from a genetic defi ciency in the enzyme glucose-6-phosphate dehydrogenase (G6PD), which infl uences the stability of the red blood cell membrane. The reaction manifests itself in haemolytic anaemia and high fever within minutes following pollen inhalation, or within the hours following the ingestion of the bean. It can be fatal within 1 or 2 days, quite frequently so in young children. If the patient survives the acute phase, he recovers within 4 weeks approximately (Aykroyd, 1982). Defi ciency is more common among men than women, and is widespread in the Mediterranean. The only protection against favism is to refrain from eating broad beans if one appears to react to them.

Afl atoxins

Afl atoxins are produced by a fungus (*Aspergillus fl avus*) and are the most potent known causes of cancer. The fungus develops on almost all grains stored in humid and hot conditions and handled without due consideration for hygiene. The quality of the grain drying is also essential in arresting the development of the fungus. Afl atoxins contaminate cereals and legumes alike, but particularly maize and groundnuts. Moreover, they can then pass into the food chain, for example through the milk of animals fed on contaminated cereals. The recommended afl atoxin ceiling level is 0.5 ìg per litre for milk, and 20 ìg per kilogram for other foods. These levels remain high if one considers that animals exposed long-term to diets containing 15 ìg of afl atoxins per kilogram of food all developed tumours. The toxicity of afl atoxins is greater among young people than the elderly, and among males than females.

Afl atoxin contamination can be avoided by ensuring that grains are thoroughly dry prior to storage. They must then be stored carefully in a dry, clean, cool place, if possible in airtight containers.

The above may suggest that the preparation and consumption of legumes is both tedious and risky. This is true only in crises, when options and means are scarce and assistance is external. It is worth stressing the fact that normally - lathyrism, favism and afl atoxins notwithstanding - people usually know how to utilize legumes, based on thousands of years' experience. Changes in lifestyle and eating habits, prompted by external interference in crises, can inhibit this knowledge. The delivery of food relief must always involve the ascertaining that recipients know how to prepare the legumes they receive; likewise, the variety that is locally known should be distributed, because preferences are usually strong in view of the always pronounced fl avour of these foods.

Legume preparation

Problems arising from the utilization of legumes require the development of indispensable preparation methods. Traditional age-old methods have resulted in the production of nutritious and tasty dishes to complement staple foods.

Soaking: The process of soaking prior to cooking is widespread. In Rwanda, nevertheless, groups met by the author refrained from soaking as they believed that the beans would thereby lose their fl avour. Soaking contributes to eliminating the envelope, reduces toxin levels, and shortens the cooking time by saturating and softening the grain. Soaking times change according to variety, and must be proportional to the storage time. A common practice is to soak the legumes overnight at room temperature; they can also be soaked in hot water, reducing the soaking time.

Husking: Husking is the removal of the sometimes hard envelope of legumes, in order to improve fl avour and digestion, but mainly to shorten their cooking. Husking consists of detaching the envelope through roasting, the application of oil and drying, or soaking and drying. The envelope is then removed by abrasion with different techniques ranging from the domestic mortar to industrial machines. In India, husked legumes are called *"dhal"*, a word that has spread and is now commonly used in reference to any husked legume. Husking is however not universal: in India, where the process is most widespread, only 75% of the legume production is transformed into dhal. In some places, husking is not systematic, or occurs automatically during soaking and cooking.

Cooking: Cooking is the most important stage to enable the consumption of legumes, because it destroys most of the toxins and enhances both fl avour and digestibility. The two main methods are wet cooking (boiling or braising) and dry cooking (roasting or frying). Wet cooking allows legumes to retain approximately 70% of their water-soluble vitamins and 80% of their minerals other than sodium (Aykroyd, 1982).

Sprouting and malting: Sprouting is common in Asia, especially in the Far East. To sprout, the non-husked grain must be soaked, then patted dry and placed on a humid surface. The process takes a few days during which the grains are frequently rinsed. Sprouting splits the envelope, which is then easy to remove, and causes biochemical reactions that improve the food value and the fl avour of the grain, while resulting in a partial degradation of the phytates, lectins and enzyme inhibitors. As mentioned above, sprouting causes signifi cant vitamin C synthesis. Sprouting can be combined with malting, which consists in stopping the process by roasting the sprouted grain. Malting enhances both digestibility and fl avour.

Fermenting: Fermenting is an age-old process involving legumes as the basis for highly digestible and tasty foods and spices; the best known is probably soy sauce. Fermentation techniques vary greatly and can be quite sophisticated; they usually concern legumes that are still not really edible after soaking, husking and cooking. This is particularly true for soybeans, which are mainly eaten fermented in some way or other, or sprouted.

Oilseeds

Finally, legumes as food plants are useful because of their grains, but also their pods, fl owers, leaves and tubers. This contributes greatly to meeting the need for vitamins, minerals and protein, and considerably enhances diet variety and fl avour. The preparation of legumes takes many forms that cannot all be discussed here. Globally, they can be eaten whole, reduced to pulp, as patties, pastes or crushed, each form having inspired a host of recipes to make the dish appealing. In most developing countries, it is the legumes and their accompanying sauce that enhances the blandness of staple foods. In industrialized countries, legumes are often treated before sale, resulting in short-cooking dry or canned legumes, ready to heat.

OILSEEDS

The listing of oilseeds follows no set rule; this manual simply describes a number of energy-rich foods whose common denominators are their high lipid content and the fact that the lipids are extracted from them. Their protein concentration is also quite high. Soybean and groundnut are sometimes associated with them because they are oil-producing legumes. This Manual adopts the botanical approach, and the latter two plants are therefore discussed in the previous section on legumes. Oilseeds can be subdivided into those that are eaten whole and whose oil is also extracted, and those that produce butters or oils only. Noteworthy is the fact that, in addition to common cultivated oilseeds, there are many semi-wild, semi-cultivated or specially protected (e.g. grasses, trees, creepers) local plants; they play a major complementary role in the diet, as well as providing a source of lipids, both during normal times and during hunger gaps or periods of scarcity. Outsiders can easily overlook such resources, disregarding the importance of picked or gathered products in the normal diet and in the mechanisms of food and economic security.

Oilseeds for consumption and oil extraction

This category includes nuts and what is commonly referred to as seeds. Nuts include walnuts, hazelnuts, almonds, pistachios, cashew nuts, Brazil nuts, macadamia nuts in addition to other, less familiar exotic varieties such as the Mongongo nut common in southern Africa. An edible portion of 100 g of dried nuts provides on average 650 kcal (2,717 kJ), for 14 g of protein, 60 g of lipids, and 14 g of glucides. Nuts are good sources of thiamine and ribofl avin, but contain little niacin and no vitamin A and C. They contain iron and good amounts of calcium. The most familiar seeds are sunfl ower, sesame and linseed, in addition to those from the many pumpkin and melon varieties. Without their envelope, the average energy value of 100 g of these seeds is 550 kcal (2,300 kJ), for 23 g of protein, 46 g of lipids, and 11 g of glucides. Their vitamin and mineral content is similar to that of nuts.

Nuts and seeds keep well. They can either be eaten as they are or prepared, or used for oil extraction, the energy content of the latter reaching 900 kcal (3,760 kJ) per 100 g. The residual meal remaining after oil extraction is protein rich and often serves as animal feed. The utilization of nuts and seeds serves different purposes: snacks, enhancing the fl avour and/or the food value of dishes, economic resource, food complement, particularly during hunger gaps or lean seasons.

The industrial utilization of oilseeds is not discussed in this Manual, which refers mainly to their domestic use.

Oilseeds as sources of lipids

Cocoa beans, Illipe nut (*Shorea spp.*) and shea nut (*Butyrospermum parkii*) are used to extract fatty matter called "butter" (cocoa, Illipe, shea butter). They are rather congealed – although their viscosity depends largely on room temperature, preparation mode and their degree of refi ning. The fruit of the oil palm provides the â-carotene rich palm oil, the fruit of the olive tree provides the healthy mono-unsaturated oleic acid, and the fruit of the coconut tree produces the (unhealthy) saturated fatty-acid rich coconut oil.

Cottonseed, rapeseed, saffl ower, grape seed, colza seed and mustard seed all produce edible oils. The energy value of all these fats is approximately 900 kcal (3,760 kJ)/100g.

VEGETABLES

Intuitively, everyone knows what vegetables are; it is however diffi cult to defi ne them from a nutritional perspective, and they escape all botanical classifi cation. They are edible plants – entirely or in part – that do not keep well, implying that they must be eaten fresh or dried or preserved, and that cannot serve as staple foods owing to their low energy density. Nevertheless, garden vegetables that are extremely cheap to produce can play a major role in the rural daily diet. Vegetables also improve the variety and fl avour of the diet, and play a decorative role. The edible parts of vegetables include the leaves (e.g. spinach, lettuce, cabbage, amaranth, sweet potato), the stem (celery, cardoon, rhubarb, asparagus), the roots (turnip, radish, onion, carrot), the fruit (tomato, marrow, squash, zucchini, eggplant), and the fl ower (caulifl ower, broccoli, artichoke). People eat vegetables for their taste and because they can produce them, rather than out of nutritional concern. Nowadays, vegetable consumption is actively promoted by health professionals, but it remains diffi cult to determine consumption trends. In the industrialized West, the proliferation of fast-food chains and the dispersion of families at mealtimes rather run counter to an increase in vegetable consumption. In developing countries, the rural exodus towards urban centres and the urban market price of vegetables are also adverse factors.

The food value of vegetables

The average food value of vegetables is approximately 35 kcal (146 kJ)/100 g of edible parts, for 1.8 g of protein. These values vary greatly, however, according to samples, origin, freshness, season, soil, and the same applies to all the nutrients of vegetables. The nutritional importance of vegetables relates to their high concentrations of â-carotene (the â-carotene content is roughly proportional to the vegetable colour intensity), ascorbic acid (of which a large proportion is however lost during cooking), and folic acid. In terms of these vitamins, vegetables are essential in balancing diets, especially those based on cereals. Vegetables also provide reasonable amounts of ribofl avin and minerals such as calcium and iron, but they are absorbed only marginally. Vegetables are also rich in fi bre. Recent epidemiological research has confi rmed the direct or indirect importance of high vegetable consumption in mitigating the risks of cancer, hypertension, and high cholesterol (role of fi bre).

The utilization of vegetables

Vegetables can be prepared in many different ways. Usually, their preparation involves rinsing and peeling to remove the fi brous or bitter parts. They can then be eaten raw with some form of dressing, or be cooked and spiced. Preparation types include boiling, braising or steaming, mixed with sauces/gravies, very brief high-temperature cooking in a little fat (scalding – the best way to preserve their vitamins). They can also be preserved by fermentation and canning.

Fresh vegetables play a crucial role in human nutrition in providing the essential vitamins and minerals required for man to lead a normal life and avoid defi ciency disorders such as anaemia and xerophthalmia (dryness of the eye that can result in blindness). This aspect does not get the attention it deserves, however, because many populations are intent only on securing an adequate calorie intake. Relief workers in nutritional crises must pay specifi c attention to the presence or absence of vegetables in the victims' diet, and take the necessary measures to ensure a balanced food intake.

FRUITS

In botany, a fruit is the ripened ovary – together with seeds – of a fl owering plant; in cuisine, the term usually refers to plant products that are sweet and fl eshy (such as mangoes, bananas, and apples). Even more so than vegetables, people eat fruit because they like its fl avour, smell, its refreshing and thirst-quenching quality and, to a lesser extent, texture. The nutritional importance of fruit arises from its high vitamin C content; most fruit are also rich in â-carotene (all except pears, quinces, lychees, citrus fruit and some berries). The energy content of fruit is low: an average 60 kcal (250 kJ)/100 g of fresh fruit, for which sugar accounts for more than 90%. Fruit also contains limited concentrations of B group vitamins. Normally, fruits contribute to a balanced diet, thanks to their â-carotene and ascorbic acid. In the harvest season, however, their importance can grow substantially, particularly among children who can literally gorge themselves on fruit. The advantage is an evident massive vitamin intake, but the downside is a protein defi ciency that can lead to dietary kwashiorkor (as witnessed in epidemic proportions in Angola during the mango season), and the risk of gastro-intestinal infection, promoted by unhygienic handling and high sugar content that can lead to fermentation. Like vegetables, fruits are rich in fi bre, thus mitigating the risk of bowel cancer and reducing blood cholesterol levels.

Two types of fruit stand out: banana and avocado. The banana energy content is approximately 100 kcal (418 kJ)/100 g, and it is easily digested when ripe. It is therefore a recommended fruit for infants as from the age of three months, and a signifi cant complement to the staple diet. The avocado energy content ranges between 160 and 200 kcal (670 and 840 kJ)/100 g, mainly of lipid origin. It contains signifi cant amounts of niacin and other B complex vitamins, â-carotene, and vitamin C. As such, it can constitute a major complement.

MUSHROOMS

Mushrooms are used mainly to vary and spice dishes, conferring on them a well-deserved distinction. But fresh mushrooms only provide 10 to 15 kcal (42 to 63 kJ) and between 1 and 3 g of protein/100 g. They cannot, therefore, contribute signifi cantly to meeting nutritional needs, even if some varieties contain B group vitamins, ascorbic acid and vitamins D and E.

FATS

Fats are lipid substances used in cooking that are not found in the natural state – they are extracted from animal and vegetable products. Fats include butter and lard (that are congealed at room temperature because of their high saturated fatty acid content), and oils (groundnut oil, cod liver oil), that are liquid at room temperature because they contain polyunsaturated fatty acids. The average energy content of purifi ed fats – especially oils – is 900 kcal (3,760 kJ)/100 g.

Fats derive their importance in nutrition from two main factors: they are a concentrated source of energy, and they contribute greatly to the taste and fl avour of foods. Furthermore, they can hold high concentrations of fat-soluble vitamins. Because fats are so rich in energy, only a small quantity suffi ces to improve the energy input substantially; they are however expensive. For those who can afford to eat enough (or more) to satisfy their hunger and choose their foods, fatty matter rich in saturated fatty acids (butter and mammal fat) promote cardio-vascular disease through the formation of atheromata.

On the other hand, the use of vegetable oils rich in mono- and polyunsaturated fats, combined with a reduced intake of red meat and an increased consumption of fi sh, has a protecting effect against atherosclerosis provided, nonetheless, that the energy intake is not excessive and that lipids constitute no more than 30 to 35% of that intake.

ANIMAL PRODUCTS

Animal products fi rst and foremost constitute an excellent source of protein for humans; they are also a signifi cant source of vitamins and minerals. However, like fats, animal products are often very expensive, and the poor are usually unable to consume them regularly in reasonable amounts. It is therefore useful to remember that animal products are not indispensable to man, who can balance his diet with vegetal products – for example by combining cereals and legumes. In addition to the animals usually eaten, many others serve as food or source of income for many populations, be it mammals, birds, fi sh, molluscs, shellfi sh, amphibians, reptiles, insects, larvae or worms. Their nutritional value is often signifi cant, especially during nutritional crises, but like gathered foods, these hunting and fi shing products often go unnoticed.

Animal products are quite popular; they improve fl avour and the nutritional properties of the diet, and thus enhance its variety. Wherever they are eaten, their social status is high, and theirs is usually a clear place in the food accompanying rites and celebrations: Christmas turkey, Easter or Eid-el-Kabir lamb, sacrifi cing a cow for funerals (the slaughtering itself often constitutes a ritual). On the other hand, their cost usually prevents them from being a staple food, other than in hunting or fi shing communities.

Meat and offal

Meat and offal constitute the edible fl esh of warm-blooded animals – although the fl esh of reptiles, where they are eaten, can also be referred to as meat. The expression meat refers to skeletal muscle, and is subdivided into red (beef, mutton, horse), white (poultry, veal, pork, rabbit), and black (game such as boar, hare, deer, dikdik, woodcock, agouti, bush rat, possum, and monkey meat). Offal refers to everything edible in an animal other than skeletal muscle, that is the internal organs (heart, liver, kidney, brain, tripe, thymus) and the rest: feet, snout, tongue, tail, ears, and marrow. As mentioned above, many warm-blooded animals other than the conventional butchery and hunting animals exist that are hunted or reared by man, and can contribute signifi cantly to the diet. Meat is an average source of energy, provided by the protein and lipids. However, the energy value of meat varies according to its lipid content, its protein remaining rather constant. Lipid variations are determined by species, the cut, the animal's lifestyle and its diet. Generally speaking, domesticated animals are fatter than wild animals, and domesticated animals subjected to industrial rearing are fatter still than those that must feed themselves. For example, at the end of the dry season, the lipid content of a nomadic (roaming) Sahelian cow is closer to that of the deer and antelope than that of industrial Angus beef. Therefore, signifi cant variations can appear in food composition tables between the reference energy value and the real value of the cut under consideration. Meat contains iron (which is very well absorbed), zinc, in addition to fair amounts of niacin and ribofl avin. Table 5.8 below indicates the values of the main nutrients contained in 100 g of meat of the main butchery and hunting species.

The high vitamin C content of offal is worth noting; vitamin C concentration in meat is minute. Liver is the type of offal that usually contains the greatest nutrient concentration, particularly iron (> 10 mg/100 g).

The nutritional characteristics of other warm-blooded animals (e.g. rodents and small birds) are similar to those listed above, except their calorie value, which can vary substantially.

Animal products

Meat preparation methods are diverse, but basic methods include simmering, roasting, grilling and frying. Fresh meat spoils quickly, and traditional preservation methods have been developed accordingly – they include drying, salting and smoking, often combined and involve the use of spices and seasoning to enhance the fl avour of the meat. Where electrical power and technology allow it, deep-freezing and canning are also excellent preservation methods.

Fish and other cold-blooded animals

The quality of the protein provided by fi sh and other cold-blooded species is just as good for man as that supplied by meat and offal. Sea fi sh and freshwater fi sh contain the same amount of protein: 17.8 ± 1.7 g/100 g of edible fl esh. On the other hand, the calorie values vary according to the lipid content, ranging from fi sh virtually devoid of lipids such as pike, tench, codfi sh, bream and sole - whose approximate energy value is 80 kcal (334 kJ)/100 g - through fatty fi sh such as lamprey, anchovy and sardine - 170 kcal (710 kJ)/100 g - to extremely fatty fi sh such as tuna (230 kcal (961 kJ)/100 g). Furthermore, the reference energy values indicated in food composition tables vary substantially, because the lipid content of fi sh is not constant, explaining sample fl uctuations. Generally speaking, the energy value of most fi sh is far lower - between 80 and 110 kcal (334 and 460 kJ)/100 g - than that of the meat of domesticated animals. Fish contains moderate amounts of iron (approximately 1 ± 0.2 mg/100 g), and sea fi sh is the richest food in iodine and also supplies a lot of fl uoride. Fritter fi sh, when eaten whole with their bones, constitute a useful source of calcium. Fish contains approximately the same amount of thiamine and ribofl avin as meat, but less niacin. Fresh fi sh also provides small amounts of vitamins A and C. Fish oil and liver is very rich in vitamins A and D, to the point of toxicity.

Crustaceans share approximately the same general nutritional characteristics as lean fi sh, while molluscs and shellfi sh contain slightly less protein and energy, but remain good sources of protein, fl uoride, zinc and iron. Frogs share approximately the same general nutritional characteristics as lean fi sh (Randoin, 1982; FAO, 1989c); so do reptiles.

The utilization and preservation of fi sh is similar to that of meat, but fi sh spoils even faster than meat, and must therefore be prepared even sooner.

Insects and larvae

Many insect species are edible: the best-known include termites, locusts, grasshoppers, crickets and caterpillars, besides many other species that constitute local delicacies. Insects and their larvae are very good sources of protein (10 to 50 g/100 g), lipids (approximately 10 g/100 g), B group vitamins and iron. They are usually gathered at specifi c times in the year, coinciding with a specifi c stage in their development or in the overall food availability. Dried, salted, smoked or crushed, they keep well. They are very tasty, especially grilled, and often serve to enhance the fl avour of other dishes. Their consumption can go unnoticed, but may account for most of the protein intake.

Blood

Blood is an important food in many pastoral societies, and is used to produce sauces and sausages; it contains high levels of iron (50 mg/100 g), as much protein as meat (18 g/100 g), and its calorie value is 80 kcal (334 kJ)/100 g.

Eggs

All bird eggs share the same approximate food value, except for energy that varies according to their lipid content. Eggs contain all the nutrients required for the development of the embryo up to hatching. For man, its greatest appeal lies in the fact that it provides best quality protein in relation to his need (13 g/100 g). Eggs also provide lipids (12 g/100 g for chicken eggs). They contain no glucides, but fair amounts of thiamine, ribofl avin, vitamins A and D and iron (but the latter is only poorly absorbed by the human organism). Eggs are digestible, easy to prepare and to obtain through home production; they are an excellent food for children as from the age of 6 months, and for the elderly.

MILK AND DAIRY PRODUCTS

Milk

Milk alone can feed mammal young from birth up to an age that varies according to species. Milk composition varies according to species and its specifi c growth requirements - all differences resulting from a functional aspect proper to the species under consideration. Milk composition further varies during suckling and the nursing. Different milk types can be substituted for one another, but none will provide the same quality as that species' own. There is no better milk for a calf than its mother's - and the same reasoning applies to humans. The latter can be fed exclusively on maternal milk until the age of 4 or 6 months, after which they require supplements to meet protein, energy, iron and thiamine needs - this is the beginning of the weaning process. For young mammals to survive and develop normally, the composition of secreted milk must remain fairly constant, in spite of the sometimes major hazards faced by their mothers in securing their own food. Milk secretion mechanisms mobilize the mother's tissues so as to preserve the quality of the milk. If the mother's diet is systematically inadequate, the amount of secreted milk will diminish fi rst, followed by its nutrient content. For a signifi cant alteration of the milk composition, the mother must herself be in a serious state of malnutrition. The quality of secreted human milk begins to drop when the mother's daily intake no longer exceeds approximately 1,200 kcal (5,000 kJ), assuming that she was not obese to begin with. Thiamine is the exception: the organism only contains slight reserves of thiamine, and immediately eliminates any ingested excess. As a result, if a mother develops beriberi, her infant will do so also quite rapidly.

The use of milk from other species in the infant diet and during weaning varies according to culture, its economy and outside infl uence. This infl uence can have serious consequences. For example, the promotion in developing countries of the Western practice of cow milk utilization, fresh or powdered, and maternal milk substitutes has had severe repercussions both on the economies of these developing countries, and on health. As a result, the World Health Organization in 1981 promulgated an international code of marketing of breast-milk substitutes. This code is one of the means devised to avoid substituting maternal milk and local weaning products with commercial alternatives. However, where their utilization is common, milk and dairy products are excellent foods, especially because of their protein quality and their high levels of calcium, ribofl avin, vitamin A and vitamin C. The only glucide to be found in milk is lactose, whose fl avour is less sweet than commercial sugar.

Lactose intolerance

Lactose intolerance is frequently mentioned – it manifests itself through abdominal pain, fl atulence and osmotic diarrhoea. It results from an activity defi ciency of lactase, the enzyme enabling the digestion of lactose. Three reasons explain lactase defi ciency. The fi rst and rarest is congenital (i.e. genetic), owing to a complete absence of lactase at birth. It is usually fatal which is why it is so rare.

The second is due to the fact that mammals usually lose their capacity to synthesize lactase some time between their childhood and adulthood, and this loss is irreversible. The problem affects Africa and Asia, mainly; human populations that grew accustomed to consuming animal milk from the early days of domestication, thousands of years ago, have been able to preserve their lactase through natural selection. They are the populations in the Mediterranean, the Middle East, India, some regions of Africa and Europe, the latter including their descendants who have migrated to America, Australia, New Zealand and elsewhere. Clearly, therefore, the indigenous populations of the Pacifi c Rim, however, face the same problem as Africans and Asians.

The associated problems are moreover quite minor: children lose the capacity to digest milk rather slowly after weaning, usually implying a fair reversibility through which, after a few days of a dairy-based diet, lactase is reactivated and permits the harmless resumption of milk consumption. Adults who have lost lactase show moderate – if any – intolerance symptoms, unless they absorb large quantities of milk at once (< 1/2 litre).

The third type of lactase defi ciency results from disorders affecting the intestinal mucous membrane, and are not further discussed here.

Dairy products

Milk is a highly perishable commodity because it is a liquid medium that can be rapidly infested by micro-organisms and because it contains lactose, free amino acids and vitamins making it an ideal culture medium for the rapid multiplication of micro-organisms. Man has thus developed milk conservation methods, the commonest being pasteurization or uperization (thermal treatments to destroy micro-organisms and allow a longer conservation in a sterile and closed container), fermentation, and the production of cheese, fats and condensed or powdered milk.

Fermented milk: Among the many types of fermented milk, the most widespread are yoghurt (resulting from fermentation mainly producing lactic acid from lactose) and kefi r (resulting from a fermentation that inter alia produces alcohol). The principle of milk fermentation involves the seeding of the milk with an adequate amount of a selected bacteria strain, for it to develop faster than the other germs contaminating the milk. By so doing, less and less lactose is available for these germs, whereas the developing lactic acid eventually inhibits bacterial growth and curdles the milk. The food value of fermented milk is similar to milk, except that approximately 1/3 of the lactose is consumed during fermentation.

Industrial transformation uses highly purifi ed strains to seed the milk, but artisan and home production involves the use of the previous day's curdled milk to seed the latest fresh batch.

Cheese: Cheese varieties are innumerable. Cheese production involves three stages: clotting, draining and maturing – the latter is not done in the case of fresh cheese. Fabrication produces curds (the cheese itself), and lactoserum, or whey, which is either discarded or used as animal feed or commonly in industrial food production. Whey contains most of the lactose lost in the process, up to 90% of the water-soluble vitamins, the uncurdled water-soluble protein, and small amounts of lipids and minerals. However, draining and maturing reconcentrate nutrients, and cheese can be a very rich source of protein, lipids and minerals (especially calcium), and a fair source of water-soluble vitamins that are synthesized during the maturing stage.

Fats: The fats drawn from milk are cream, butter and ghee (butter oil). The cream is separated from the milk either by spontaneous concentration or by centrifugation. The result is skimmed milk, and cream – the latter is no more than milk with a fat content ten times higher. A 100 g portion of

Animal products

30% fat cream contains 300 kcal (1,254 kJ), approximately 3 g of protein and 4 g of glucides. Butter is extracted from cream by churning, or beating, which results in separating the lipids (the butter) from the cream's watery phase, called dasher. Butter consists of more than 80% lipids, approximately 15% water, less than 1% protein, and less than 1% glucides. Its calorie value is approximately 750 kcal (3,135 kJ) for 100 g. Butter also contains fair amounts of carotenoids precursors of vitamin A, and vitamins A and D. Removing the remaining water, protein and glucides results in ghee, by decantation or centrifugation after heating. The calorie value of ghee is close to 900 kcal (3,760 kJ)/100 g. The advantage of ghee over butter is its tolerance to high cooking temperatures, since it has lost the protein and glucides that carbonize when butter is overheated.

Condensed and powdered milk: The crucial importance of water quality and hygiene in reconstituting milk is discussed below. Powdered skimmed milk keeps better and is considerably cheaper than full milk. For use in humanitarian action the former, nevertheless, must be enriched as discussed below. It is also worth noting that the use of powdered milk in humanitarian action is restricted.

The concentration of milk by evaporation produces condensed milk (sweetened or unsweetened) or powdered milk (skimmed or full). Condensed and powdered milk preclude micro-organism development, and are therefore long-conservation commodities.

Powdered skimmed milk no longer contains fat-soluble vitamins (especially vitamins A and D); it must therefore be enriched at least in vitamin A, and preferably in vitamin D also, as per the following enrichment rates:

- vitamin A: 1,500–3,000 ìg (5,000–10,000 IU)/100 g of powdered skimmed milk.
- vitamin D: the rate must be 10 times lower than vitamin A, based on international units.

This amounts to 12.5–25 mg (500–1,000 IU)/100 g of powdered skimmed milk. (European Commission, 1991).

Powdered milk must be reconstituted in a way that produces a liquid with an energy density identical to liquid full or skimmed milk. Such reconstitution demands impeccable hygiene conditions and the strict application of the manufacturer's instructions (usually expressed proportionately: "*x level measures of powder to y identical measures of drinking water*").

In the absence of such instructions, the following can be applied.

- Measure 130 g of powdered full milk using scales, place powder in a volume-graded container, top it up to 1 l with clean water (boiled for 10 minutes if the water quality is not guaranteed), and stir. This produces 1 l of milk containing approximately 650 kcal (2,720 kJ). To reconstitute 1 l of milk weighing approximately 1 kg, therefore, 130 g of powder are completed by 870 g of water (i.e. 870 ml of water, since the density of water is 1 kg per litre in standard conditions). This implies that milk containing approximately 65 kcal (272 kJ)/100 ml is produced by mixing a given mass (x g or kg) and 6.7 times this mass of drinking water. Indeed, 130 g of water mixed with 6.7

times 130 g of water, (i.e. 871 g of water) produces the same result as completing 130 g of powder up to 1 l with water. The translation into mass can prove useful in the absence of a graded container indicating volume.

- In the absence of both scales and volume-graded containers, full milk can be reconstituted by mixing one measure (e.g. a cup) of milk powder and four measures of water – this produces a slightly lower (by a few percent) energy density milk than that produced with the above method of topping 130 g of milk powder up to 1 l with water. Tests have shown that 130 g of milk translate into a volume of 220 ml; consequently, adding 4 times 220 ml of water to 220 ml of powdered milk, the powder is mixed with 880 ml of water (instead of the 870 ml used in the illustration above). The difference is negligible.

In the absence of instructions provided by the manufacturer, powdered skimmed milk should nevertheless result in an energy density of approximately 340 kcal (1,420 kJ)/l of reconstituted milk, equivalent to entirely skimmed fresh milk – 94 g of powder should be topped up to 1 l with drinking water. In other words, 1 mass unit of powder to 9 mass units of water, or 1 volume measure of powder to at least 4 and at most 5 volume measures of drinking water. The lack of accuracy between 4 and 5 measures arises from the variations in the density of powdered skimmed milk, ranging between 400 and 550 g/l of powder.

SUGARS

Sugar, syrup, honey and treacle are popular because of their sweetness, their preservation qualities, their digestibility and their high energy value. However, they provide nothing besides calories in the form of glucides and their excessive intake is deleterious for health (risk of diabetes, cardio-vascular disease, obesity and dental decay).

Commercial sugar comes from the sugarcane and the sugar beet; both contain approximately 16% sugar (saccharose). Industrial extraction methods result in chemically almost pure products, whose calorie value is 400 kcal (1,672 kJ)/100 g. Honey is produced by bees from the sweet nectar found in fl owers, and its calorie value is approximately 300 kcal (1,250 kJ)/100 g, provided by fructose and glucose. Maple syrup also contains 75 to 80% sugar, with similar calorie values to honey. Hydromel is an alcoholic beverage produced by fermented honey mixed with water. Hydromel can be distilled to produce a strong spirit. Treacle is a syrupy residue of sugarcane or sugaı beet production with a calorie value of approximately 250 kcal (1,045 kJ)/100 g. Honey and treacle are believed to be particularly healthy and to have medical virtues, but this is not supported scientifi cally. Preserves and jams are a convenient way of keeping fruit, by mixing them with an equivalent amount of sugar, and heating and stirring them until the mixture thickens to the desired texture. The calorie value of jams is of the order of 250 kcal (1,045 kJ)/100 g; their vitamin C content varies greatly according to the treatment of the fruit prior to preparation and preparation time.

BEVERAGES

Man needs only still water for his hydration. He nevertheless prefers other beverages, be they natural or chemical, for their fl avour and because many have pharmacological effects. This explains the popularity of sodas, alcohols, sweet or chocolate drinks, tea, coffee and fruit juice, and the huge diversity of artisan and industrial beverages. This popularity often translates into habits and social or religious rituals, which are sometimes deep-rooted and can have major economic and political repercussions. The consumption of some beverages, especially alcoholic, causes psychosomatic dependencies and health disorders that often reach public health proportions. In addition, it sometimes entails an economic cost that can be exorbitant at household level and within the society itself. The production and sale of these beverages is of course a major source of income for the private sector and for the State through tax channels.

Alcohol consumption is a source of individual enjoyment, and can play a social binding role. But these two aspects sometimes have signifi cant repercussions on humanitarian action: the absorption of alcohol can generate violent behaviour, and the need for alcohol provokes it – this causes major security problems; the economy of victims of armed confl ict or natural disaster obeys its own rules: humanitarian aid can be diverted to produce alcoholic beverages intended for sale, or to purchase tea or coffee and sugar, which, in some settings represent the key to any economic negotiation – this behaviour is often frowned upon by relief agencies who react tactlessly as a result; it is however easy to explain by the survival conditions of households confronted with a hostile environment – rather than drawing hasty conclusions, the reasons underlying such behaviour must be understood before reacting.

In addition to hydration, and excluding maternal milk, the nutritional role of beverages is secondary, even if some provide substantial amounts of energy and vitamins. Sweet drinks such as sodas, syrups and beverages containing cola nut extracts consist mainly of sugar and aromas. Their energy value varies between 40 and 50 kcal (170 and 210 kJ)/100 g. Their excessive intake is one of the main causes of obesity among children. Fresh fruit juice contains the same nutrients as fruit, and provides a good source of vitamin C, but the nutritional quality of industrial fruit juice varies greatly. Coffee and tea are popular for their aroma and their stimulating effect. In alcoholic beverages, a distinction should be drawn between beers, wines and spirits. Beer is produced from cereals (barley, sorghum) or bananas. Its calorie content varies according to its alcohol and sugar concentration. The energy value of common pale and dark ales with an average alcohol content is approximately 45 kcal (190 kJ)/100 g. The same value applies to commercial ciders and hydromel. Levels vary greatly however in the case of artisan products or specialities. Wine is produced from grapes and its energy value likewise varies according to its sugar and alcohol levels. Common white and red wines contain approximately 70 kcal (290 kJ)/100 g; this value can double in the case of sweet or dessert wines. Wine is also produced from palm juice and fruit other than grapes. Spirits are strong alcoholic beverages produced from fruit, cereals or potato. The alcohol produced by the fermentation of glucides is concentrated through distillation. Commercial 40% alcohol/volume spirits contain some 250 kcal (1,045 kJ)/100 g and thus constitute a signifi cant source of energy – but this is usually not the purpose of their consumption.

HERBS, SPICES AND SEASONINGS

Herbs (e.g. thyme, rosemary, laurel, oregano and tarragon) are leaves, whereas spices (nutmeg, pepper, cumin, chilli, cinnamon, ginger, saffron and vanilla) are seeds, fruits, pistils, bark or roots. Seasonings are preparations such as mustard, chutney or stock in cubes, but salt is a seasoning too. These three categories of condiments serve primarily to enhance and fl avour dishes. They play virtually no nutritional role other than to make food appetizing - and this in no way diminishes their culinary importance, explaining why even the poor use them widely. This aspect is too often neglected in emergency food relief for already malnourished groups receiving tasteless food rations. But it is precisely those groups that most need the means to enhance their food to render it appetizing when malnutrition-related anorexia is already rampant. Furthermore, the author has observed everywhere that groups requiring signifi cant food assistance sacrifi ce part of their ration to secure these means; this behaviour must therefore be anticipated and the use of herbs, spices and seasonings (especially salt) encouraged, by providing it in some way. In this context, salt is not indispensable to cover chloride and sodium needs (except in cases of extreme perspiration); food in fact provides enough of these minerals. The average individual daily intake of salt varies greatly according to population groups and individuals, but 10 g is an average.

ADDITIONAL INFORMATION REGARDING FOOD

Understanding food composition in terms of its nutritive value is useful in several respects. First, it enables the extrapolation of nutrient intake from food consumption data and it then facilitates the defi nition of diets and food rations to provide the specifi ed nutrients. Food composition is found in tables or in computerized databases. Data is expressed in weight (g, mg, ìg) for 100 g of edible portion of the commodity under consideration. Data is "representative" of the nutrient content of a given foodstuff. The values are by no means absolute or unchanging; likewise they are not overly specifi c to the method applied or the sample under scrutiny, in order to remain representative. The development of databases encounters two main diffi culties: biological variability that is characteristic of life, and the nutritional content of specifi c foodstuffs, which varies considerably according to soil, cultivation and rearing methods, age of the plant or animal, freshness and hydration. As a result, the analysis of different samples in different locations produces different results. Bearing these limitations in mind, tables nevertheless provide invaluable working tools, providing the user is prepared to apply the required fl exibility to ranges and average values rather than absolute values. For example, the deviation between the real calorie value of a given foodstuff and the reference value indicated in the table can reach 10% – far more in the case of meat, whose fat content varies considerably. Protein deviation is in the order of 5%, and the deviation can be signifi cant in the case of vitamins and minerals. Values provided by tables should, therefore, enable observers to determine what diet is most likely to supply this or that element beyond defi ciency thresholds, rather than accurately calibrating the intake in this element.

FOOD PROCESSING AND COOKING

Food processing is defi ned here as including cooking; processing is intended to improve digestibility and appeal, preservation and transport, and enrich the foodstuffs thus treated. Processing methods are innumerable and highly interesting – this Manual restricts itself to discussing the effects of the commonest methods on food. Losses are largely proportional to the duration and intensity of exposure, but they are diffi cult to quantify.

The nutritional value of processed foods can be affected as follows.

1. Cereal refi ning can be disastrous for their B group vitamin content.
2. Soaking and washing can remove water soluble vitamins and minerals.
3. Cooking in water (e.g. boiling or simmering) can dissolve water-soluble vitamins and minerals and thus waste them, unless the cooking water is consumed. Furthermore, boiling usually reduces the energy density of basic foods (see below).
4. Cooking can waste 30 to 60% of the vitamins – in the case of vitamin C, the loss can be complete.
5. The ambient acidity affects vitamin stability. Vitamin C and thiamine are unstable in neutral or alkaline mediums, but stable in acid mediums. Retinol is unstable in acid

mediums, vitamin D is stable only in neutral mediums, and ribofl avin is unstable in alkaline mediums. Vitamin E, niacin, and vitamins B_6 and B_{12} are unaffected by the ambient acidity.

6. Only ribofl avin, niacin and vitamin B_6 are stable in the open air (that is, they are not oxidized by atmospheric oxygen).
7. Only thiamine and niacin are stable to light.
8. Only niacin and vitamin B_{12} are stable to heat.
9. Unsaturated fatty acids are unstable at high temperatures and oxidize resulting in potentially toxic products. This is a problem only if the fat under consideration is overheated and smokes, and is used repeatedly (e.g. frying oil, which oxidizes slowly). In the case of butter, it is not the fat that blackens during cooking, but the protein and lactose residue contained in the minute whey content in butter. Clarifi ed butter does not present this problem (see above, regarding fats).
10. If foods are cooked normally (i.e. not burnt), the food value of glucides, protein and lipids is not or only slightly affected by cooking.
11. Cereals and legumes are substantially enriched in vitamin C when sprouted (30 to 50 mg/100 g of dry matter).
12. Fermentation through non-toxic germs raises acidity, and thus prolongs the preservation of foodstuffs by inhibiting the growth of other micro-organisms that can be dangerous. It also enhances fl avour and digestibility, enriches the foods thus processed – and is part of alcohol production.

FOOD TOXICITY

Food can cause poisoning or infection for a number of reasons.

1. The plants or animals that they are derived from naturally produce toxins:
   - cassava contains cyanide;
   - *Lathyrus sativus* (grass pea) contains a neurotoxin that causes lathyrism (see above); q other legumes contain

haemagglutinins that attack red blood cells and intestinal cells; q some sea fi sh contains potentially lethal neurotoxins; q some fi sh, such as tuna, must be rapidly processed after its catch, or its protein deteriorates and produces histamine causing headache, palpitations and diarrhoea; q vegetables in the cabbage family potentially cause goitre; q some mushrooms produce toxins (sometimes lethal, such as Death Cap, *Amanita phalloides*), or hallucinogenic substances (e.g. Fly Agaric, *Amanita muscaria*).

2. Some foods are contaminated by toxin-producing organisms, such as mussels that feed on a type of plankton producing the potentially deadly saxitoxin, which causes tingling (or paraesthesia), muscular weakness and vomiting; or oil produced from mustard seeds collected together with other seeds containing sanguinarin, an alkaloid that causes serious heart muscle infl ammation (cardiomyopathy) identical to that associated with wet (or cardiac) beriberi.

3. Food can be contaminated by bacteria or parasites: q bacterial infection:

   - the commonest are caused by salmonella (*Salmonella typhimurium*), *Clostridium perfringens* and yellow staphylococcus (*Staphylococcus aureus*), causing acute gastro-enteritis;

   - *Eschericia coli* also causes acute gastro-enteritis among children and traveller's diarrhoea;

   - *Clostridium botulinum* produces one of the most potent toxins (1 ìg/kg is a lethal dose); it thrives in cans and ham, and its growth is forestalled by adding nitrite – a bloated can, or a can that releases gas upon opening should be disposed of with its contents; its contents should never be eaten – contamination is not absolutely certain, but prudence should take precedence in view of the risks;

   - brucellosis causes fever, with peaks and remission; it is caused by bacteria infecting cows and goats, found in their milk and derived dairy products, unless the milk has been pasteurized – the infection is common among people who drink the milk fresh or eat dairy products made from fresh milk;

- bovine tuberculosis is easily transmitted through fresh milk – it causes lesions in the lymph glands, joints and bone; q parasite infection:
- the commonest arise from the consumption of beef infested by bovine tapeworm (*Taenia solum*), pork infested by porcine tapeworm (*Taenia saginata* and *Trichinella spiralis*), freshwater fi sh infested by broadfi sh tapeworm (*Diphyllobothrium latum*), saltwater fi sh and crustaceans infested by Oriental liver fl uke (*Clonorchis sinensis*) and Oriental lung fl uke (*Paragonimus westermanii*) – infection results from insuffi cient cooking or raw consumption of these animals;
- raw vegetables, such as lettuce and watercress, can be contaminated by trematodes (fl ukes), and by intestinal roundworm (*Ascaris lumbricoides*), whipworm (*Trichuris trichura*), and giardiasis (*Giardia lamblia*).

4. Food can be contaminated by mould that produces toxins such as afl atoxins (mentioned above in relation to maize and legumes), or the toxic alkaloids produced by rye ergot (*Claviceps purpurea*), a parasite fungus.
5. Food contains substances that cause reactions in some individuals (gluten and lactose intolerance, favism, specifi c food allergies).
6. Food is contaminated by substances used in agriculture and stock rearing (fungicides, insecticides, hormones and antibiotics), or by environmental pollution (dioxin, mercury, cadmium, radioactive substances).
7. Food contains deliberately added chemicals that can prove dangerous, such as some preservatives used to excess in the delicatessen industry.
8. Food produced from sick plants or animals.

The major health problems associated with food toxicity are those caused by bacterial and parasite contamination, and those related to the toxins contained in some foods. Contamination commonly occurs through direct contact (hands, food, soiled objects, fl ies and other insects, rodents and domesticated animals); faecal-oral contamination is frequent.

Food is also an excellent culture medium for pathogenes (especially milk, both natural and reconstituted from powder). Infection resulting from food contamination can be serious and accounts for most cases of infant morbidity and mortality. Poisoning from toxins contained in basic foods or regularly consumed foods can take on serious proportions, as it usually affects the entire population.

Strict hygiene measures are required to forestall these problems, throughout the food chain from producer to consumer, and to ensure water cleanliness and the appropriate processing of waste and vectors. Moreover, consumers must be informed regarding potentially toxic foods, and the methods of preparing them safely and healthily.

National and international regulations govern food quality by specifying quality criteria. The best known are those provided by the FAO's *Codex Alimentarius*, and the European Commission (European Commission, 1991), in addition to specifi c domestic regulations. Humanitarian action has a major responsibility in adhering to these regulations, given that some producers consider humanitarian assistance as a convenient channel to dispose of products considered to be sub-standard in the country of origin.

FOOD MEASUREMENT UNITS AND THE EFFECTS OF COOKING

The mass (effective weight) of solids and the volume of liquids must be measured in order to calibrate food consumption. Food composition tables then provide the tool to determine nutrient intake. Possible food processing – and its impact on food value – is integrated into this analysis. Humanitarian action sometimes lacks the measuring tools and conversion factors required to measure food and appraise the effects of specifi c processing. Some benchmarks are provided below; they are not all absolute, but nevertheless provide useful approximations.

Boiled foods tend to absorb some of the cooking water, and thereby dilute their energy content. A conversion factor can thus be applied to the weight of cooked foods *versus* raw foods. For example, the conversion factor of white fl our into bread is roughly 1.4 (i.e. bread prepared with 100 g of fl our weighs approximately 140 g).

Conversion factors, obviously, are not absolute values - they vary according to the quality of the ingredients and cooking methods. But they do give an idea of the impact of cooking on the weight of raw food. Where required and feasible, it is better to calculate values on the spot through practical experimentation. Table 5.10 below provides conversion factors for staple foods and the energy density of the raw and cooked food.

7

The Feeding Process

INTRODUCTION

Nutrition is the exchange of matter and energy between the organism and its environment. This exchange results from a need, and occurs in the course of the feeding process, the subject of this Chapter.

Living organisms must, according to their specifi c characteristics, continually fi nd matter and energy in certain states in their environment, and their survival depends on it – this is the essence of the nutritional need. But living organisms are fi nite entities and must therefore excrete matter and energy that they cannot recycle, or risk bursting – excretion must occur in proportion to the absorption and transformation of matter and energy (including the renewal of specifi c structural elements). From this standpoint, excretion is the second vital need arising from biological determinism. Thus, the nutritional need is met by matter and energy found in the environment in the course of a process called the nutritional flow.

DETERMINISM SET BY ORGANISM AND CULTURE

The feeding process is determined by the phenomenon of organized association. This determinism is related to the preconditions for a specific behaviour, and to the requirements of association. The fi rst level of association, that of the living organism, obeys biological determinism; the second is that of society as defi ned by its culture, and obeys cultural determinism as an extension of biological determinism. These two determinisms manage human life, which means that the latter must satisfy specific needs.

Biological determinism

Biological determinism is specific to life and expresses itself fi rstly in vital needs. In higher animals it subjects individuals to largely involuntary functions such as breathing, rest, nutrition, excretion and reproduction. Man has however gradually departed from his initial lifestyle, in which he was a "naked ape", and his biological determinism thus translates into the concept of basic needs. Malinowski defi nes this concept as "*the system of conditions in the human organism, in the cultural setting, and in the relation of both to the natural environment, which are suffi cient and necessary for the survival of group and organism*" (Malinowski, 1994).

These conditions are the following:

1. Metabolism
2. Reproduction
3. Bodily comforts
4. Safety
5. Movement
6. Growth
7. Health

As mentioned above, meeting these conditions gives rise to largely involuntary phenomena. But it also prompts deliberate phenomena, such as the search for and the consumption of food, reproduction, and the quest for bodily comforts and safety. These phenomena infl uence one another insofar as each requires time and minimal resources for them to be carried out - and, thus, for allowing the survival of the individual and the group. As a result, voluntary (or deliberate) phenomena associated with the feeding process belong to the overall satisfaction of vital needs, and discussing them individually is pointless.

Cultural determinism

Cultural determinism appears as soon as individuals resort to social organization to increase their chances of survival and, if possible, to improve their living standards through an enhanced coverage of their basic needs. In principle, society is an organized association, implying that the behaviour of the individuals that make it up is itself organized and regulated in all its forms of activity. This behaviour is nothing more than the culture that defines the society under consideration, since culture is the sum of the behaviours acquired within that society. Basic needs can therefore be matched by cultural responses (Malinowski, 1994), as follows.

Basic needs		Correspondin
1. Metabolism	->	Commissariat[4]
2. Reproduction	->	Kinship
3. Bodily comforts	->	Shelter
4. Safety	->	Protection
5. Movement	->	Activities
6. Growth	->	Training
7. Health	->	Hygiene

Organized and regulated organization (i.e. culture) implies that the conduct of activities satisfy the four conditions discussed in Chapter II, that is:

- anchorage on a material support enabling the coverage of basic needs;
- compliance with standards of behaviour that satisfy these needs;
- presence of an educational system to ensure that the young can take over from the retiring elderly – in its absence, the risk is cultural erosion;
- subjection to an authority that enforces standards of behaviour.

These conditions provide the foundation for any culture, and give rise to new needs called instrumental imperatives, or cultural needs (Malinowski, 1994), as follows.

1. The cultural apparatus of implements and consumer goods must be produced, used, maintained, and replaced by new production.
2. Human behaviour, as regards its technical, customary, legal, or moral prescription must be codified, and regulated in action and sanction.

3. The human material by which every institution is maintained must be renewed, formed, drilled, and provided with full knowledge of tribal tradition.
4. In society, authority must be defi ned and endowed with the powers and means to enforce its orders.

These cultural needs are just as demanding as the basic needs arising from biological determinism, being bound to them by an instrumental relationship. For example, man may not necessarily have to use a tractor-drawn plough or a combine-harvester to obtain his bread; but if such practices arise from his cultural development, the implements involved become indispensable and vital to the society's supply. In other words, it becomes necessary to produce, maintain and replace them, to train mechanics and engineers, to extract petroleum, which are essential subsistence conditions. Farmers also need to own land or have the possibility of cultivating it, to buy and use the necessary implements, spare parts and fuel without which they cannot perform the actions required to live in society. Likewise, members of society must have housing that complies with specific standards, and they must resort to sometimes costly transport systems to commute between their home and their workplace. This is the nature of cultural needs arising from the conditions governing the organized behaviour common to all cultures. The instruments providing the foundation of a culture and the resulting cultural needs represent the cultural determinism of a given society.

DETERMINISM SET BY THE ENVIRONMENT

The determinism imposed by the environment is different from both biological and cultural determinisms insofar as it arises from confrontation rather than organization. Society attempts to free itself from environmental constraints by responding to its own needs and familiar environmental limitations as effi ciently as possible. This shapes the culture itself: lifestyle, architecture, technology, neighbourhood relations, social structure and hierarchy, spirituality, etc. In terms of the feeding process, culture develops ways of producing and securing food, and – in order to avoid crisis – other means of adapting to known constraints. For example, the organism adapts its cardiac rhythm and its metabolism in order to strengthen its immune system. The natural and human environment shapes the behaviour of society and organisms, because they must take specifi c measures to survive.

In short, the feeding process is man's response to his nutritional need: biological response of the organism (interior) and cultural response of the society (exterior). Man is subjected to the determinisms thus created, and takes his chances with his environment, and must survive and reproduce within it.

FEEDING PROCESS ACTIVITIES

The feeding process is the practical expression of the nutritional fl ow. Theoretically, the nutritional fl ow is continuous within the organism: if it ceases, the organism dies. In reality, however, stops and starts occur well back from where the elementary thermodynamic reactions take place. For example, the liver works continuously, as does the brain, but man only drinks and eats a couple of times per day - and he only cultivates his land twice or three times yearly. This discontinuity results from the feeding process being made up by separate activities organized in a specifi c sequence. Activities of the feeding process begin in the cultural and environmental framework of the individual, and end in the biological framework of the organism. Arising from an organized behaviour, they are thereby determined. They must moreover perform suffi ciently well to respond to the demands of the nutritional need and its coverage.

ACTIVITY SEQUENCE

The activities of the feeding process follow a specifi c sequence, from the individual confrontation with the natural and human environment to secure food, to the excretion of stool and urine, and the release of carbon gas and thermal energy.

These activities all share causal relations in the following sequence.

1. Securing food
2. Preparing food
3. Sharing food
4. Consuming food
5. Digesting food

6. Absorbing nutrients
7. Biologically utilizing the nutrients
8. Excreting waste

THE ORGANIZATION AND DETERMINISM OF ACTIVITIES

The activities of the feeding process are organized and determined, because they occur within the framework of the organism and culture. They therefore rest on a specifi c material base, comply with execution standards, and submit to some form of control; these are all conditions that express the determinism of activities.

ACTIVITY PERFORMANCE

Each activity of the feeding process must be performed effi ciently enough to enable the organism to live. Performance is thus associated with specifi c conditions, which are diffi cult to meet because the organism (interior) does not control them, no more than the individual (exterior). As a result, effi ciency is not automatic, and the organism, the individual and society must develop adaptation mechanisms to face risks of poor performance (or counter-performance itself). It goes without saying that activity ineffi ciency can have serious consequences for other activities, especially if it occurs at an early stage of the feeding process. Unfortunately, success is diffi cult to ensure early in the process, precisely where adaptation mechanisms must be especially effective.

STAGES OF THE FEEDING PROCESS

Some activities of the feeding process are shared by all humans. They include the digestion and absorption of food, and urinating, and they result mainly from biological determinism. Others tend towards a common objective, for instance the securing of food, but can differ signifi cantly in nature or manifestation: these relate mainly to cultural determinism. This Manual proposes a model for the feeding process within any society, in spite of differences. This provides a tool to facilitate, among other things, the analysis of nutritional crises within the cause and effect relations and, consequently, to suggest relevant action.

To this end, the activities of the feeding process are divided into three main stages, and discussed accordingly; these stages are defi ned by the structure that accommodates them.

1. The securing of food is always determined by the cultural and natural environments of the individual concerned. It is sometimes determined by the "outside" human environment when this interferes with the human environment specifi c to the individual concerned. The securing of food is the stage during which man faces outwards to confront his environment (society and natural environment). Man is forever competing for available resources; for this, he resorts to his own resources, and makes an effort that costs energy and can be unpleasant. This also implies that he is healthy and adequately fed, in other words, that his previous efforts have proven effective in every way.
2. The consumption of food (i.e. preparing, sharing, actual consumption) is determined by the successful completion of the previous stage, culture and health. This second stage is one of intimate social interaction, that is, within the family - the smallest sustainable social cell. If the family has secured enough food during the fi rst stage, it prepares it, shares it among its members, and eats it. This provides the enjoyment both of social interaction, and of satisfi ed hunger.
3. The biological utilization of food (digesting, absorbing, biological utilization and excreting) depends on the two previous stages, but also on the health status of the subject. This stage is one of satisfaction associated with satiety. With the exception of its last phase (excretion), it takes place inside: man stores energy, and outside activities are replaced by internal chemical and mechanical processes.

Within the feeding process, this Manual pays specifi c attention, to the securing of food (i.e. stage 1); securing food is the crucial stage within the feeding process, because life depends on its effi ciency or ineffi ciency. Ineffi ciency can result from individual elements that tend to be dismissed as social cases and are of interest to humanitarian agencies whose mandate includes this aspect. But such ineffi ciency can also affect entire communities or trade categories owing to perturbations preventing them from securing food - sooner or later resulting in disaster. In terms of nutrition, humanitarian agencies are confronted mainly with generalized cases of ineffi ciency or failure to secure food; this failure in turn entails an ineffi cient consumption and biological utilization of food. Generalized failure in later stages (i.e. in the consumption or utilization stage) where people do not actually lack food suggests that the problem is mainly medical and sanitary. An adequate response must then involve health services and those concerned with the quality of water and habitat. In-depth understanding of the securing of food is especially important today because humanitarian agencies are changing their approach to nutrition problems. In the past, this approach was alas frequently confi ned to malnutrition and food distributions once the disaster was widespread. Nowadays, the trend is to develop a broader understanding of nutrition (integrating economic, political and social factors), thus enabling a more timely and preventive approach. This implies a better understanding of the lead-up to crisis, and closer interaction with its possible victims. In terms of humanitarian operations, therefore, more attention must be paid to the fi rst stage - that involving the securing of food - than the two others.

Each stage of the feeding process is made up of organized, determined activities that are linked to performance, and each stage is thus discussed according to these elements.

8

The Securing of Food

The securing of food involves activities aiming at obtaining food from the environment. The performance - or success - of such activities is crucial, because the rest of the feeding process depends on it. It is therefore a key stage in terms of the nutritional functioning of a given society; it has also, in man's recent history, undergone changes with fundamental consequences on the functioning of society and the relation between man and his environment.

The search for food has evolved with the development of different cultures and their instrumental imperatives such as economics, social control, education and political organization; many lifestyles exist side by side today. The food securing activities of the Amazonian hunter-gatherer, the Senegalese farmer, the Russian miner, the Afghan businessman and the CEO of a French car manufacturing plant differ greatly. But they all respond to the same physiological demands and consist in fi nding matter and energy in the environment, at a specifi c frequency, with the means that are adapted to the individual culture. The matter, energy and means involved pertain to the "*cultural apparatus of implements and consumer goods must be produced, used, maintained, and replaced by new production*" (Malinowski, 1994) - economics provide this response in any culture. As a result, the securing of food is associated mainly with the economy of a given society according to its culture; an economic approach is required to understand this mechanism in any society, and also provides a basis for comparison.

A brief discussion of the evolution of food securing activities also sheds light on the development of economics and its consequences.

THE EVOLUTION OF FOOD SECURING ACTIVITIES TOWARDS MORE ECONOMIC ACTIVITIES

For hundreds of thousands of years, man was a hunter-gatherer who found his food by collecting, hunting and fi shing whatever the environment produced spontaneously. In terms of the securing of food resources, the human diet was quite similar, to that of many other higher animals.

The Neolithic revolution allowed man to manage his environment in order to secure his food through production activities such as agriculture and stock-breeding; this shift was caused by a sometimes variable combination of opportunity, comfort, ingenuity, and sometimes insecurity caused by the shrinking of natural resources. For the fi rst time, man was faced with food surpluses that he could exchange for non-food commodities produced by non-farmers. In some conditions, agriculture is a guarantee for survival, but it also imposes greater cultural determinism on its derived activities: implements must be made, maintained and replaced, infrastructure must be built, and a security system must be created and maintained to produce, preserve and store food. This shift is associated with the sedentary settling that appeared at the time in densely populated areas. Such village or town groups promoted the assembly of specialized production activities other than agriculture (e.g. commercial, administrative, political and military), which indirectly promoted the securing of food. The discovery and the utilization of metal defi ned a new evolution of tools, trade and armament, and further promoted this trend. Agriculture nevertheless long remained the predominant activity to ensure subsistence, because productivity was still too low for surpluses to accumulate and enable signifi cant population segments to conduct other activities.

The agricultural revolution of the 17th and 18th centuries eventually overcame this hurdle in Europe (this had been achieved centuries before in Asia, but on a lesser scale owing to the absence of an industrial revolution); it resulted in the production of signifi cant agricultural surpluses to respond both to the nutritional demands of the major part of society that was not involved in agriculture, and to set aside the stocks required to face the normal variations of any agricultural production. Production increases were determined by implements, and thus resulted in major demands on metalworking for the production and maintenance of such implements. The production of metal required the smelting of ore, which in turn implied the use of coal, itself extracted from mines, and operating the mines involved steam engines. This development introduced the industrial revolution, followed by the intensive use of cotton in the textile industry – promoting the rapid development of this major segment of the urban economy. Cotton is considerably better suited than wool to the constraints of mechanization, and so responded to the high textile demands in Europe (Bairoch, 1983). Man's access to and mastery of fossil energy (coal and, later, petroleum) provided the basis for the industrial revolution. Combined with agricultural production, the use of fossil energy generated societies where production activities are varied and often highly specialized, resulting from an intensive (and not always judicious) exploitation of the natural environment. This is not food production in itself, but enables the securing of food through appropriate exchanges; such a change entails major lifestyle upheavals.

As indicated above, economics provide the cultural response to the increasing complexity of food procurement; in other words, as the network of material interdependencies develops, man sacrifi ces some of his material self-suffi ciency and subjects his diet to economics. This evolution consists of the following sequence:

the appearance of production – through production activities, man secures goods that nature does not provide spontaneously (i.e. without his intervention); the diversifi cation of the cultural apparatus of implements and consumer goods; the specialization of production activities, and their association with the three familiar sectors of the modern economy – primary (i.e. agriculture, forestry, and hunting and fi shing), secondary (transformation), and tertiary (the provision of services such as trade, banking, administration, transport, health, education, and insurances). The diversifi cation of implements and consumer goods and the specialization of production activities have two major consequences for the securing of food: the increase of cultural demands and the need for transactions.

The increase in cultural demands

The diversifi cation of the cultural apparatus of implements and consumer goods increases dependency on these implements and goods, and cultural demands therefore grow proportionately. This infl uences the coverage of all basic needs that depend on the economy (i.e. basic economic needs) including food, according to the income available to cover all associated expenses. The following example drawn from the Swiss Federal Statistics Offi ce illustrates the average budget proportion devoted by Swiss households to their main basic economic needs in 1993:

- transport and communications 11.2%
- education and leisure 9.6%
- beverages and tobacco 6.8%
- clothing 4.2%

The Swiss example is an extreme in terms of the proportional attribution of expenses between basic economic needs that are unrelated to food and those related to food. The above data is based on the average available household income in Switzerland – the same calculation based on average gross household revenue shows that the proportion allotted to food is in fact well below 17.9%. Clearly, the budget percentage allocated to food varies according to available revenue; wealthier Swiss households devote proportionately less of their budget to food than the poor. This phenomenon is expressed by Engel's law: with given tastes or preferences, the proportion of income spent on food increases as income diminishes.

This confi rms what seems self-evident: basic economic needs that must be met with an available budget follow priorities – food ranks high, but only up to a given point: Engel's law shows that it is impossible to allocate 100% of the budget to food. Direct observation in many countries has led Lipton to note that food practically never accounts for more than 80% of the total expenses (Lipton, 1982). This appears to be a critical threshold beyond which people behave as if there were no further alternative: they can no longer save on non-food commodities, and yet cannot survive on less food. If their available revenue falls, then they reduce their food and non-food expenses in the same proportion (Pacey and Payne, 1985). This means that, even in cases of malnutrition, people do not devote their entire resources to food, and every incipient famine bears out this fact. In diversifi ed economies, the threshold of 80% of resources being allotted to food can be considered as the threshold of absolute poverty.

The need for market transactions

The specialization of production activities causes a loss in self-suffi ciency to varying degrees. Social partners thus accept mutual dependencies in order to meet their basic economic needs: those who produce food need implements, those who produce implements need food, and both need the clothing they purchase from suppliers; the latter in turn must secure food and implements, and so on. These interdependencies call for transactions during which commodities produced are exchanged for commodities required. Social partners therefore account for both supply and demand. As the specialities entailing interdependencies multiply, it becomes impossible to resort to the direct exchange of commodities in the form of barter. This problem is addressed by the following parameters:

- money as a means of exchange;
- the market, where supply and demand meet within transactions;
- the trade-offs that set transaction prices or terms.

Money

Money appears in all societies based on economic specialization; it deprives specialized partners of their independence in terms of meeting their basic needs, making them dependent on services. Money nevertheless provides a standard, and also a form of payment. It is a purchasing power reserve, because one of its main functions is to separate individual exchange operations.

Expressed in prices, it also indicates the value attached by consumers and producers to a given commodity. Initially, therefore, money is a technical instrument; it however rapidly became an instrument of power (by generating new power relations in which the shrewder dominates the physically stronger) and hence the object of envy. Indeed, it confers power by providing the means of buying practically anything at a favourable moment, and permits the exploitation of weakness.

The market

The market is an arrangement allowing supply and demand to meet in transactions. It fi nds a compromise between the confl icting interests of producers who attempt to fetch the highest price, and of consumers aiming at the lowest price. Such arrangements can be made in the market-place. Understood as an arrangement, however, the market does not necessarily suggest a specifi c location, and there are as many markets as there are transaction types: the goods and services market, the labour market, the exchange market, and so on.

ECONOMIC ACTIVITIES

The activities

Economic activities are those required for survival, i.e. to meet all basic economic needs, including food. Typical activities enabling survival today - alone or in combination - are the following five.

Tapping the natural environment

This consists in collecting the food resources produced directly and without signifi cant human intervention. Such activities include hunting, gathering, and fi shing. Hunter-gatherers depend on this, and their survival depends directly on the renewal of natural food resources, and on the extent of the territory available. Some groups still rely exclusively on hunting and gathering; they are however disappearing because they lack the means of defending both their culture and the vast expanses required for their livelihood against technically more advanced competitors. Collecting nevertheless persists in most cultures, and its dietary importance ranges from essential (e.g. the Sahelian farmer) to recreational (the French weekend mushroom collector).

Non-industrial animal and plant production

Subsistence agriculture and pastoralism are livelihoods in which the direct product of agricultural and pastoral activities provides the basis for the diet. These livelihoods are vanishing in highly industrialized countries; elsewhere, subsistence agriculture and, more still, pastoralism, are increasingly eroded owing to the deterioration of the environment by man and modern forms of globalization.

Activities generating a purchasing power

These activities enable people to acquire the goods and services produced by others, in cash or kind. Purchasing power in kind results in barter based on agreed trade-offs. Purchasing power in cash results in purchases; this facilitates access to various goods and services, but the trade-off is accordingly more complex than for barter. Production activities that generate purchasing power are highly varied and include the following:

- the production of raw materials through agriculture, forestry, horticulture, fi shing, etc. – profi t is derived from the supply of raw materials;
- transformation: artisanal or industrial production from raw materials: extraction, refi ning, assembly, fi nishing – profi t is derived from the value added to the product at each transformation stage (mineral becomes metal, metal becomes specifi c parts, parts are assembled into implements; animals are slaughtered and the meat thus produced is butchered, the hides are tailored into clothes, shoes, etc.);
- services: transport, trade, distribution, banks, insurances, health professions, administration, education – profi t is derived from services that facilitate, preserve or improve the life of consumers (letter or person delivered to their destination, ownership confi rmed by legally recognized documentation, individuals in better health or professionally trained, etc.).

Such activities are conducted by private or public companies. From an economic perspective, those owning the company must be distinguished from its employees. Specialization can be quite high, both for the company and for its employees: the greater the degree of specialization is, the more complicated it becomes to streamline its network of interactions.

These activities appear at the same time as production activities differentiate, work is divided and market trends become the main infl uence on production. They are typical of market-oriented and nationalized societies that rely heavily on the input of paid labour for production, distribution and the provision of services. This means that the food supply of the segments of society that are not involved in its production must be ensured by industrial food production, by the return on other activities allowing the import of foreign food commodities, or external food aid. Therefore, households whose main economic activities lie outside the food production sector rely on their society's feeding system for their supplies. The feeding system engulfs production, imports, and food assistance, in addition to the distribution of both export and domestic commodities. Where imports and/or foreign food aid account for a signifi cant proportion of the available food, the country depends on food availability on an international scale. The feeding system of a given society or country is illustrated in Figure 6.7 below (see also Section 3.8 below regarding the synoptic approach to the securing of food).

These prompt individuals (or the society) to refund, donate or lend food, or the means to secure it. Such behaviour is dictated by kinship, reciprocity, pity, interest, bad conscience or charity, or by a mutual assistance contract. Examples include the protest of infants, the deliberate subservience of a beggar, the fl attery of a customer intending to take advantage, the threats issued by a crowd to guarantee the price of bread, the fl ight from famine of a starving migrant, the waiting for assistance of a refugee in a camp. These are all more or less successful attempts at invoking social obligations. To donors and lenders, the strength of such obligations is directly proportional to their psychological, social, economic, cultural and political proximity to the social cell under consideration (e.g. family, corporation, clan/tribe/ethnic group, or State), and their motivation to act. Inactive members of the family have probably contributed already, or will eventually do so. But for most of society, production activities (or their absence) that involve the activation of social obligations are sustainable only in the presence of an effective social welfare system – based on the prerequisite that all members of society contribute towards it, and thus benefi t from the system when they become inactive.

Tapping the human environment

This consists in stealing food or the means to secure it. Within a given society, petty larceny (such as stealing fruit or eggs) may be forgiven; but systematic theft is usually not tolerated because it entails no viable reciprocity. However, it can be imposed out of fear of the thief or his background, for example. Theft can thus be more or less accepted, but it always implies some form of reciprocity, and certainly never provides the basis for subsistence. History has in fact demonstrated that no society can develop if its own culture is exclusively based on looting.

Described as an activity, theft amounts to gathering, except that the fi eld of activity is not the natural environment, but the product of the activity of other individuals, even humans in the case of slavery in many ancient societies – and even today in some countries, or cannibalism – e.g. in pre-Colombian America (Harris, 1978).

In short

To sum up, modern man resorts to these fi ve types of economic activity to secure his food and other essential goods and services; he attempts to combine them as best he can so as to reduce the dependency caused by excessive reliance on one type alone as discussed in Section 3.7 below.

The necessary means for the activities

Economic activities imply the use of means to produce economic resources in a regular manner. These means are the household production assets, and are referred to here as "means of production".

Means of production are those enabling the continuation of production activities, in a way consistent with the rate of consumption of goods and services. In other words, they provide access to food and all essential goods and services in a renewable way. They consist of a basic resource and the inputs required for its utilization. Inputs are usually associated with a basic resource in some way; in some cases however the required input can fulfi l different functions, such as a car, used both to commute to work and for leisure. These means of production are:

labour is the fi rst and most important, and is common to all forms of economic activity; it is determined by the general health condition, and its inputs are food and hygiene; land and water that are useful in terms of food collection and animal and plant production, and mining; its necessary inputs include implements, machines, draught animals, spare parts, fertilizers, pesticides, seeds, power, labour, and time; professional training and the inputs required to produce saleable commodities or goods (e.g. a shoemaker's training, combined with the required material and tools, or a doctor's education and his practice); capital to establish or develop transactions; required inputs relate to the securing of customers (for example, an oil merchant seeks to purchase oil in the countryside for sale in the city – this requires cash to actually buy the oil and rent a stand at the city market, in addition to transport and possibly storage); the professional training and corresponding inputs that enable a specialized salaried activity (e.g. an engineer's training and the budget to cover the cost of transport and professional clothing, or a tradesman's training and the necessary implements and clothing); today, employees are less expected to provide the tools of their trade in developed economies, and employers allow a specifi c budget for this; capital that generates interest (e.g. cash investments, breeding stock, leased land) and the inputs required to attract customers, maintain the herd, and maximize the land's market appeal; status that facilitates the activation of social obligations – the main input is either a legal status for the unemployed, the retired, the disabled among others, or an image that inspires pity, bad conscience, fear or compassion.

People are not all equal in their economic activities between and within societies, depending on the quality, the quantity and the appropriateness of their means of production and their ability to use them.

THE ORGANIZATION AND DETERMINISM OF ECONOMIC ACTIVITIES

Economic activities carried out through the use of means of production must take place within a culture. They can thus be analysed by following their organization and determinism schemes.

The function of economic activities

Man resorts to economic activities in order to meet his essential economic needs (including food) directly or indirectly. However, the relation between this activity and the covering of needs is not automatic; the observation of individual economic behaviour must therefore always involve an understanding of its underlying reasons, and resulting expectations.

Community

The community involved in economic activities depends mainly on the use of its resources and its culture. However, all economic producers share two characteristics: they must participate in activities, and each family unit must include at least one producer. Families are understood here as households, the smallest sustainable social unit: individuals living alone or groups living together voluntarily. The household unit is central to this Manual, being the smallest common denominator for a range of activities that are logically and closely connected:

- it determines food-securing activities, which in turn shape the subsequent stages in the feeding process for all members of society;
- it is central to the preparation, sharing and consumption of food, because it accommodates dependants such as infants and the elderly in addition to its productive members;
- it infl uences other elementary needs (such as reproduction, and the search for shelter and safety) – as discussed below, these needs determine activities and the food securing performance; the link between reproduction of the species and survival of its culture, on the one hand, and nutrition on the other, is close because of imperative reciprocal obligations.

Individuals do not always form a family with children; this is unimportant here, because they must nevertheless obey the same rules in order to secure economic resources.

The concept of household tends to suggest a solid nucleus, in which interests and resources are both shared. However this may be misleading, because the active members of a household can have strongly diverging interests and obligations; even so, the household is the strongest social unit, considerably more so than the individual, the group or the nation.

Structure

The structure is the basic organization unit required to fulfi l a function. The structure that supports the active economic contributors is determined mainly by the means of production available to households to meet their basic needs (in turn shaped by the economic development and the social structure of the society). In practical terms, hunter-gatherer families each represent a structural unit, because each is self-sufficient in satisfying its own basic needs. The same comment still applies to some pastoralists and subsistence farmers; in this case, however, the relation is not as clear because pastoralists and farmers may not actually own the herd or the land they look after, but are paid to do so. Therefore, not owning the produce of their labour, they must resort to the market to cover their economic needs, like any artisan or wage earner.

In short, the greater the self-suffi ciency at household level, the more its close society (i.e. the family, clan or tribe) provides the basic structure determining its economic activity. The lower the household's self-suffi ciency, the more the "Tribe-State" takes over the different economic segments that ultimately enable everyone to meet their needs through exchanges. In this case, the integrating structure is too remote from daily concerns for households to identify with it; they therefore gather and organize themselves to defend their interests against other economic groups. In fact, wherever the organized behaviour of a society is highly divided in this way, social classes appear in direct or indirect association with the economy; the degree of association is determined by their activities and real power within the economy. This explains the existence of associative professional structures such as artisan corporations, trade unions, associations, and castes: they all provide a real structure for economic activities and, thus, for the means of securing food. Such associations all design charters or standards that are superimposed with the political norm, in order to regulate the group's specifi c activities in both content and form. They also generate their own teaching systems accordingly. The strength of its structure determines the group's capacity to voice its concerns towards the central authority, and to secure its status and employment - this capacity determines its survival. Indeed, the social status of all such structures or units is a refl ection of their economic power, be it direct (i.e. activities that are indispensable to the economy) or indirect (activities that are recognized as vital for the culture, or associated with the exercise of power). They are also bound to one another by dependencies or interdependencies that are often complicated by the fact that modern States result from the blending of several cultures that must be reconciled by means of a political authority, with all the problems of interest and power that this suggests. Nowadays, particular attention must be paid to the meaning of such structures in view of globalization; the power of some of them reaches well beyond that of national political leaders, and they regulate human life with the sole objective of profi t, with no further thought to the social contract that the economy needs in the long term, or the other instrumental imperatives that are indispensable to the existence of any culture.

Norm

The concept of norm defi nes what can be done, and how.

Acceptable activities

The relationship between man and the cultural apparatus of implements and consumer goods is based fi rst and foremost on ownership; the ultimate objective is to appropriate existing economic resources. In every society, anything can only be appropriated in relation to one's own available means, which must be recognized by the rest of the community as one's own, thus conferring upon them a varnish of legitimacy. The means of production described above must comply with this norm – they must either belong to the individual and his family, or be communal goods whose relevant access is clearly regulated. In short, the legitimate ownership of means of production entails the right to secure resources through recognized activities. It is in this sense that looting and theft are usually not recognized appropriation activities – this being said, in the complexity of modern economic relations some types of appropriation are accepted when they are in fact akin to theft or looting.

The normative dimension in securing economic resources is crucial, particularly in crises: households or entire segments of society can starve alongside resources that they cannot appropriate because of the social contract that binds them to the rest of society. Breaking the rule would prompt

The Tribe-State comprises only one cultural group, as opposed to the Nation-State that can consist of many. Either way, this situation means that the society under consideration has lost its primary function, that is, of increasing the chances of survival through the organization of individuals into a group; thus offenders no longer have much to lose. This can result from the fact that their life itself is at stake, or that society lacks the means and the will to react. The great Irish famine of the 19th century illustrates this to a large extent (Gray, 1995).

Rules of conduct and implementation techniques

Every type of effective activity has to be organized in one way and one way only, through which it becomes culturally stabilized, that is, incorporated into the cultural heritage of a group (Malinowski, 1994). This implies the presence of an educational apparatus, which is just as differentiated as production activities are. In any culture worthy of the name, this apparatus is not confi ned to teaching techniques only; it also aims at conveying a set of ethics, rules of conduct and moral values, without which technology tilts culture towards technocracy. "*Science without conscience is but the ruin of the soul*" said Rabelais, in 16th century France. The main component of the educational apparatus is therefore the family, in which codes of general conduct and the cultural taboos of the society are taught - these provide the indispensable basis for the implementation of specifi c activities according to the accepted cultural norm. Specifi c activities can be taught as such. Each culture has its own coherence and deep roots that provide the foundation for the form and substance of activities. Respect for this form and substance are just as indispensable to the survival of the culture as culture is indispensable to the survival of the individuals that make it up.

Enforcement

All societies give themselves strong means (authorities and representatives) to ensure that the securing of resources obeys the ownership norms that it (or the power in place) has recognized; it can deal with non-compliance if necessary. The great Irish famine resulted from this phenomenon: the State rejected the survival mechanisms that threatened to violate existing rules, and instead allowed millions to starve or be forced into exile. This shows that in crises (certainly at their onset), survival mechanisms are limited to what is permitted, according to what personal possessions are left. This is an important concept in attempting to understand the conduct of victims of incipient crisis.

Norms, but above all the authority that enforces them, are rather stable elements whatever the circumstances because they ensure the survival either of society (when it is culturally homogenous), or of the segment of society that holds power (when society is culturally heterogeneous). In the latter case, it is both politicized and heterogeneous, therefore uneven from an economic perspective.

FACTORS DETERMINING ACTIVITY PERFORMANCE

The economic resources required and the timeframe can be viewed as the two major constraints forcing households to produce a given minimum quantity of resources, at a rate that is consistent with their possibilities.

Factors determining the economic resources required (denominator)

Economic goods and services required for the coverage of basic needs can be quantifi ed to a certain extent. This should enable the appraisal of the economic resources required for this coverage to be adequate, that is, to set an objective to be met with the production of resources in cash and kind. Special attention must nevertheless be paid to the fact that needs vary between and within cultures (and according to the environment), and such variations fall into fi ve broad categories: cultural variability, the magnitude of needs, economic status, behaviour and the conjuncture.

Cultural variability

The cultural apparatus of goods and services, like the set of values specifi c to each culture, entails expenses that vary from one culture to another. Marriage can involve a cost here, and a profit there; housing and schooling do not involve the same constraints everywhere; political, economic, and social status may – or may not – entail obligations involving an economic cost; furthermore, cultural value can make some commodities indispensable when, at fi rst sight, they are not. Similarly, it may be vital to take part in traditional or religious rituals involving considerable expense.

The magnitude of needs

The need for clothing, shelter, heating and food depends on climate. Transport costs depend on the distance between the home and the workplace. Finally, household needs will also vary according to the evolution of the family.

Economic status

As illustrated by Engel's law, the proportion of the budget allocated to different needs varies according to the resources that are available to the household, that is, according to the economic status within the culture and the range of choices that result from it.

Behaviour

The economic behaviour of individuals in the same economic bracket varies according to their spending habits (i.e. wasteful or sparing). Lifestyle does not have the same meaning for everyone, translating into different preferences or priorities (i.e. utility) and, thus, different costs. Households do not all seek the same forms of wellbeing and safety. This behavioural aspect is particularly relevant to the nutritional need. The full spectrum of nutritional needs can be covered with different foods whose costs vary greatly. Consequently, the direct observation of individual normal food behaviour is indispensable to defi ne accurately the food resources required within a given timeframe. A household can meet its nutritional need adequately from very diverse foods, provided it has the choice. Within set limits, households can consume varying amounts of the same products without health or functional problems, but with a different nutritional status.

Economic circumstances

Economic situations vary according to season, the markets of goods, employment, capital, dividends and exchange rates, and according to politics. Such variations lead to different types of budget utilization and needs coverage behaviour; a given expense may be considered exaggerated and unnecessary today, and normal tomorrow.

This highlights the differences in the economic needs of households, social groups and cultures, but also how these vary over time. The concept of basic needs may appear to be straightforward, but its reality is far more complex; only its economic aspects are discussed here. One major diffi culty arises in attempting to appraise individual basic needs: there is no general rule, and each must be considered separately. A common pitfall is the ranking of basic needs, and the setting of minimum thresholds in order to quantify the economic resources required to achieve minimum sustainable living standards. This is subjective, and can become judgmental and elitist:

- ranking his needs reduces man to his involuntary needs, ignoring his psychological, social and cultural identity – this mistake is common both in development programmes and in so-called humanitarian operations.
- in addition, the question arises as to setting poverty thresholds rather than wellbeing, or even wealth thresholds – this mistake may be common in development programmes, but is almost standard in humanitarian operations.

In short, individuals and groups set their own priorities and defi ne their own concept of needs, and both are related to their culture. Economic needs can always be quantifi ed, but only with the direct participation of those who are under scrutiny. The overall economic performance of households can therefore not be fi tted with a universal quantitative and qualitative denominator.

Factors determining timeframe

The timeframe in which performance is appraised is determined by the time unit specifi c to the production rate, related to the renewal of economic activities: hunting, fi shing, gathering, and agricultural seasons, paydays, the time required for the production of a given good or the provision of a service, or the recovery of capital interest. Households sometimes conduct several economic production activities simultaneously: performance is in this case determined by the production cycle of the activity that accounts for most of the revenue. However households can also set timeframes for themselves, according to the evolution of both the family and its needs. This entails a division of time into intervals that are not necessarily regular.

Factors determining the economic resources produced (numerator)

To produce resources regularly, economic activities must allow for means of production. Production is determined by:

- the return on, or productivity of, activities (return, or yield, is defi ned as the output per input unit of a specifi c means of production);
- the number of production units activated.

Thus, resources produced within a given timeframe correspond to the resources produced per input unit, multiplied by the number of input units - in other words, the output multiplied by the number of input units.

Such an approach to economic resources produced may appear cumbersome, but it involves the scrutiny of the underlying analogous mechanism of the production of any type of resource: a standard must be applied to both exchanges and production.

The yield of production activities

The basic defi nition of productivity, or yield, is simple: it is the ratio of output to a selected input. In the case of household economy, yield is not so obvious because households can usually secure their economic resources through various activities, involving different means of production, to produce different types of resources according to their degree of self-suffi ciency. As seen above, most households must produce economic resources in both cash and kind. In the fi rst case, productivity is a direct result of man-hours or any other relevant measurement unit, such as cultivated surface. In the second, the production of cash resources usually involves the production yield of goods or services per relevant unit, and a cash conversion yield of this production. For example, a cereal farmer calculates his yield in terms of weight per surface unit (this calculation is particularly relevant in terms of the farmer's domestic cereal consumption).

He also calculates the yield (from which he derives his profi t) of the surplus sale, expressed in monetary unit per weight unit. An abundant harvest thus translates into a high production yield, but market prices can be low owing to the resulting available cereal excess; the sale yield is then accordingly reduced. In such a case, the farmer may fi nd it diffi cult to balance his budget, in view of his unavoidable expenses in order to survive. On the other hand, a mediocre harvest in shortage situations can prove quite profi table in terms of sale, if demand is strong enough to raise prices. For wage-labourers, the form of compensation plays a central role in terms of yield, depending on whether the salary is related to time or to output.

Here again, the law of supply and demand is crucial, both on the labour market and on the goods and services market, to determine the yield of production activities. Moreover, it is usually possible to choose different ways of utilizing resources in order to obtain the greatest yield or productivity, depending on the household's own appraisal of its circumstances, sometimes involving gambles as to economic trends. Returning to the above example of the cereal farmer, if his harvest is excellent but market prices are low, he may choose to borrow money to cover those needs that require economic resources, and store his harvest for sale in the following season at a better price. His knowledge of climate and market trends enables him to anticipate developments with good prospects of success; however, such a gamble may also be a last, desperate resort, heralding destitution if it fails.

The examples above show that the best concrete approach to yield or productivity calls for the scrutiny of the general and specifi c parameters of the fi ve types of activity that defi ne economic activities and the securing of food.

General parameters: Four parameters can infl uence the yield of household production activities, but they may not all peak together.

1. The value of activities on the labour market and the goods and services market.
2. Productivity inputs.
3. Individual factors.
4. Contextual and structural factors.

Activity value: Clearly, resources produced within the same timeframe but by different professions vary considerably.

The capacity of a given profession to produce economic resources is determined by what is referred to here as its qualitative value in the economy of the culture under consideration. This value determines the trade-offs between what is sold and what is bought in exchange for this production.

It is defi ned by three main types of power.

1. The economic power associated with the activity is linked to demand for the production specifi c to this activity on the goods and services market – that is, that value is set by the rarity of the profession, its production, and the inelasticity of demand for this production.

2. The political power held by the community resorting to a specifi c activity is linked to the means of pressure it can exert to defend its interests (such as compensation rate and form, work-time, etc.), and its position in economic, political and social power relations. For example, in the early days of the industrial revolution in the 19th century, mining was essential to industrial and trade developments, and demand was thus strong. The economic power of miners was weak, however, because their social status was among the lowest, and their political weight insignifi cant. This status is refl ected in the way they were exploited (imposed working hours, compensation). Upheavals, strike and union assemblies proved the only way to exert pressure effectively and afforded them the political power to improve their salaries and social status.

3. The cultural power arising from the carrying out of a specifi c activity, conferring social status upon whoever exercises it. This type of power refl ects the cultural values of the society and is usually elitist, that is, bound to a feature that is not commonly shared within society, but acquired by the individual or inherited, and enjoys the esteem of society in general (the arts, medical or religious activity, superior erudition or professional expertise, high-level responsibilities, political stature).

Often, one of the above types of power alone confers recognition upon the activity, but they can also accumulate: producing something rare and necessary, within a powerful and socially prestigious guild, is a reliable formula for a comfortable income.

Productivity inputs: Productivity inputs infl uence the yield of production activities per production unit. They permit the increase of production per time or surface unit. The household, or economic unit in charge of the activity, must secure them and cover the costs associated with their utilization. Table 6.5 below provides some examples of productivity inputs.

Individual factors: In spite of identical activities, means of production and health condition, major productivity differences can appear, because individuals are not equal in terms of their own capabilities (will, manual and intellectual capacity), nor are they in terms of their professional training. Moreover, the compensation for equal work can nevertheless refl ect discriminatory inequalities according to the social status attached to individual factors such as racial or ethnic segregation, and gender discrimination; women are usually paid less than men.

Contextual and structural factors: Contextual and structural factors are independent of the will of the individual, of their activities and their productivity inputs. They include, in particular, geo-climatic parameters, and the conditions of supply and demand that set the market forces and the terms of trade at both micro- and macro-economic level.

Parameters specifi c to activities: The yield of gathering activities is determined by climate and the availability of game and plants; the input unit refers to the surface covered.

The yield of food production is determined by the cultivated species, climate, natural soil fertility, and agricultural techniques. The input unit refers to the cultivated surface.

The yield of activities that generate purchasing power is determined by what can be obtained in terms of sale price, salary, fees, interest rate, savings or loans. Input units refer to the units sold: respectively, time or production units (depending on the form of compensation) in the case of salaries, service units in the case of fees, monetary units in the case of savings or investments, and monetary or in-kind units depending on the nature of loans.

The yield of social obligations is determined by, on the one hand, the strength of social status to "impose" an obligation upon the benefactor, and the performance of the benefactor's production activity in terms of satisfying his own needs, and contributing to the coverage of those of one or several benefi ciaries, on the other hand. The input unit refers to the benefactor. The yield of activities preying on the human environment (such as theft) is determined by power relations; the input unit refers to the producer of stolen commodities.

The yield of economic activities poses increasingly acute problems to more and more societies whose economy, ecology, and demographic growth are close to saturation and breaking point.

The concept of security

Economic security is achieved when a household has the sustainable means to obtain all the goods and services that it requires to meet its basic economic needs, according to its cultural and physiological standards. The economic security of a given household is therefore determined by its access to consumable goods and services, and the conditions for security demand that this access be adequate and stable.

Adequate access

As discussed above with respect to the denominator of performance in Section 3.6, the notion of adequacy is very diffi cult to outline in terms of basic needs, including the nutritional need.

This being said, and assuming the household is well aware of this diffi culty, adequate access is determined by four main parameters.

Performance security

1. the means of production (or productive assets), in terms of quality and quantity to achieve the required economic performance;
2. the market availability of the consumable goods that the household cannot itself produce – this availability is infl uenced by:

- the capacity of the society or country to produce goods, services and currency to fund imports; q the aid received from other countries or organizations; q the distribution system;

3. the physical proximity of labour markets and the goods and services markets that the household depends upon;
4. the economic reserves and social obligations that protect against possible economic counter-performances.

Stable access

Access stability is determined mainly by the sustainability of the household's means of production - in other words, on the condition that the means of production permit the renewal of access to resources: the land, thanks to sun and rain, provides one or several harvests per year; labour regenerated by rest and food, is able to conduct paid activities every day; invested capital produces regular interest; herd reproduces. But the stability of access is also infl uenced by the stability of availability or supply, which in turn refl ects the vitality of the regional or national economy that softens production and import fl uctuations.

Thus, the economic security of a given household is determined by the sustainability and adequacy of its means of production and reserves, but also by the economic security of its partners in the market, in turn infl uenced to some degree by the national economy.

Specialized literature all too often discusses economic security from the restrictive angle of food security, as if households only consumed food. This Manual deliberately chooses the broader approach of studying the overall economic performance that is required to meet all the basic needs that involve economic resources (goods or services). Indeed, the allocation of resources to the coverage of basic needs is determined by the inelasticity of demand for the goods and services required to this end. The more limited the resources are, the more the priority of their allocation goes to goods whose demand is most inelastic and renews most rapidly; in this case, when the limit of survival has been reached, it is found to be food (and very possibly water in future).

This radical perception of needs leads economists, nutritionists and politicians to discuss food security before addressing economic security. Their approach is pragmatic regarding poverty and disaster, considering that at least access to food resources (Sen's "food entitlement" - Sen, 1981) and food availability must be suffi cient. However, when the nutritional need has become acute to the point of eclipsing all other economic concerns, then an advanced stage of famine has already been reached, and the victims of such situations have only their lives to lose.

The terminology of food security implies that food is the minimum commodity to which people must have access; it quickly turns into a priority objective, for households, societies, nations and the politicians and economists that govern them. Such an approach is overly restrictive as discussed above (Lipton, 1982; Pacey & Payne, 1985; Gillespie & Mason, 1991; Maxwell & Frankenberger, 1992).

"Suffi cient access" and "acquisition" are both determined directly by the means of production by which households produce the resources for exchange or consumption. This in fact means that the key to food security lies in the means of production, in their productivity and their sustainability: these provide durable access to food and the other consumable goods and services.

The concept of "economic security" is thus preferable to that of "food security", because it allows for human wellbeing according to culture, and is not limited to the digestive tract.

Security mechanisms

Economic security concerns all households, without exception. However, households are usually bound to others by family, economic, cultural or political ties; while at the same time, public or private enterprises have the mandate to ensure the security of specifi c groups. In other words, different groups set up different security systems - they are grouped as follows: individuals, households, communities and professional groups, non-governmental organizations, States and their services, international institutions and donors.

When security mechanisms are ranked, it appears that households (defi ned as the smallest social common denominator) and the individuals they include cannot always ensure their self-suffi ciency alone - and the same comment applies to some extent to the economic and social sub-structures surrounding them. They therefore require relays at higher or external levels of organization. Households can therefore resort both to their own security mechanisms, and external ones; these are discussed below, but some important ger . ~al aspects require clarifi cation fi rst.

Origins of security mechanisms

Security mechanisms are not improvised, they refl ect an accurate knowledge of the hazards that usually threaten economic performance. They arise within a culture in response to events registered in its collective memory. They usually correspond to an organized behaviour specifi c to each culture, where they form part of tradition and are specifi cally carried over from one generation to the next. The purpose of such mechanisms is to reduce or remove vulnerability to possible events that could harm the collective economy. They are generally related to the variations whose amplitude is considered normal by different economic groups. When the magnitude of unfavourable phenomena exceeds the norm, then diffi culties arise.

For example, in central Mozambique, the oldest farmers claimed that drought never occurred in two successive years, resulting in their habit of constituting reserves for two years at most. In 1992, however, drought struck exceptionally for three years in succession, causing scarcity. Village elders thereafter adapted their position to allow for three-year reserves. Another example is provided by the Western European unemployment security system. Resulting from the Great Depression of the 1930s, it was mainly put in place after World War II, in a time of great economic growth. This system was perfectly adequate to respond to the minimal contextual unemployment that existed until the 1970s. However, this system is inadequate in addressing massive structural unemployment arising from neo-liberalism, because the issue is no longer to assist a few individuals in times of prosperity, but rather to redefi ne the terms of the social contract, for which "growth generations" are ill-prepared. In cultures rooted in strong traditions, it is easy to analyse and understand the intrinsic security mechanisms. But the sometimes rapid changes in lifestyle can render such mechanisms obsolete or irrelevant exposing the population to unforeseen problems.

The corporatism of mechanisms

Security as defi ned above constitutes an ideal that is only rarely attained. Households strive for it, but its prerequisites are numerous, complicated and often impossible to satisfy. This holds true within cultural groups whose cohesion appears to be strong, but in which the specialization of roles and activities leads to corporatism, diverging opinions and consequently the appearance of social classes competing for political power. These factors are nothing but manifestations of the security construction performed by every economic corporation, sometimes to the detriment of others. The labour market and the goods and services market provide the meeting point of societies, where power relations express themselves between the different economic partners of a given culture.

Partners know exactly what to expect from one another, and each fi rmly intends to profi t. The exploitation of weakness expresses itself here discreetly or openly, depending on whether such weaknesses are temporary or structural. Tourists enjoy the exoticism of local markets; they are not always aware that, for many partners in poorer countries, the market constitutes a combat arena.

Households' quest for economic security today is no longer confi ned to national boundaries, and this complicates the analysis further. Every village arena can be infl uenced to some extent by developments on global stages such as the New York, London, Paris or Tokyo stock exchanges. The latter are dominated by a handful of private companies whose power is greater than that of nation States. These companies are clusters of many smaller enterprises and likewise result from the construction of economic security at individual and private level. This construction ensures the security of those who belong to the company, in addition to its shareholders, but at the same time it is detrimental to that of countless households, as refl ected by the growth of unemployment statistics resulting from restructuring.

HOUSEHOLD SECURITY MECHANISMS

Foundations of household security mechanisms

Between World War II and the 1980s, the industrialized West provided a unique example of economic stability and social security, in which most of the active population only performed one economic activity (in the form of wage labour) during most of its working life. Relatively low unemployment rates, the reasonable price of basic consumer goods, and insurance against unemployment, accidents and sickness ensured stable living standards. The State played a major role in price stabilization policies and in the egalitarian management of social security systems. As a result of all this, households ceased to ensure their own security, because it was guaranteed by the State, which made it compulsory and automatically deducted the required premiums and taxes. However, most of the world's population live in conditions that neither the State nor anyone else cares about. The fl ow of consumer goods is unstable, prices are not controlled, there is no social security system or employment guarantees. This means that performance varies greatly, that economic accidents are frequent and that households are left to their own devices to face these factors, accidents, and sickness that strike them directly. Incidentally, wishes for good health that are common in many cultures are not simple courtesy, but refl ect a real concern. An individual suffering long-term illness or disability cannot cover his needs and can face destitution together with his family. It is therefore crucial for households exposed to common hazards in their environment to secure their own response mechanisms.

Household security mechanisms in terms of the security concept

The security mechanisms that households can resort to are limited to the parameters that they can infl uence:

- in terms of the parameters determining the adequate access to the consumable goods and services described above, households can infl uence only the management of their means of production and the constitution of reserves – they cannot, individually, infl uence the availability of employment opportunities, nor that of goods and services on the market;
- in terms of access stability, households determine the sustainability of their means of

production, but not the stability of the availability of employment opportunities, nor that of goods and services on the market – as a result, they cannot infl uence demand and supply trends that set prices that, in turn, defi ne employment opportunities and compensation rates.

This means that security mechanisms can be limited when it is a case of facing economic stress. Nevertheless, they are indispensable to reduce dependency on external mechanisms that are often non-existent or slow in reacting.

The purpose of security mechanisms

Security mechanisms clearly serve to ensure the stability of an adequate access to consumable goods and services. The underlying concern, however, reaches well beyond the immediate coverage of basic needs: it is a matter of preserving the active and passive household assets as the only real guarantee for survival. The plough, the land, the tool, the herd and the store are more important than food or clothing, because the former are required to obtain the latter. In diffi cult circumstances however, the plough, the store or the land may have to be disposed of in order to obtain food. This abnormal economic behaviour occurs in all famine situations; it allows the individual to secure food for a time but deprives the household of its means of production, and thus results in destitution and dependency. Security mechanisms are intended to avoid this. From this standpoint, and as described above, it is not so much food security that is sought as the preservation of the means of production, which is a precondition for household economic security.

The functioning of security mechanisms

Security mechanisms protect active and passive household assets according to a strategy revolving around the three following axes.

1. Managing the means of production to ensure a suffi cient and stable economic performance.
2. Constituting reserves in order to face possible counter-performance periods with minimal damage.
3. Establishing and using social obligation networks, for the same purpose.

Managing the means of production: Ensuring a suffi cient and stable performance is the overall priority in the survival of a household; economic performance, as discussed above, is primarily determined by the means of production enabling basic economic activities. Means of production can suffer a loss in productivity, or may even become unusable. This happens when droughts reduce the yield of agricultural production, or when competition grows intolerable on the labour market or the goods and services market. To face this hazard, productive assets must be reinforced in favourable times, and the means of production must be diversifi ed. This enhances the choices of the most appropriate means of production in times of stress, and also facilitates the compensation of productivity loss of given means of production through the use of other means. Diversifi cation rests upon two major preconditions: alternatives must exist, and households must be both fl exible and adaptable enough to resort to them. The concept that is central to diversifi cation applies to economic activities, but also to the manner in which they are conducted.

A common example in rural settings is the organized use of the following means of production: subsistence agriculture, stock-breeding on different scales, artisanal production of usual consumer goods and charcoal, wage labour of one family member (on site or in the nearest city, seasonal or permanent), gathering of natural resources (especially food-related, but also fuel for domestic use). The resources thus produced are intended both for domestic consumption and for sale. Agriculture provides examples of diversifi cation in the form of inter-cropping, the use of varieties with different maturing cycles, taking advantage of microclimates, and the successive use of different plots of land to save water. In this framework, large families initially face a problem, insofar as they include many "idle" mouths to feed, but these may soon become productive and develop into a signifi cant labour force that will strengthen the diversifi cation of economic activities. The diversifi cation and accumulation of jobs are likewise common in towns, often entailing signifi cant involvement in the informal economy, be it legal or illegal. Diversifi cation thus offers options for subsistence. Their utilization complies with the organization of the workforce in order to obtain the best possible yield at the right moment. The tactic of utilization of the various options aims fi rstly at avoiding the utilization of household reserves (see below). It usually follows a "normal" pattern to face variations, likewise considered as "normal", of the production of economic resources and the basic economic needs. Thus, in normal circumstances, a certain proportionality of work distribution applies. Any change in this proportionality is tantamount to perturbation, be it positive or negative.

Managing the means of production in order to ensure suffi cient and stable performance in fact consists in putting in place mechanisms of adaptation to the normal fl uctuations of the yield of production activities, and to the normal fl uctuations of the needs to be covered. The implementation of these mechanisms is likewise considered as normal and is in no way pathological, because it consists in avoiding a rise in the economic vulnerability level of the household. On the other hand, three comments apply to the diversity of choices and to security:

- diversity of choice is not to be confused with the need to utilize all possible options to their maximum – the former is synonymous of security, while the latter indicates crisis or poverty, hence vulnerability;
- crisis victims are often forced into production activities that would be considered unacceptable in normal circumstances – here again, this behaviour can easily be misinterpreted as the utilization of a diversity of alternatives, when it in fact refl ects a crisis behaviour;
- in a precarious natural and human environment, it is possible to accept excessively low salary conditions and to restrict the scope of alternatives, as a counterpart for the contractual guarantee provided by even a limited employment security.

These three comments illustrate the importance, when assessing economic security, of identifying why people conduct a specifi c activity, and its qualitative cultural value. The three types of behaviour listed above do not constitute the development of a security system nor its utilization by a coping mechanism, they are survival mechanisms. The difference between coping and survival mechanisms is that the former maintains performance without loss, whereas the latter entails a cultural, economic or physiological penalty.

The constitution of reserves: The constitution of reserves is essential to the protection of the household's means of production and assets. Reserves (or passive assets, or fi xed household capital) include anything that can be consumed, exchanged, or sold to meet basic needs, when the means of subsistence do not permit a suffi cient economic performance. The constitution of reserves is possible when the production of goods and services is equal to or higher than what is required. As long as production is suffi cient, it is less risky to reduce consumption deliberately and constitute reserves with the resulting balance. The constitution of reserves follows various channels:

- limiting consumption in order to generate surplus;
- increasing food consumption in order to constitute fatty reserves;
- increasing production in order to generate surplus;
- saving surplus or exchanging it for goods with a high market value or a high exchange value (e.g. savings accounts or life insurance policies);
- purchasing, keeping or investing only with respect to what has a market value – for example, it is preferable to purchase corrugated iron rather than tiles to cover a roof, because the iron sheets can more easily be removed and sold if necessary.

The constitution of reserves is a long-term process, often spanning generations. In this view, family jewels are not simple ornaments, they represent an economic security (they can be pawned or sold in times of economic diffi culty). Fixed capital represents an economic buffer for use when the means of production and resorting to diversifi cation no longer ensure minimal living conditions. When production is insuffi cient, reserves protect the means of production, because the latter do not then need to be sold for survival. Clearly, after a poor harvest it is preferable to sell off some jewellery rather than the plough or draught animals. The constitution of reserves in fact amounts to securing coping mechanisms to compensate counter-performance: thus the use of reserves to compensate counter-performance entails impoverishment.

Establishing and using social obligation networks: In terms of security mechanisms, social obligations form part of mechanisms that are external to the household, since they exist for it and are directed towards it from outside. Households nevertheless play an active role in this framework, as follows:

- fi rstly, on an individual level, by invoking these obligations and being able to demonstrate that they amount to a right;
- secondly, by using and creating them on a participatory basis: the household associates with others in a more or less organized structure – association and organization are two potential strengths relative to those who are solicited; trade unionism, demonstrations, membership of professional societies with the power to demand are all activities that allow social obligations to be established and exploited – the common form of participation in industrialized countries is the (usually compulsory) contributory membership of the social security system (see below);
- fi nally, by contributing to these structures as a donor, on the basis of reciprocity that provides the basis of the development of social obligations within a culture.

As a reminder, subsistence means are defi ned in this Manual as those enabling the production of economic resources on a continuous basis. Therefore, they do not include reserves, because they dwindle as they are used.

Social obligations provide access to refunds, gifts, loans, credit, and exchanges. They are an important security mechanism because they offer additional alternatives when performance is poor, and when the diversifi cation of economic activities – or the use of reserves – cannot improve it. However, in response to poor economic performance, households can adopt different tactics: for example, they may prefer social obligations to reserves or to the diversifi cation of economic activities. As a result, one should not draw hasty conclusions regarding a given economic situation from the choice of a specifi c security mechanism: only thorough behavioural analysis will clarify the situation. Usually, the social obligations that households can invoke belong to the culture of their society. They relate to responses that are clearly named and are associated with clearly defi ned problems (e.g. loss of herd or harvest, unemployment, accident, sickness, widowhood, or loss of one or both parents). Social obligations can also contribute to increasing assets, and thus reinforce security. Those based on custom or law are compulsory – within the limits of the conferring entity's possibilities – and therefore well deserve the name of obligations. Their associated reciprocity is worth noting, be it based on written contract (e.g. private and public insurance) or verbal tradition, known, respected and enforced by all the members of the community on pain of expulsion. Reciprocity guarantees that all community members can enjoy similar measures in case of need; without it, it is likely that social obligations would be much more limited. Reciprocity and enforcement are two concepts central to social obligations: they guarantee both sustainability and survival. When social obligations are based on moral values rather than on a norm, reciprocity can lead to blackmail or abuse. The benefi ciary may be relieved for the moment, but at a considerable price that increases his dependency.

The constitution of reserves and the establishment and use of social obligation networks both in fact extend the diversifi cation of possible options at the level of the means of production. They are nevertheless quite different in nature, because their sustainability is considerably more limited, particularly in facing a crisis that affects the entire population. The separation of the establishment of social obligation networks from diversifi cation may be challenged; indeed, many poor families often include at least one member whose production activity is begging. Likewise, many families draw part of their income from remittances in cash or kind from relatives who are wealthier or whose position obliges them to do so. The diversifi cation of subsistence means and the remittance system traditionally form part of the means of production in some cultures. The establishment of social obligation networks on the other hand entails a dependency towards the donor, and is only available in case of demonstrated need, with very different social, cultural and economic implications.

The many famines of the past thirty years amply demonstrate that household security mechanisms are often insuffi cient to protect individual households against crises that extend to the community as a whole. Larger entities must provide a relay, or accept responsibility for household security; security mechanisms thus become external to the latter.

External security mechanisms

External mechanisms have been mentioned above; they result from the same concerns and follow the same purpose as household mechanisms. Household mechanisms are overall quite similar, to the point of providing scope for a set formula; external mechanisms on the other hand vary considerably depending on the country, the region, and the economic group under consideration. They must therefore always be appraised individually. Variations result mainly from the political, economic, ideological and social parameters that characterize individual States; they also result from the interest of the international community in those States and their population, in compliance with international regulations, or because of its own economic, political, and social agenda. The expression "international community" refers here to private and public organizations such as the World Bank (WB) and the International Monetary Fund (IMF), the United Nations Food and Agriculture Organization (FAO), the United Nations Development Programme (UNDP), the World Trade Organization (WTO), the International Labour Organization (ILO), the World Food Programme (WFP), offi cial bilateral cooperation agencies, non-governmental development agencies, and human rights and environmental protection agencies. The means and the methods resorted to in order to ensure or improve economic security vary greatly, as do their results. Consequently, the subject is very broad, and can only be mentioned here in passing. Globalization has boosted the importance of external mechanisms because of the (not always reciprocal) dependencies that it implies. These mechanisms are described below.

Ensuring adequate economic performance

At local and regional level, workforces, resources and negotiating groups (e.g. trades unions) are associated in order to increase the productivity of economic activities, and to ensure an equitable allocation of produced resources.

At national level, the role of the State is crucial. Stabilizing prices, implementing a participative growth policy, exerting economic power over weaker States, authorizing unions and negotiating with them, promoting employment, providing and maintaining distribution, health and education services, guaranteeing freedom of the press (which operates both as a detector and as a means of pressure), setting up early warning systems, etc. These are all examples of the means at the disposal of the State to improve or ensure the economic security of its citizens.

At international level, macro-economic policies associated with structural adjustment, trade liberalization and the exploitation of comparative advantage are currently viewed by those who devised and imposed them as indispensable means to ensure the economic security of all countries. This has raised serious doubts. The United Nations have attempted repeatedly to promote food security and adequate nutrition for all (First International Conference on Nutrition (FAO/WHO, Rome, 1992) and World Food Summit (FAO, Rome, 1996). In spite of the media attention attracted by such events, their short-term positive effects are diffi cult to see, whilst in the long term their effect may be positive in sensitizing the public and the media. The discouraging aspects of these summits are manifold, in particular because of the contrast between the stated intentions aimed at defending rights, and the weakness of their recommendations and the means available for their implementation. Besides, a host of development agencies have attempted, more or less successfully, to raise the economic security of social groups ranging from villages to States themselves.

The constitution of reserves

At local and regional level, the reserve constitution mechanisms lie in the hands of small highly traditional communities who have been able to preserve communal granary systems or stocks to be shared in times of crisis. Such mechanisms however tend to disappear, because of the growing infl uence of national economies on such private systems. This tends to promote individual interest to the detriment of collective interest, and leads to reluctance in pooling resources that could otherwise be invested individually.

The constitution by the State of monetary, energy and food reserves provides a relative security in case of crisis. However, if the crisis becomes nationwide, its associated needs are such that regular supplies depend entirely on market and production dynamics (in other words the stability or growth of economic production). On such a scale, in addition, the constitution of signifi cant reserves (both public and private) is less and less encouraged by the facility of exchanges, taxes on existing stocks, international trade agreements, and consumption rates. There is a rough divide between industrialized countries, where consumption is high and food self-sufficiency is almost total, and non-industrialized countries, which are usually too poor to constitute reserves (with some notable exceptions). However, in the long run, industrialized countries are probably more liable to serious crisis than poor countries. This is due to the major challenges such as the exhaustion of fossil energy, world economic competition, the automation and specialization of production, the frailty of distribution systems, and the confi nement of agriculture to a minute proportion of the population. In industrialized countries, the State only has limited reserves, and households keep virtually no stocks, and have practically no alternative means of production to face durable crisis. In poor countries, on the other hand, households must fend for themselves entirely, and therefore set aside reserves and resort to diversifi cation – this often enables them to overcome a crisis in a remarkable way. Non-development is in fact possibly a security for the future, while over-development is stretched to the limit.

At international level, the constitution of reserves is in decline. International trade agreements on agriculture, the reduced importance of the public sector in favour of the private sector, and the concentration of most of the world's industrial food production in a handful of multinationals have all reduced the world availability of food stocks. At the same time, the demand for them has risen considerably. This is a kind of dead-end, because the food defi cit of many developing countries is worsening, while food production subsidies in surplus-generating countries has dropped considerably – this does not augur well for the worldwide improvement of food security.

Establishing and using social obligation networks

At local and regional level, solidarity is expressed through social obligations relative to family, corporation or tribe (or clan).

At State level, social obligations correspond to what is called social security. This security can be determined by the public or the private sector, frequently in combination, and may be compulsory. The principle is one of mutual insurance to which all active members contribute, in order to obtain a fi nancial cover in case of accident, sickness or unemployment. Moreover, the State may also set up security systems in anticipation of crisis, such as the creation of jobs, subsidizing the price of staples, the distribution of food ration cards and food-for-work type projects.

At international level, the United Nations system (in particular the WFP), together with non-governmental organizations (NGO) and the international donor community have set up early warning systems and constitute contingency food stocks, in order to respond to economic counter-performances affecting regions or countries in crisis.

In short, security mechanisms defi ne the resilience of a given society, community or household to the risk of crisis and crisis itself. Security mechanisms - permanent cultural behaviour phenomena - are not to be confused with coping mechanisms, which take advantage of the alternatives offered by security mechanisms momentarily when economic performance is insuffi cient. Security mechanisms are set up in favourable circumstances; coping mechanisms appear in incipient crisis.

A SYNOPTIC APPROACH TO THE SECURING OF FOOD

All the above elements illustrate the complexity of the fi rst stage of the feeding process (i.e. the securing of food); this fi rst stage must be considered within the modern context of diversifi ed economies. It is nevertheless possible to apply a relatively simple model to all households. In order to achieve its purpose (i.e. to provide a set formula for the securing of food), the model is quite general and suggests a number of concepts that are valid in all circumstances, containing all the key elements that must be taken into account. Clearly, no two situations are identical; but each can nevertheless be described with accuracy. For example, the population of central New York, Paris or London secures its food according mainly to its purchasing power; on the other hand, in the great marshlands of the White Nile, in southern Sudan, the securing of food is determined by fi shing. In many situations, however, the securing of food is highly diversifi ed, and changes according to seasonal and economic circumstances. The model is thus general because it offers the full range of possibilities to be investigated in considering a given population. The same comment applies to the variables infl uencing performance. All do not apply everywhere, but they must all be mentioned in order to investigate a problem anywhere.

First concept

The securing of food is an essentially economic phenomenon. When man distances himself from nature by evolving from the status of hunter-gatherer to that of producer, he develops the cultural apparatus of implements and consumer goods - that is, his economy. He also generates cultural needs in the wake of his elementary needs; he diversifies his production activities, specializes and so loses autonomy in terms of meeting his elementary and cultural needs (shortened here to his basic needs). In other words, he creates societies of individuals that are interdependent in terms of meeting their basic needs. From an economic perspective, interdependency revolves around the labour market, the goods and services market, currency as standard of exchange value, and around demand and supply. As activities specialize, these factors soon turn food into just another economic good - with the difference that food is an absolutely essential good. This means that demand for this commodity is constant whatever the circumstances (i.e. inelastic demand), and that priority must be given not to food itself, but rather to the means that permit it to be secured regularly. Such means also allow the securing of other necessary goods and services through exchange. As a result, households (understood here as the smallest social common denominator) must include the securing of food in their overall economic strategy. The latter enables it to acquire all the goods and services required to meet its basic needs, and preserves this capability in the long run, according to the forces of the economic environment.

Second concept

The securing of food rests on the resources that enable economic production activities. Economic production activities that permit the securing of the goods and services required to meet basic economic needs must be sustainable; to this end, both time and production means (or active assets) are necessary, and the latter are made up of basic resources and inputs. "Sustainable" is understood here as responding regularly to the renewal rate of needs in the long run. Goods and services are acquired through direct production for domestic consumption (i.e. consumption by the producing household) and/or through exchange. In the case of exchange, the idea is indeed to acquire fi rst a form of purchasing power in exchange for the goods and services produced, and then the goods and services required in exchange for this purchasing power. Production means represent the basic condition for the durable economic sustainability of households. Referred to as basic economic needs when they are determined by the cultural apparatus of implements and consumer goods. The general sustainability conditions of the main types of activity represent the crux of household economy assessments.

1. Hunting, gathering and fi shing must not deplete the production capital (plant and animal), and must allow it to regenerate by tapping resources elsewhere. Sustainability is determined here by the fertility of the productive species and the available area.

2. Agriculture, stock-breeding, horticulture, forestry and fi sh farming must regularly provide an amount suffi cient for domestic consumption and sale (in order to cover the other basic economic needs through exchange). Sustainability is determined by the productivity of utilized surfaces and volumes (and its ecological preservation), the terms of trade to convert the production into purchasing power, and fi nally the ratio between that purchasing power and the desired goods and services.

3. The acquisition of purchasing power (manufacture, transformation and the provision of goods and services) must provide regularly a means of exchange whose value is at least equal to the cost of all basic economic needs. Sustainability is determined by hourly productivity, the cash yield of what is produced, the exchange between purchasing power and the desired goods and services, and the labour supply for the production under scrutiny.

4. To invoke social obligations, the social status must be strong enough to impel the donor to provide the necessary contributions, and the donor's own performance must be suffi cient to cover his own needs, in addition to those of his benefi ciaries.

In the case of industrial production and forestry, domestic consumption is unusual.

The following general points are equally important.

1. The means of production of households are recognized as legitimate. The same comment applies to their production activities, and the goods, services and purchasing powers that these activities allow to acquire. This amounts to the concept of "entitlement" as discussed by Sen: an individual's ability to secure commodities is determined by the legal relations that govern the ownership and utilization of resources in his community (Sen, 1981).
2. Production activities are subjected to an organizational scheme and determinism specifi c to the culture of any type of society, and of any group that is economically active within it. This means that such activities always have a specifi c function, that the smallest social common denominator that conducts them is the household. The household exists within an economic structure, as defi ned by the cultural norms in force, and under the supervision of a specifi c authority.

THE CONSUMPTION OF FOOD

The securing of food is the most crucial stage in the feeding process, because inadequate performance at this level results in insuffi cient consumption. Moreover, to secure food, man must come to terms with his environment, which can be more or less hostile to him. Individual and household behaviour is by no means the determining factor at this stage, it is rather the availability of resources. On the other hand the activities associated with the consumption of food are mainly infl uenced by behaviour or factors that affect the individual directly (such as sickness). Humanitarian operations often address problems related to resources – this is their main purpose after all – and thus avoid potentially dangerous survival economy behaviours; they however have little infl uence on behaviours resulting from cultural practices or culture shock. Humanitarian operations can at best mitigate the effects by protecting and restoring health. Exerting direct impact on the consumption of food by changing behaviour is diffi cult; it is however possible to infl uence consumption by intervening earlier in the process, at the level of resources, and later in the process, at the level of healthcare services, in addition to acting upon water and habitat.

THE ACTIVITIES ASSOCIATED WITH FOOD CONSUMPTION

The consumption of food consists of a series of activities that range from the choice of food to its ingestion.

The choice of food

The choice of food is infl uenced by the following parameters:

- the performance of the securing of food, which is mainly determined by purchasing power, and food production and gathering;
- culture-specifi c eating habits;
- foods available locally;
- personal attitude, as determined by the interest in food, preferences, priorities in the allocation of resources, level of education, dietary knowledge, and trends and fashions in feeding.

Most of the world's population is limited in its choice of food by its economic performance and, thus, its ability to secure the food. People eat what they can produce, buy or gather in the framework of their eating habits; they often limit the budget they devote to food to the strict minimum. Their dietary knowledge is sketchy or non-existent – it is anyway unimportant in the absence of the means to apply it. In the Western world, the luxury of choice promotes a diversifi ed diet and removes defi ciency; but it also results in disorders due to excess (those that are the most serious in terms of both morbidity and mortality) and in clinical or sub-clinical defi ciencies, when choice results in the systematic selection of the same type of food. The Western diet is in fact tending to become uniform and lose its social connotations (eating is performed like any other somatic function), and this contributes all the more to the development of disorders due to excess.

The processing of food

The processing of food is limited here to household practices, and includes the following:

- treatment and storage after harvest or purchase;
- cooking or other culinary preparation;
- serving;
- storage of prepared food and leftovers.

Food processing methods are important on several accounts (especially in terms of culinary preparation), but their major aspect in terms of humanitarian operations is their infl uence on food hygiene, food conservation, and the preservation of nutrients.

The sharing of food

The sharing of prepared food is a fundamental activity in the feeding of dependants. It refl ects the social structure and hierarchy, and the cultural norms in force – bearing in mind that standards may change in case of crisis.

Feeding infants, children and other dependants

Dependants are defi ned here as individuals who are incapable of feeding themselves independently. Such individuals therefore require someone to take charge and do so properly; possibilities include the following:

- households themselves in the case of infants, small children, the sick and elderly living under the same roof;
- institutions such as hospitals, homes, orphanages and prisons.

Households

Clearly, this is where the feeding of infants and small children is crucial, with breastfeeding or its substitute, terminated by the weaning process.

Breastfeeding: Breastfeeding is an activity that pertains to biological determinism and, to a certain extent, to cultural determinism. Indeed, although mothers are naturally inclined to breastfeed their infant, some societies have developed artifi cial feeding methods, by resorting to wet-nurses or to substitutes for maternal milk, usually administered in a feeding bottle. Breastfeeding provides the fi rst food: maternal milk. The latter alone covers all nutrient requirements in a balanced manner and simultaneously protects the infant against infection. Maternal breastfeeding is the most appropriate manner of feeding children up until the age of 4 to 6 months; from then on, maternal milk no longer suffi ces to cover infant energy, protein, iron and thiamine requirements. At this stage, therefore, the diet must begin to diversify and weaning sets in.

Weaning: Weaning follows breastfeeding, and replaces it (or bottle feeding) with foods that are increasingly those of adults. But weaning is not only a change in diet; it is also a fundamental transformation in the child's lifestyle and its relation to its mother. This shift can be traumatic, especially if it coincides with the arrival of a sibling. In developing countries, weaning is the most crucial period in the survival of infants for the following reasons:

- their exposure to infectious disease increases, through a growing contact with their social and natural environments, and through their change in diet – weaning foods are easily contaminated, while the protection against infection previously provided by maternal milk wanes;
- their diet is changed, and this shock itself must be overcome;
- the quality of this diet is not always adequate, especially if breastfeeding ceases abruptly;
- the affective bond with the mother is seriously frayed.

Feeding other dependants: This category includes the elderly, the sick and the helpless wounded. The determining factors in the diet of the elderly are appetite, the specifi c care they may require, and the portion of food allocated to them. The same factors apply to the sick and wounded, in addition to the dietary requirements of their condition.

Institutions

Institutions call for a service that ensures food of adequate quality and quantity. In the case of specialized facilities such as hospitals, they must also provide an appropriate response to the dietary needs of their patients.

The factors determining institutional food consumption include the budget available, possible domestic food production, kitchen equipment, and the quality and availability of their staff. This is important here, because humanitarian operations sometimes involve the taking over of the food supply of institutions such as hospitals and psychiatric facilities, orphanages, homes for the elderly and prisons. This need usually arises from lack of funding and/or equipment, but it can also result from corruption (fund or food diversion) and the ostracism against some inmates. The problem in

The ingestion of food

The ingestion of available food is determined by appetite, which in turn depends on physical and emotional health, the appeal of the diet and the quality of its processing and, fi nally, the social environment. The ingestion of food is the culmination of all the earlier activities (both deliberate and involuntary) in the feeding process.

THE PRECONDITIONS FOR CONSUMPTION

These include fi rstly the means of storage and preservation that enable the keeping of food after harvest, slaughter, catch or purchase. The storage quality of staples is essential. Hazards such as rodents, birds, insects, mould and bacteria must all be protected against. Foodstuffs must also be protected from excessive moisture, light, and heat; they must be stored in a closed but ventilated place, sheltered from humidity, weather, and infestation. Time must also be given to the supervision of stocks and the elimination of parasites and of foods that have become improper for consumption. It is not easy to fulfil all the requirements for the quality storage of staples such as cereals and legumes (especially in the form of fl our) while limiting losses; as a result, most losses in subsistence agriculture after harvest usually occur during storage.

Food preparation must involve equipment and the water and fuel necessary to cook meals. In stable situations, equipment does not damage easily, and is thus not a limiting factor. On the other hand, access to water poses increasingly serious qualitative and quantitative problems; population growth and concentration, erosion, deforestation, desertifi cation and pollution all aggravate these problems. The search for fuel for cooking often results in ecological disaster. Crisis exacerbates water and fuel problems. Another diffi culty is related to kitchen equipment, particularly in case of population displacements, when heavy material such as pestles and mortars or modern stoves must be left behind. The quality of prepared food always suffers, and hazards associated with pathogenic contamination or insuffi cient detoxifi cation result. Insuffi cient quality also has the most serious repercussions during weaning, when infants are less shielded or lose the protection of maternal antibodies and are exposed more or less abruptly to pathogens.

THE ORGANIZATION AND DETERMINISM OF ACTIVITIES

Like the securing of food, the conduct of activities associated with consumption is always set by a given culture and its acquired behaviours; they can therefore be analysed by following their pattern of organization and determinism.

The function of food consumption activities

Activities associated with food consumption complete those related to the securing of this food, in order for man to satisfy his nutritional need. This function involves, fi rstly, the selection of foods among existing resources, then their preparation to make them more comestible, then their sharing among the members of the community and, fi nally, their ingestion. But meals usually have a social and sometimes political additional role.

As seen above in relation with the securing of food, the community involved at the consumption stage is confi ned to the household, or to several related households. But an institution can also be regarded as a community in this way.

Structure

Structure is the elementary organization unit required to perform a function; as such, it is often merges into the community.

Norm

The food consumption norm is defi ned mainly by eating habits, which also set the following:

- the choice of food (where possible);
- the different ways of preparing food;
- the sharing of food;

- the ingestion of food;
- the nutritional care provided to dependants, particularly breastfeeding, infant feeding and weaning methods.

Eating habits also include dietary taboos that can affect the choice of food and its attribution to different family members, in addition to the weaning and feeding of small children. The understanding of taboos is important for two reasons: avoiding mistakes in nutritional intervention, and detecting possible vulnerabilities.

Behaviour towards food is an attitude associated with the personal daily relation to food, and with the various behaviours observed by the individual in his vicinity, which result from habits and culture. These are external factors. But behaviour towards food is also related to physiological, psycho-sensorial and symbolic motivations, and these are internal factors.

The integration of factors infl uencing the behaviour towards food implies, *inter alia,* a process of memorizing tastes, odours, circumstances and sensations perceived consciously or unconsciously around meals, and which later determine the affi nity for a given food, according to its preparation and the circumstances surrounding its consumption. For example, food poisoning involving agreeable foods can lead to repulsion (sometimes defi nitive) from such foods, because the disagreeable feeling of indigestion takes precedence over the initial liking. Thus, behaviour towards food is also infl uenced by psycho-sensorial motivations some of which arise from the subconscious, giving eating habits a normative character much stronger than may be thought.

This aspect is also very important for humanitarian operations. In cases of anorexia caused by physiological disorder, patients only accept specifi c familiar foods, and then only in minimal amounts. They have no appetite for new foodstuffs and reject them. This is particularly spectacular in severely malnourished children also suffering from related disorders. They become anorexic, and they must above all not encounter unfamiliar foods at that stage.

Another interesting aspect of eating habits relates to consumption modes. Man does not view his food in terms of its nutrient content, but in terms of ingredients. He has succeeded empirically in combining the different ingredients required for his dietary balance, and has also developed appetizing preparations. He has conferred a symbolism upon his foods, and this symbolism is a determining factor in human relations. He has succeeded in feeding himself while developing his taste for food. These considerations are also important in humanitarian operations, as they must allow for a human outreach that goes well beyond the simple delivery of balanced rations.

In Western countries, the control of food consumption is primarily a private domestic matter, and only to a certain extent is it individual. But in more traditional societies, this control can also be enforced by religious and lay authorities. Furthermore all countries have food quality control mechanisms and associated regulations at national level; these regulations must be respected strictly when importing foodstuffs to assist populations in crisis.

ACTIVITY PERFORMANCE

The performance of food consumption is expressed in the following equation:

nutrients consumed ---------------------------------- / timeframe nutrients required to satisfy the nutritional need

This equation is infl uenced fi rstly by the analysis of activities related to the securing of food, in order to determine whether the food thus obtained is suffi cient for a given family or community. A positive answer does however not necessarily suggest that each individual receives a portion that is adequate to cover his nutritional need. Performance must therefore also be verifi ed in relation to the various members of the community, particularly the most vulnerable. It must be done, all the more, if performance is insuffi cient, in order to detect possible discrimination – bearing in mind, however, that humanitarian action has only little infl uence on cultural behaviour patterns.

Nutrients required to meet the nutritional need

The sum of nutrients required to meet the nutritional need in fact represents the nutritional need itself. Nutrients must therefore be expressed as available amounts of food, once prepared and directly ready for consumption (in other words, when they have already lost some of their initial nutrient content through storage, refi ning and cooking). The calculation is not complicated but requires the use of food composition tables, a limited number of basic dietary rules and the application of appropriate correction factors according to the probable losses incurred during the food processing stages, particularly cooking. It is also worth noting that a balanced food ration, suffi ciently rich in energy, usually also contains enough protein, vitamins and minerals. Iodine and zinc provide two exceptions, because their concentrations in foods vary according to soil and water composition.

Timeframes

Man usually consumes food on a daily basis, and timeframes are thus usually set for 24 hours. This does not mean that a nutritionally healthy individual must absolutely eat every day although, if he does not, he must then compensate for the resulting reserve loss.

This is rather easy for adults, whatever the available foods; but it can be impossible for small children fed on low energy-density foods such as cassava, during weaning. When people eat less frequently than once a day, it is due to famine, sickness or personal decision.

The nutrients that are actually consumed are determined by the following factors.

1. The overall economic performance in the securing of basic economic goods, which in turn infl uence:
   - the quantity, quality and diversity of the regularly available food, in turn affecting appetite;
   - the material means necessary to prepare food;
   - in part, the time required to prepare and distribute food to the family members;
   - the mental disposition to prepare attractive food and share it within the family.
2. Appetite defines the amount of food that individuals can ingest; it is determined fi rstly by the individual's physical and mental health, and then by his preferences and the quality of the food.

3. Eating habits, which in turn influence:
   - the amount of food allocated to each family member;
   - food taboos;
   - discrimination;
   - sharing priorities which do not necessarily refl ect discrimination;
   - the atmosphere surrounding meals and their role in the cohesion of the family system;
   - food quality;
   - food given to infants and small children (breastfeeding and weaning).
4. The care provided to vulnerable groups or dependants; these partly infl uence their physical and mental health, and thus their appetite. This care is defined by the provider's (usually the mother) education and skills, attitude, motivation, and available time and resources – both of which are frequently the most important limiting factors.
5. The quality of the food preparation; this infl uences the micro-nutrient content and appetite, is determined by culinary practices and means, and the skills, motivation and health of the cook, and fi nally the time available to do so.

PERFORMANCE SECURITY

It is accepted that to varying degrees all peoples who have survived had eating habits and cultural behaviours that ensured an adequate, suffi cient, balanced and comprehensive diet. The notion of varying degrees introduces that of vulnerability for those on the brink of sustainability in terms of means and customs. There is no direct security mechanism that ensures food consumption. The latter can, however, be ensured indirectly by the mechanisms that govern the securing of food, by the quality of the care given to dependants (e.g. education, economic growth, the fi ght against discrimination, etc.), and by the means of preservation of health (access to healthcare, water, habitat and safety). The mechanisms that govern the securing of food are described above, the care that must be given to dependants is discussed in Chapter XV, and the main conditions allowing health to be preserved are briefl y listed below.

Conditions for physical health

Good physical health is determined by the following factors:

- a good nutritional status;
- a healthy diet, that is, supplying all the required nutrients in suffi cient quantity but without excess and in a balanced manner – foods that provide them must not be harmful, they must be prepared in a way that preserves nutrient quality and prevents toxicity; fi nally, their processing and handling must be hygienic;
- the integrity of the organism in order to consume, digest, absorb and utilize the foods, and fi nally to excrete their waste;
- the absence of illnesses that may interfere with nutrition or mental health;
- adequate care of dependants;
- sufficient access to preventive and curative healthcare;
- sufficient education to make the most of healthcare services, particularly in terms of prevention;
- good water and habitat hygiene conditions, themselves set by:
- sufficient access to drinking water, implying that sources are sufficient in number and that catchments and distribution networks are in good condition and protected from contamination;
    - environmental sanitation in order to control the risk of contagion that may be associated with it, as follows:
    - the adequate evacuation and treatment of human, domestic and water waste;
    - the control of vectors of contagion (i.e. fl ies, mosquitoes, parasites, and rodents), by direct eradication and reducing the chances of human contact – this is already partly achieved by waste disposal;
    - adequate shelter from cold and weather.

Conditions for mental health

Mental health is fi rstly determined by physical health, and then by living conditions. Children need affection and a reassuring environment; adults need security – political, economic and social – in order to be able to cope with the long-term diffi culties they face.

THE BIOLOGICAL UTILIZATION OF FOOD

Man's biological utilization of food is involuntary, because it is subjected to biological and thermodynamic determinism. Humanitarian action can infl uence it indirectly by addressing the conditions that defi ne it; these include, mainly, health, domestic food availability, and care of dependants. The infl uence of humanitarian action can also be direct, in the form of therapeutic nutrition measures.

ACTIVITIES ASSOCIATED WITH THE BIOLOGICAL UTILIZATION OF FOOD

The activities associated with biological utilization can be classifi ed in four major stages: digestion, absorption, functional utilization and excretion. These activities are not particularly relevant to humanitarian operations, and are only discussed briefl y here.

Digestion

Digestion is defi ned as the sum of the chemical and mechanical transformations undergone by food in the digestive tract. Digestion transforms food into its basal molecular units, thus allowing it to be absorbed. The digestive tract includes the mouth, the oesophagus, the stomach, the small intestine and the colon or large intestine.

- In the mouth, chewing allows a fi rst rough crushing of the foods. Dental condition is important in this respect. Saliva moistens and lubricates the food and thus facilitates its swallowing into the oesophagus. Saliva also contains ptyalin, an enzyme that begins the degradation process of starch.
- In the stomach, food is mixed and reduced to a pulp called

chyme. It is at the same time exposed to the action of hydrochloric acid, which dissolves it and promotes the action of digestive enzymes, particularly pepsin (which acts upon proteins), and lipase (which acts upon lipids).

- In the small intestine, chyme is subjected to the action of:
- gall, originating in the liver through the gall bladder, which emulsifi es the fatty elements contained in the food into fi ne droplets; q pancreatic juices which contain the major digestion enzymes that act upon proteins, starches and fats; q enzymes secreted by the intestinal mucous membrane, which terminate the fragmenting of macro-nutrients into their essential components: simple sugars, fatty acids, glycerol and amino acids, which can then be absorbed.
- In the colon, digestion is practically complete. Only food residue (fi bre, partly digested nutrients), cell residue, bacteria (that form the intestinal fl ora) and water (largely reabsorbed) remain.

Absorption

Absorption is the transfer of the nutrients contained in the intestine into the organism through the intestinal mucous membrane. Most nutrients are transported actively through their own mechanisms - regulated mostly by their level of intake and their concentration in the organism. In addition, passive absorption can set in beyond a certain intestinal concentration. Nutrient absorption is complex and is not yet fully understood.

Functional utilization

After their absorption, nutrients are stored and/or transported to the organs to be utilized according to their respective functions. Some, such as sugars, are consumed in metabolism and must therefore be replaced as fast as they are consumed. Others, such as iron, are recycled regularly and effi ciently; they are however lost sooner or later, be it specifi cally through metabolic pathways, or through the unavoidable losses that result from "organic leakage" and tissue renewal. They must therefore be replaced according to the average time they spend in the organism.

Excretion

Having fulfi lled their function in the organism, or when they are present in excessive concentrations, nutrients or the produce of their degradation are excreted through urine, stool, perspiration and the gases produced by breathing. Furthermore, the "leakage" of some metabolic pathways, intestinal and skin desquamation, and hair and nail growth are also forms of nutrient (or their metabolites) excretion; as such, they also constitute unavoidable losses. Urine contains most soluble metabolites (e.g. salts, nitrogen group amino acids in the form of urea, excess vitamins, and other degradation products). Stool contains gall salts, trace metals and other products excreted by the organism into the intestine, in addition to the undigested food residue mentioned above. Breathing expels carbon dioxide and water, mainly. Carbon dioxide is produced by the combustion of carbon molecules utilized as a source of energy (sugars, the carbon framework of amino acids, lipids). Perspiration expels water, in order for it to be vaporized and thus refresh the body (the transformation from liquid to gas consumes heat). Perspiration also expels salts, particularly sodium chloride.

THE ORGANIZATION AND DETERMINISM OF ACTIVITIES

The organization and determinism of activities in the biological utilization of food have been discussed above. There is no need to dwell on the points that are not particularly relevant to humanitarian action.

ACTIVITY PERFORMANCE

The performance of the biological utilization of food can be expressed as the ratio of the use by the organism of consumed nutrients, on the one hand, and what it should be in order to achieve an adequate nutritional and health state, over a given period, on the other. At this stage in the activities in the organism, such an approach to performance makes little sense, because it cannot be used in practice, except in laboratory conditions. However, attention must be paid to the factors that affect this phase in order to maximize its effi ciency.

The biological utilization of food is determined by the following:

- the amount of food consumed;
- the quality of food consumed, in terms of balance between nutrients, be they Type I or Type II nutrients;
- the quality of food consumed, in terms of hygiene;
- the reserves of the organism and its nutritional status;
- health in terms of any possible infl uences on the activities of biological utilization, mainly:
- the condition of the digestive tube in terms of digestion and absorption;
- the liver function in terms of storage and metabolism;
- the metabolic function throughout the organism;
- the kidney function in terms of metabolism and excretion.

Intestinal parasites and bacterial and viral infection have a major impact on digestion and nutrient absorption. They profit from chyme nutrients (thus contributing to defi ciency), and cause sometimes serious malabsorption and nutrient loss through diarrhoea and lesions to the intestinal membrane. Parasite and infectious diseases are common, and thrive in crisis situations. Nutritional interventions in such settings must always include control measures for these diseases.

Furthermore, food hygiene is directly related to the spread of infectious disease. The ingestion of contaminated food is widespread, particularly in crisis situations. A particularly dangerous food commodity in this respect is reconstituted powdered milk, used as a substitute for maternal milk and bottle-fed: the quality of the water (or the cleanliness of utensils used in the process) used to reconstitute the milk is often doubtful or poor.

The biological utilization is thus determined early in the feeding process, and by health; as a result, intervention that aims at promoting the biological utilization of food must focus on these two aspects.

PERFORMANCE SECURITY

Like food consumption, there is no direct security mechanism for the biological utilization of food. The only way of achieving this security is to ensure an adequate nutritional status and mental and physical health at individual level. The conditions for this are themselves related to the performance achieved during the two previous stages of the feeding process (the securing of food and its consumption), the integrity and security of the family and social structure, suffi cient access to preventive and curative healthcare, and satisfactory access to water and habitat.

NUTRITIONAL STATUS

The living organism must meet its nutritional needs through a feeding process. The degree to which these needs are met defi nes the nutritional status of a given organism. The nutritional status, in other words, is set by the performance of the feeding process, and the factors that infl uence it. Together with health, the nutritional status however also defi nes the functional capacity of the organism, which in turn infl uences the biological utilization, the consumption, and the securing of food; this is illustrated in Figure 6.17 below.

NUTRITIONAL STATUS AND ITS MEASUREMENT

The picture that springs to mind in relation to the nutritional status is one opposing "thin" and "fat" persons, neither of whom is considered "normal". This image refers to the status of the lean mass (i.e. muscle and organs) and the fatty (or adipose) tissue. But this approach remains restrictive, because the nutritional status relates to the condition of all the parts of the organism. The "thin/ fat" image in particular ignores the vitamin and mineral status – it is not necessarily related to lean mass and adipose tissue. Fat individuals may lack vitamins and minerals, while thin ones may be amply provided. How, then, can all the parts of the organism be measured? No single method provides the answer, and several must be combined to do so, bearing in mind that some parts cannot be measured with accuracy. Assessment methods are briefl y discussed below.

Investigation of clinical signs

Clinical signs include those that are visible at the level of the skin, eyes, hair, the mouth lining, of palpable organs such as the liver and the thyroid, and of the reaction (or absence thereof) to stimulation. These signs provide sometimes useful defi ciency indicators and permit the quantifi cation (to a certain extent) of defi ciency, because they usually appear when defi ciency is advanced. The absence of such signs suggests the absence of obvious defi ciency, but does not rule out defi ciency itself: defi ciency may still be at a sub-clinical stage, and suddenly become visible. More than fi fty clinical signs have a nutritional meaning. Some are unambiguous, easy to observe and interpret, such as goitre or pellagra dermatosis; others are diffi cult to isolate and interpret, such as diffuse facial or hair discolouring. The appraisal of clinical signs must be left in the hands of skilled staff.

Nutritional anthropometry

This method consists in measuring the physical dimensions of the organism and, often, in combining them in order to determine the adequacy of growth or nutritional status with respect to the lean mass and adipose tissue, on the basis of reference data. Anthropometry however only provides an estimate of the lean mass and adipose tissue and, like clinical signs, does not enable absolute quantifi cation of the fat and protein reserves available to the organism. Resorting to nutritional anthropometry and investigating clinical signs are the two approaches preferred by humanitarian agencies.

Biochemical tests

Biochemical tests applied to blood and urine samples in particular can, directly or indirectly, provide a fairly accurate idea of the status of many constituents. Humanitarian agencies do not use them widely, however, because they are not suited to most encountered fi eld conditions; their use must be left to well-equipped laboratory facilities.

Biophysical methods, like the extrapolation of lean mass from the potassium isotope 40 content, are even more accurate than biochemical tests, but they cannot be applied in humanitarian operations.

It is thus worth noting that the nutritional status of individuals cannot be assessed comprehensively; for assessments to be as accurate as possible, a full battery of methods must be applied, most of which are impractical in the fi eld. Clinical defi ciency signs and anthropometric measurements (related to reference values) are ultimately the only realistic tools, and as such do not provide absolute answers.

ADEQUATE NUTRITIONAL STATUS

An adequate nutritional status may be described as one that is not improved by administering essential nutrient supplements. This defi nition implies a satisfactory functional capacity of the organism, because it is determined by the nutritional and health states. Functional capacity is determined by the presence of all the components of the organism, in suffi cient amounts, and according to specifi c proportions. Furthermore, functional capacity must be defi ned according to performance criteria in terms of growth, pregnancy and breastfeeding, physical work, emotional stability, resistance to sickness or recovery following sickness. Resistance to infection is not necessarily determined by the same parameters as resistance to cancer and cardio-vascular disease.

An adequate nutritional status can also be described as the quantity and proportion of the components of the organism associated with the smallest mortality risk (or the greatest chances of longevity) in good mental and physical health conditions. Mortality risks cannot be quantifi ed accurately in terms of the relative component proportion (except in case of defi ciency or lethal excess of specifi c constituents); on the other hand, life-insurance statistics indicate that, below minimum lean mass and above maximum adipose tissue thresholds, mortality risks increase owing to defi ciency and excess disorders respectively. In adult males, for example, the mortality risk increases exponentially as soon as the body mass index (BMI) falls below 16 or rises above 30. Between these two extremes lies a mortality risk area that is equivalent for BMI between 20 and 25, amounting to an approximately 15 kg variation for a height of 1.75 m. This shows that differences in nutritional status can be associated with an identical longevity, thanks to the organism's ability to regulate its homeostasis (i.e. the stabilization of various physiological constants). It is also likely that within this low-risk area, functional capacity is satisfactory.

It may seem that functional capacity and mortality risk go hand in hand, but they can in fact be opposed. Muscular mass and height can be useful for heavy physical work, but shorter, less robust individuals may face lower risks of mortality and of degenerative illness related to age, and be more vigorous (Pacey & Payne, 1985).

Moreover, the association between mortality risks and nutritional status varies according to situation, because mortality is not only determined by nutritional status, but also by the synergic interaction of this with other factors such as infection. Mortality risks related to nutritional status can therefore not be extrapolated from one situation to another. During the great Ethiopian famine (1983–1986), considerable variations were observed in the mortality risks for a given nutritional status between the Tigre highlands in the rainy season and the desert fringe in the dry season. Highland children

The body mass index expresses the ratio between weight (kilograms) and height (metres) squared (weight/height). whose weight-for-height index lay below 60% of the median had practically no hope of survival in therapeutic feeding centres, whereas desert children practically all survived because they were not much exposed to infectious disease. However, the mortality risk variation was smaller in the case of mid-upper arm circumference (MUAC) for height measurement: different anthropometric indicators do not have the same meaning.

The above comments show how diffi cult it is to defi ne an adequate nutritional status: it cannot be measured accurately, and it is not a set entity.

It can, at best, be defi ned as the absence of clinical defi ciency signs, the absence of manifest illness, and a given status of lean mass, adipose tissue and growth – this can be approached through anthropometry. But the latter only provides an estimate of one aspect of the nutritional status (reserves of adipose, muscular and visceral tissue), itself only an estimate of the actual nutritional status. However, the status of the adipose tissue and, to a large extent, that of the lean mass, refl ect the organism's energy reserves, and the energy need is the most demanding. In nutritional crises, inadequate coverage of the energy need (through insuffi cient intake or anorexia) most rapidly and usually causes complications; as a result, the combination of anthropometric measurements and clinical examinations provide a fair estimate of the nutritional status, and shed light on whether it is good or degraded.

9

A Conceptual Approach to Crises

A CONCEPTUAL FRAMEWORK FOR CRISES

A defi nition of the word "crisis" must fi rst be agreed on. Among its different meanings, that of a "grave phase" in the evolution of events appears to be most fitting to the intuitive notion of a crisis in terms of humanitarian intervention.

GENERAL CHARACTERISTICS OF CRISES

A crisis does not arise from nothing, nor is it due to chance. It develops more or less rapidly according to a cause and effect process, referred to as the crisis process, which is characterized by specifi c conditions.

The crisis process

A crisis process develops in the course of events which, in turn, makes history and blends into it. The limits of the process must therefore be identified, and to do this, three phases are defi ned.

1. The preliminary phase, in which the crisis emerges and develops. During this phase, to a certain extent, adaptation occurs and, if necessary, is followed by the utilization of reserves and defence mechanisms.
2. The acute phase, which amounts to the crisis as such. Reserves and defence mechanisms are exhausted fi rst, and a growing functional degradation then gradually leads to the failure – and, ultimately, death – of the system under consideration. The system can be the economy, an organism, or a society.

3. The recovery phase, in which the crisis is resolved for such elements as have survived it; this includes resuscitation, followed by recovery or rehabilitation and, ultimately, consolidation or strengthening.

The preliminary phase

This phase is frequently unobtrusive, and it might even go unnoticed when the primary causes for the crisis are such that they result directly in crisis, or when they occur without obvious warning signals – this is sometimes the case in earthquakes, tidal waves, or volcanic eruptions. The duration of this phase can vary. It is contingent upon circumstances and/or events integrated into the crisis process, and which herald and prepare the acute phase. From a prevention perspective, the preliminary phase thus warrants the attention of humanitarian organizations, although the line between the preliminary and acute phases is sometimes diffi cult to draw in the causality chain.

The preliminary phase is nevertheless always crucial, because events preceding the crisis are less serious than those occurring in acute crisis. This is, in fact, one of the major challenges facing humanitarian intervention in terms of prevention, as crisis processes often subside by themselves. For instance, it is rare for an isolated drought episode in an arid setting to threaten the population seriously; indeed, the latter can usually resort to adaptation mechanisms in reaction to a phenomenon which is both familiar and suffi ciently recurrent to be anticipated. However, if several drought episodes occur in such rapid succession as to deplete adaptation mechanisms, this population will be under threat. The fi rst episode is thus the trigger factor for the crisis process. It equates to the preliminary phase but, at this early stage, the event of crisis itself remains uncertain. The distinction is made both by the population experiencing drought, and the humanitarian agencies, offi cials, the media, donors, and the general public. Illustrations include the repeated failure of early warning systems intended to arrest the crisis process. During the preliminary phase, most gamble on a spontaneous reversal of fortune towards normality – especially as damage is still invisible, and this frequently discourages many prevention efforts. However, it is during this phase that resistance to crisis factors develops, and sometimes collapses.

The acute phase

This is the crisis itself, the phase of real threat for those experiencing it. Its duration is variable, and the crisis develops according to the nature and progress of its causes, according to the appearance (or not) of new crisis factors, and to available reserves and defence mechanisms. This development can take several forms as follows:

- a rapid shift to recovery, thanks to appropriate assistance measures;
- stabilization through coping mechanisms, but this entails increased vulnerability owing to their exhaustion;
- deterioration, possibly leading to disaster.

The recovery phase

This phase can take many forms, but can only begin when the causes of the crisis have vanished or diminished substantially. The recovery phase is contingent upon what remains of the victims' coping mechanisms and potential outside assistance. Possible scenarios include rapid and sustainable improvement, a restored status (roughly equivalent to that preceding the crisis), or a resumption of precarious but suffi cient living conditions, with an aggravated weakness (increasing the chances of a resumption of acute crisis as soon as its causes reappear).

Distinguishing three phases, albeit somewhat artifi cial, enables us to model crisis processes, to approach them in an analytical manner, and to defi ne needs for humanitarian assistance. Thresholds between the three vary from one situation to the next, but are always linked to the appearance of a more or less immediate threat between the fi rst and second phase, and are bound to the more or less gradual disappearance of the causes for the crisis between phases two and three.

Conditions leading to crisis

1. In the cause and effect chain characterizing the crisis process, one or several causes must stand out at some stage as crisis factors. To use the terminology developed by Dr Pierre Perrin, we shall refer to such causes as "phenomena" (Perrin, 1996) or, to borrow from physics, "perturbations".

2. For a phenomenon to result in a crisis, it must fi rst strike a target.
3. The target must be vulnerable to the phenomenon. The action of the phenomenon on the target then amounts to aggression.
4. The effect of aggression must manifest itself through damage.
5. For damage to precipitate a crisis, it must constitute a problem whose seriousness characterizes a crisis situation. In other words, those confronted with it lack the means to respond to it adequately (either by direct action or by evasion), thus exposing themselves to a critical situation, or critically increasing their vulnerability.
6. Inability to respond adequately results from the abnormal magnitude of the problem and/or vulnerability.

This chain of conditions indicates that the emergence of a crisis is related to two levels of vulnerability: the fi rst is providing the initial phenomenon with a foothold, the second is the inability to respond adequately to the impact of the phenomenon. For example, if the infl uenza virus (phenomenon) propagates and meets a vulnerable individual (target), the individual will suffer an infl uenzal infection (impact, amounting to the damage for the system and creating the problem).

In this case, the problem is usually surmountable because the immune system is activated and eventually rejects the virus. Thus here there is no crisis, strictly speaking. If, on the other hand, the individual is abnormally vulnerable to the impact, if he or she is unable to fi ght the virus once the infection appears, the individual faces an insurmountable (or diffi cult to surmount) problem which endangers his or her life. He or she is thus clearly in a crisis situation, and probably requires medical assistance.

Furthermore, in a cause and effect relationship, the impact clearly also represents a phenomenon which can meet with incapability to confront it (second vulnerability level). The resulting invasion is all the more signifi cant, and the patient's weakness increases. This increased weakness then amounts to a new impact (and, at the same time, a new phenomenon) which can encounter, for instance, pulmonary vulnerability, while another phenomenon may appear (for example, the presence of bacteria causing pneumonia).

FORMULATION OF CRISES

From a conceptual perspective, the occurrence of crises obeys the following principles.

1. The crisis process develops following the combination of a phenomenon and vulnerability, generating an (adverse) impact: phenomenon × vulnerability = impact

   This formula (Perrin, 1996) demonstrates that impact is directly proportional to the magnitude of both the phenomenon and vulnerability. It also means that one or several phenomena can act on different types of vulnerability, and that this can result in several impacts.
2. The impact constitutes damage which, in itself, poses a problem.
3. The victims of the damage attempt to respond to the problem, according to two different scenarios: q their response is adequate, and crisis is thus averted;

- their response is inadequate because they are vulnerable to the impact, and crisis results. In case of crisis, the inadequate response can be due to either short-sightedness, or incapability of reacting. However, the resulting situation is critical in both cases:
- a problem addressed inadequately results in crisis.

4. Damage without adequate response increases vulnerability, or leads to new types of vulnerability.

Owing to the multiplicity of cause and effect reactions, crisis is characterized by increasing problems, combining to aggravate the deterioration of the situation; this can result in disaster.

This means that the crisis phase itself can present different stages of gravity by involving more and more people. Similarly, pauses can occur between the appearance of new phenomena and that of new types of vulnerability, or between the appearance of a new phenomenon and its impact.

NUTRITIONAL CRISES

The human being's nutritional need is met by the feeding process. Nutritional crises can thus only develop if the feeding process is unable to cover this need (unbalance between needs and means as illustrated in the scale model above). Nutritional crises can therefore be explained as follows.

A nutritional crisis is a serious situation that results from the inadequacy of the feeding process performance, to the point of creating problems which those confronted with them cannot independently resolve in a satisfactory manner.

From this, it becomes obvious that nutritional crises can vary in nature and affect isolated individuals as well as entire populations, according to phenomena, vulnerability, and the feeding process level where performance is inadequate. Moreover, owing to cause and effect reactions, an insuffi cient performance (or one that cannot be compensated for) at a given level will result in inadequate performance at other levels of the process. This shows both that crisis is dynamic, and that it can be contingent upon (or result from) a specifi c problem or an accumulation of problems. Such a defi nition is not easily grasped from the onset, but has the advantage of avoiding the classic pitfall restricting nutritional crises to the realm of catastrophes such as famine or severe malnutrition. This restrictive approach likewise results in limiting humanitarian intervention to curative measures applied to the latest problems in the process, in contradiction with the general principle that humanitarian intervention aims at least as much at prevention of suffering as its alleviation.

In a crisis situation, the feeding process performance is inadequate, owing to the combination of phenomena and vulnerability – producing impacts. These three factors of crisis are discussed below.

THE PHENOMENA

A phenomenon is anything amounting to the aggression of factors determining the performance of the different steps of the feeding process. Phenomena inducing nutritional crises affect the following:

- the resources that are necessary to carry out the activities;

- the implementation of these activities;
- the resources produced by these activities.

Phenomena can come from two sources. the human community and the natural environment. Those originating in the human community relate to war, economic, social and cultural crises, and disturbances to the environment resulting from human activity (given forms of erosion and desertifi cation, the resulting drought, global warming and pollution). Those originating in the environment relate to natural climatic phenomena (drought, fl oods, hurricanes, or erosion), non-human predators and geophysical phenomena (earthquakes, volcanic eruptions, tidal waves).

Provided that the currently observed trend in warming is indeed mainly due to human activity.

In the framework of nutritional crises, phenomena related to the obtaining of food are those which can possibly infl uence economic production activities and their produce. Indeed, any signifi cant reduction in production or return will, most frequently, have major consequences on the performance of securing food. Any phenomenon infl uencing the securing of food will likewise affect its consumption and biological utilization, since these two steps are contingent upon the fi rst.

Phenomena regarding, primarily, food consumption will also have an impact on its biological utilization. But they may also alter the securing of food, by impairing the functional capacity due to the more or less rapid degradation of the subject's nutritional status.

Phenomena regarding primarily the biological utilization of food, other than those affecting its consumption, result in illness that impairs principally the system (illnesses of the vital functions and organs, metabolic congenital malformations, some cancers). Such phenomena are likely to affect the obtaining and consumption of food as well, since they impair functional capacity.

Human phenomena

Among political phenomena, war is the main trigger of nutritional crises. Looting, destruction, danger, restrictions of access and movement, population displacements, confi nement, occupation, terror and harassment, compulsory levies, embargo and conscription... all these elements may undermine the household economy and, thus, the securing of food. Indeed, they directly infl uence the means of production, production activities and the resources thus generated. War also indirectly affects activities aimed at obtaining food owing to its impact on the domestic economy, on the environment and on the different forms of authority. Furthermore, the insecurity often resulting from war can cause farmers to cultivate only the absolute minimum, to avoid unnecessary expenses in the probable event of fl ight (this has been observed in Rwanda, for instance), or if they fear that their harvest may be looted. It must be noted, nevertheless, that when the danger related to war is not fl ight, but rather the levying of contributions, farmers take this factor into consideration when planning their production to avoid resource shortages or possible violence (similarly, businessmen subjected to fees levied by the mafi a increase the commodity price to cover this tax).

Acts of war may also modify the consumption and biological utilization of food, particularly by the wounded, but also by communities themselves. Indeed, they may infl uence feeding and food preparation customs and generate post-traumatic stress disorders (PTSD) which in turn affect both the individual's appetite and the family cell, and the behaviour of those responsible for dependants (particularly mothers). In displaced persons' camps on the Cambodian border, it was observed that malnutrition increased in parallel with food availability; this in itself seemed absurd, all the more so considering that the incidence and prevalence of infectious diseases remained stable. On the other hand, the population under scrutiny had been displaced several times and had been subjected to severe abuse, bringing the mothers to a psychological breaking point manifested in the neglect of their children. Humanitarian agencies responded to the ensuing malnutrition by increasing food rations which, of course, resolved nothing.

The side effects of war, such as the displacement of populations, may foster the development of epidemics with direct consequences on the consumption and utilization of food, either among specifi c groups (e.g. measles), or within the entire population (e.g. cholera, tuberculosis or other viral or bacterial infections). The latter will then also reduce the production potential of existing economic resources.

Governance and government authority can also infl uence the securing of food. Drèze and Sen have demonstrated that measures to control famine are taken by democratic governments in countries accommodating an opposition and where freedom of the press prevails (Drèze & Sen, 1989). Furthermore, lifestyles chosen on an ideological basis and imposed by force can lead to catastrophic famine, as in the USSR in the 1930s, and in Cambodia under the Khmer Rouge.

The weakness of institutions, especially professional, may also constitute a risk factor for some groups whose vulnerability increases owing to their incapability to react to economic or political orientations, or simply competition.

Similarly, some development choices can foster nutritional crisis and a general weakening of the economy, amounting to the preliminary phase of the crisis: the exploitation of the Aral Sea basin in the former USSR is an example of this.

Some aid policies can also have negative effects potentially leading to crisis. In spite of their political origin, they are discussed below in relation to economic phenomena.

Economic phenomena

Economic phenomena are major factors of nutritional crises, either by causing famine directly, or by inducing poverty and restricting choice. Several types of phenomena exist among which the most important relate to (or result from) the market and speculation, competition or economic subjection, economic policies imposed by the State or international economic bodies, adverse economic development, competition over scarce resources, and international aid, in particular food aid. All these phenomena infl uence the household economy directly and, consequently, food availability and consumption – but they also impair living standards. This generates other phenomena affecting the consumption and biological utilization of food directly.

The impact of phenomena related to the market and speculation can be deleterious by raising the price of essential commodities such as food. Such phenomena result from the combination of shortages and power struggles. They can trigger famine when the terms of trade are reversed for major segments of the population who, to survive, would need to spend more than the income they can actually secure. The phenomenon can be even more devastating insofar as demand is determined not only by the victims of the reversal of the terms of trade.

Consider for instance farmers who, in a given region, sell a good harvest massively to private traders whose clients reside outside the region under consideration, or even abroad. If the farmers have sold too much (thus undermining the necessary reserves), or if the following year's harvest is poor, they will need to purchase food, thereby generating an abnormal demand. If this food can be subjected to speculation, or simply if it is exported for a higher price than what the farmers can afford, they will risk famine. Another serious degradation factor is currency devaluation for those whose income is fi xed and not adjusted, such as pensioners. It has been observed that, following a devaluation of the currency and a price infl ation in Abkhazia, the price of bread had increased approximately ten thousand times, putting pensioners in a dire situation. They continued to receive the same, unchanged pension, they were no longer productive, and it was therefore impossible for them to adjust their income.

Phenomena related to economic subjection aim at rendering domestic economies dependent upon crucial inputs. The most typical example is that of hybrid or genetically modifi ed seeds: on the one hand, their use requires repeated, yearly purchases as their properties are not maintained following reproduction. On the other hand, they also demand considerable yield inputs such as fertilizers, pesticides and controlled irrigation. In Angola in 1999, the living conditions of a specifi c community deteriorated following its abrupt isolation due to the war. Depending on this type of seeds and its related necessary inputs that it could no longer secure, this population would rapidly have faced catastrophe in the absence of humanitarian aid.

Harmful phenomena related to the policies currently imposed by international economic bodies, particularly structural adjustment, liberalization and globalization based on the theory of comparative advantage, are increasingly well understood. This is particularly the case for structural adjustment, whose impact is more strongly felt by the poor than the wealthy (Azoulay & Dillon, 1993; Salih, 1994). Furthermore, privatization excludes major segments of the population from services indispensable to their wellbeing. Cost-recovery policies have the same effect when applied indiscriminately.

Adverse economic development can lead to environmental deterioration (erosion, desertifi cation, soil salinity, deforestation, resource depletion and pollution). The impact of such phenomena spins into a vicious circle between available resources and the environment's support capacity (reduced by excessive exploitation); it thus contributes to rural exodus towards urban centres, and to the impoverishment of both migrants and residents who prefer to remain in their areas of origin in spite of the diffi culties they face. The overall degradation of living standards and public hygiene also affects food consumption, not only owing to an inadequate performance in obtaining food, but also *via* the effects of infectious diseases on appetite, and by the deteriorating quality of the attention devoted to those who require it. Moreover, the excessive exploitation of the environment gives rise to risks of fl ooding and landslides whose consequences can be catastrophic.

An increasing number of people depending on the informal sector also imply increasing poverty, in terms both of the resource base and of the affected population. Poverty is understood here as a combination of precarious living conditions and a greater vulnerability both to adverse economic phenomena of any type, and to phenomena potentially infl uencing food consumption.

Food aid can itself cause more damage than good if delivered indiscriminately and without relation to a need assessed with a view to preserving or supporting the local economy. This applies to so-called "emergency" food aid, delivered in crises, as well as to "project-related" food aid, delivered to "vulnerable" groups, and to "programme" food aid. The latter is intended to be sold in order to secure resources (counterpart funds) for the government to fi nance development projects, among others. It is now recognized that aid can compete with and discourage local production; it can discourage local initiatives aiming to improve economic security by inducing a dependency syndrome. In such cases, food aid usually does not provoke famine directly, but contributes to increasing the vulnerability of the local economy by weakening it, and increasing the danger that it will be seriously affected by the next aggressive phenomenon.

Social phenomena

Population (or demographic) growth is beyond doubt the most worrying phenomenon. Already in the 19th century, Malthus had predicted that if the planet's population adjustment did not occur in a managed way (birth control), it would occur through famine and war, because population grows geometrically, while the production of resources grows arithmetically. In industrialized countries, Malthus's theory has not yet been verifi ed, because industrial and agricultural development has kept up with, even overtaken, population growth - which itself has tended to stabilize - at the cost of the massive use of fossil energy. In countries where this development has not taken place, the Malthusian dilemma remains strongly valid. It often results in competition for scarce resources; this translates into a high confl ict risk and contributes to adverse development, and thus to the deterioration of the environment and its support capacity, to pollution, to rural exodus and an increasing precariousness of living conditions.

Geometric progression: progression in which each term is a fi xed multiple of the preceding one (e.g. 1–4–16–64). Arithmetic progression: progression in which a constant is added to each term in order to obtain the next term (e.g. 2–4–6–8).

A manual dealing with nutrition and humanitarian assistance cannot ignore the negative side-effects of food aid. Although intended to be social in nature, food aid nevertheless can cause the economic repercussions discussed above.

The deterioration of the social fabric, linked to the evolution of specifi c lifestyles, is another phenomenon inducing anomalies in food behaviour, in water and habitat hygiene, and in care given to dependants. Its impact is therefore also felt on the consumption and biological utilization of food.

Cultural phenomena

Distinguishing between social and cultural phenomena is not easy. Social phenomena can be observed in any society, while cultural phenomena relate to specifi c acquired types of behaviour. For example, the Somali individualistic and clanic behaviour resulted in a confl ict which caused one of the last century's most devastating famines. This behaviour is acquired, and thus eminently cultural. Some cultural weaning and infant care practices also have serious consequences on the consumption and biological utilization of food. For instance, the Baganda children in Uganda are weaned by abruptly changing from maternal milk to mostly starchy food, low in protein and other nutrients, and poor in energy. They suddenly lose the immune protection of breastfeeding, the weaning food exposes them to new forms of bacterial contamination, and their appetite is satiated without their nutritional needs being covered, resulting in many cases of severe malnutrition.

Accidents and illness

Accidents resulting in massive pollution (Minamata in Japan, Bhopal in India, and Chernobyl in the former USSR) can make entire regions improper for human settlement, or contaminate resources and result in serious problems in terms both of the economy and health. However, the most common accidents affect individuals: workplace and traffi c accidents, mainly. Such accidents can infl uence all three steps of the feeding process, and endanger the survival of the household when the victim is a parent, particularly in the absence of social security. The same applies to non-infectious and infectious diseases (the latter are discussed briefly below as phenomena, and in further detail in the section devoted to malnutrition and infection).

Climatic environmental phenomena

Climatic environmental phenomena generally have the greatest consequences on the primary sector of the economy. Therefore, they affect primarily those who depend upon it for a living, and then those who depend on it through exchange. Some climatic phenomena owe their importance – even their existence in specifi c regions – to the deterioration and pollution resulting from the growth of human activity. It is therefore no longer easy to differentiate with certainty between climatic phenomena that are in fact natural accidents, and those whose origin is also human.

Drought

Among natural climatic phenomena, drought causes the

greatest number of nutritional crises. Combined with war - and, occasionally, non-human predators - it can be absolutely devastating, as seen in Ethiopia, Angola, Mozambique, Somalia and Sudan. Drought is fi rst and foremost a climatic occurrence. These occurrences show three types of variation:

- yearly variations, involving short time scales;
- pendulum systems, where periods of relatively humid years alternate with other, relatively dry spells;
- climatic change, which either develops over centuries or results from accidents (meteorites, solar spots or human activity as a whole), and can thus occur more rapidly.

An increase in the frequency of drought spells in sub-Saharan Africa has been observed since the late 1960s, but it is diffi cult to attribute this to a pendulum system or climatic change owing to persisting uncertainty as to the nature of global warming. It is however possible that we are witnessing climatic change aggravated by a pendulum movement. In northern Mali, some areas are completely dry yet contain shell residue; these areas accommodated permanent ponds until 1972, and have not contained water since. Terrestrial warming may have played a major part in this development. It must nevertheless be borne in mind that pendulum variations are considerable in the Sahel (10 to 18 years), while they are shorter in southern Africa, where dry spells do not exceed fi ve years (Glantz, 1987). In Angola, since the early 1980s, the altitudes at which endemic malaria begins have been observed to be rising, thus indicating warming. Since the late 1980s, dry spells have also become more frequent, while they were previously unknown in the country. In Mozambique, an old traditional leader stated in 1992 that for the fi rst time in his life he had experienced three consecutive dry years, and that he intended to modify his safety mechanisms accordingly. Drought can also result from human environmental over-exploitation, particularly deforestation.

Most frequently, populations are prepared for climatic variability, and have introduced cultural safety mechanisms to respond to it. However, at the negative extreme of a pendulum phenomenon, or when the frequency and intensity of variations abruptly exceed the norm, cultural mechanisms can prove insuffi cient. A famine is likely to develop in the absence of timely governmental and humanitarian intervention. When war combines with this type of situation, famine obviously becomes diffi cult to avert, as local authorities frequently lack the means or the will to intervene, while humanitarian agencies often face major acceptance and security challenges.

In semi-arid areas, drought is a relatively frequent feature, for which people are usually prepared because the rainfall variability is up to 30% around the annual mean. Therefore, the frequency and/or intensity of the phenomenon must be excessive to give rise to crisis. Usually, climatic or agronomic data cannot offer this threshold – it is indicated rather by the economic and social behaviour of the victims, as well as the terms of trade prevailing on the market. As a result, in most cases one cannot predict a nutritional crisis from an isolated drought episode, or from the episode considered at the moment of the enquiry. It must be placed in the context of past episodes, in the prevailing economic context, and be observed and analysed through the eyes of those experiencing it. In some cases, years of reasonably serious drought are required to precipitate famine; in others a single episode will suffi ce, as was the case in Irian Jaya in 1997, following El Niño.

Moreover, while exceptional droughts, sometimes combined with war or other deleterious phenomena, can be the predominant cause for nutritional crises, the social, cultural demographic, economic, political and ecological context also plays a major part. The resulting vector can differ substantially from what the drought episode, considered in isolation, may have suggested. It is therefore possible for a seemingly minor drought episode to launch a crisis, while several consecutive droughts may not.

Floods

Floods result from abnormally abundant rainfall saturating the soil's absorption capacity, or from spates provoked by rainfall or erosion upstream, sometimes very far from the fl ooded area. Generally, fl ood is less of a crisis factor than drought, although this depends on duration, the time of year, the speed of the waters and the available means to confront it and mitigate its effects. In Somalia, fl oods in the Shabelle and Juba River basins usually have serious consequences because they occur during the main planting season in a geographic (and sometimes political) environment that is unfavourable to effi cient intervention. Paradoxically, fl ood often follows drought: fi rstly because the latter can be followed by abnormally abundant rainfall, secondly because drought hardens the ground and thus fosters surface fl ow. Floods, like drought, can also result from human activity, such as deforestation upstream, which causes erosion and signifi cant runoff, in turn provoking unusually fast and large spates.

Hurricanes

Hurricanes are less frequent than drought and fl oods, and their consequences are usually more short-lived. More frequently, the danger arises from the risk of injury. Nevertheless, hurricane Mitch, combined with torrential rains, has demonstrated the high damage potential of such phenomena; they can push large areas into precariousness, thus increasing the danger of disaster related to any aggravating phenomenon.

PHENOMENA LINKED TO NON-HUMAN PREDATORS

Predators of production activities

Man is increasingly his own worst predator; however today some societies and regions still fall prey, for lack of control capacity, to predators that can massively threaten agricultural production, be it in the form of crops or harvest. The well-documented devastating damage of locusts can result in famine. Similarly, some insects and caterpillars can destroy agricultural production, as observed in southern Sudan in 1989 and 1994. Birds are likewise feared, particularly in areas where millet and sorghum are staple crops, because the ripened grain is literally proffered to the birds. Great fl ights of birds, similar to cricket swarms, can in fact be observed. Insects and rodents also attack the harvest once it is stored, and can cause signifi cant losses that seriously weaken the economy. Predators of animals can also endanger the pastoral economy: nowadays, those are mainly epizootics caused by parasites and infectious diseases affecting livestock.

Predators of man

In the food relations of ecology, man is indeed a formidable predator and destroyer, but he also accommodates predators who threaten to kill him through viral, bacterial or parasitic infection. Illness therefore also plays a major part in triggering nutritional crises. Those of specifi c concern to humanitarian intervention include infectious diseases, owing to their potentially devastating consequences on entire communities. Diarrhoea and infant diseases can cause individual nutritional crises: infection, anorexia, malnutrition, etc. But they also infl uence maternal health, as the natural reaction to high infant mortality is an increase in birth rate, for which women pay the highest price. Illnesses fi rst modify the consumption and biological utilization of food. However, they lead to an alteration of the functional capacity of the organism, which can impair performance in securing food. Malaria, river blindness (onchocercosis), sleeping sickness (trypanosomiasis), tropical sores (leishmaniasis or *kala-azar*), cholera, not to mention HIV/AIDS are illnesses that not only seriously undermine the household economy, but also, when they reach epidemic proportions, threaten to hinder the overall economy. Epidemics thrive in concentrated populations and deteriorated living conditions.

Geophysical environmental phenomena

Geophysical environmental phenomena – such as earthquakes, volcanic eruptions and tidal waves – are brutal occurrences that can cause many casualties both human and infrastructural in mere seconds. Governmental and humanitarian response, in terms of nutrition, is usually required and signifi cant for only a very brief period immediately following the catastrophe and until its survivors have recovered from the initial shock. Thereafter, recovery programmes – or resettlement and integration elsewhere, if the area is so badly affected that it precludes permanent human dwelling – become more important. Such phenomena do not themselves lead to famine, but may impoverish populations that must resettle or have lost their assets to the point of dependency and poverty.

The review of the various phenomena directly causing nutritional crisis indicates that many raise the propensity to crisis by creating or increasing vulnerability, and by paving the way for other phenomena. Furthermore, these phenomena can combine in many ways to exploit both existing vulnerability, and the vulnerability they cause. All these phenomena do not necessarily amount to an aggression but may turn into one as defences fail, prevention proves ineffective, non-existent or impossible, and when alternatives and reserves diminish. The evolution of the crisis process therefore depends on the time required for this failure, ineffectiveness and diminution to be evident.

Generally speaking, phenomena triggering nutritional crises can:

- vary in nature;
- combine together and exploit existing vulnerability;
- attack diverse entities;
- affect several activities within the feeding process;
- have a trickle-down effect by opening the way for new phenomena, by themselves growing, or by generating new types of vulnerability;
- have multiple and different impacts according to the type of vulnerability they encounter;
- take advantage of several types of vulnerability.

VULNERABILITY

Vulnerability expresses the susceptibility or weakness of a given entity confronted with aggression, and indicates a defi ciency rather than something tangible. Indeed, for a phenomenon not to constitute an aggression, a system must preclude it from occurring by preventing or destroying it; or it must be evaded while relying either on the means to wait for it to end, or on activities which do not provide it with a hold. As a result, vulnerability that provides a hold for the phenomenon arises from the absence of preventive measures, and the inadequacy or lack of defence mechanisms, reserves, and/or alternatives. Vulnerability is relevant only with respect to the presence of risks, that is, the probability of an aggressive phenomenon manifesting itself and undermining the affected entity. Vulnerability is therefore proportional to these two probabilities. Similarly, it makes sense only with respect to the nature of its relation to events. Thus, vulnerability must be qualifi ed. Economic vulnerability is only meaningful in relation to phenomena which can generate an aggression on the economy. Furthermore, if one can qualify vulnerability, and demonstrate the existence of a threshold beyond which the phenomenon will produce an impact, then it follows that below this threshold the system is not vulnerable. The concept of vulnerability is thus relative to the magnitude or scope of the aggressive phenomenon, and fl uctuates with it.

Nutritional vulnerability

In human nutrition, "vulnerable groups" is a common concept. It encompasses small children, pregnant and lactating women, sick people and the elderly, in the context of nutritional vulnerability. Indeed, within the population, these categories or groups are the most vulnerable to malnutrition, but their vulnerability is universal because its nature is above all physiological. However, restricting nutritional vulnerability to physiological vulnerability indicates a narrowness of mind which, combined with other controversial issues, can have serious consequences on humanitarian intervention (Mourey, 1995; Mourey, 2002).

Physiologically vulnerable groups are the same everywhere; however, the members composing such groups do not necessarily all suffer from their vulnerability, far from it. It turns out that those who suffer from it have an individual vulnerability by far superior to the norm and/or they belong to areas, communities, groups or households experiencing ecological, economic, social, cultural or political types of vulnerability before physiological vulnerability. Specifi cally, one can differentiate societies by the following distinctive features regarding the prospect of malnourishment for the physiologically vulnerable (sometimes the entire population):

- the capacity of the productive means to satisfy essential economic needs and, thus, secure food;
- hygiene, water and habitat conditions;
- access to health services;
- the level of care devoted to dependants, specifi cally the attention given to small children.

In other words, economic capacity, the natural environment, the level of development, culture and the political environment are all determining factors in distinguishing between societies with respect to their nutritional vulnerability. This shows that vulnerability types vary signifi cantly in human nutrition. In crisis, it is not uncommon to encounter several of these vulnerability types, which can combine and lead to tragic outcomes. As a result, the observer concerned by the nutrition of communities must set himself apart from what is traditionally referred to in nutrition as vulnerable groups, if he wishes to understand the concept of nutritional vulnerability as a whole. He must fi rst seek possible vulnerability types related to the distinctive nutritional (and, more generally, lifestyle) features of the society under scrutiny before investigating physiological vulnerability. The latter is to be found everywhere, but will manifest itself more or less strongly depending on vulnerability types located earlier in the feeding process.

To reinforce the notion of diversity and multiplicity of vulnerability types, it must be remembered that – for a phenomenon to qualify as aggressive and cause crisis – two different vulnerability levels must necessarily combine, whatever the affected activity:

- the inability to prevent or evade the phenomenon;
- the inability to confront or evade the impact of the phenomenon once it has occurred, for lack of resilience.

Generally speaking, regarding the three steps of the feeding process, the main vulnerability types are linked to the following dimensions.

1. In terms of obtaining food, vulnerability is linked to:
    - poor health, affecting functional capacity;
    - poverty, being the opposite of economic resilience;
    - war, which can infl uence all factors determining economic performance;
    - the level of domestic development, which determines the capacity of the economy to perform on the international market;
    - the type of government, which chooses what assistance to extend in case of harmful phenomena affecting the overall economic performance of communities or regions;
    - climate, infl uencing harvests, hunting and collecting, and fishing activities;

- lack of integration or social support, undermining resilience;
- production activities, depending on the nature of the aggressive phenomena;
- dependency on institutions (prisons, hospitals) for access to food;
- cultural practices, when they lead to passivity or deleterious reactions towards new phenomena.

2. In terms of food consumption, vulnerability on the one hand ties in with other types of vulnerability occurring before and related to the obtaining of food; on the other, it results from poor health (reducing appetite), but also from the neglect of dependants (in terms of care and food), particularly children and the elderly. Poor health, as well as sub-standard healthcare can stem from different types of vulnerability (see below).

   Furthermore, persons living alone are vulnerable because, more often than not, they deprive themselves of, or are precluded from, a favourable social environment: those particularly affected are the elderly, social cases and addicted persons (alcohol, drugs).

   Changes in lifestyle can also result in vulnerability in terms of food consumption: the elderly, increasingly idle and lonely, teenagers and students breaking out of the family circle, displaced persons who cannot (or do not know how to) take advantage of existing resources, impoverished populations who cannot adapt to an inferior lifestyle, and migrants. Finally, access to new, unfamiliar types of food that are not always healthy but are appetizing and can lead to real dependency phenomena, is also a source of vulnerability.

3. In terms of the biological utilization of food, vulnerability arises from other types of vulnerability occurring before and related to the obtaining and consumption of food, and from poor health condition (impaired functions of the organs and metabolism).

Clearly, the higher (i.e. earlier) in the feeding process the vulnerability is located, the greater the probability that it will be faced by many; whereas vulnerability related to dysfunctions of the metabolism and located further down (later) in the process rather affect specifi c individuals, even exceptional cases. This trend should, nevertheless, not be regarded as an absolute rule.

Political vulnerability

Political vulnerability is related to the risk of confl ict, repression or discrimination, the lack of appropriate measures to arrest the crisis process, and disregard for the provisions of international humanitarian law and other legal instruments aiming at securing acceptable living conditions for man. It also relates to the inadequacy of services which usually depend on the political system functioning properly, such as public transport, and health and education services. Defi cient transport leads to economic vulnerability; poor health services result in physiological vulnerability, and inadequate education services cause social vulnerability, *inter alia*. Political vulnerability can promote all the above phenomena, and its mere existence can infl uence the entire feeding process.

Economic vulnerability

Commonly, economic vulnerability allows phenomena to undermine economic productive activities and their yield. It can be caused by human and natural phenomena, as described above. It can infl uence human groups or entire regions, depending on whether the phenomenon affects geographic zones or specifi c productive activities. This type of vulnerability is inversely proportional to the household's means of production and resilience. It infl uences the securing of food and, thereby, the following stages of the feeding process directly, but it can also modify the attention given to dependants, access to health services, and hygiene, with indirect repercussions on the consumption and biological utilization of food.

Ecological vulnerability

Ecological vulnerability is shaped by the environment's support capacity, and to the danger of environmental hazards. The environment's support capacity is inversely proportional to the intensity of production activities exploiting it. Environmental hazards such as drought, locusts or endemics like trypanosomiasis weaken the productive capacity as well as the organism. Ecological vulnerability often accompanies economic and physiological vulnerability, and can thus affect the feeding process as a whole.

Social vulnerability

Social vulnerability generally refers to the weakness of individuals, households or groups, due to ignorance, isolation or behaviour, and diminishes them within a society by, for example, excluding them from solidarity mechanisms and preventing them from countering aggression adequately. However, social vulnerability also arises from dependency on external assistance for survival. This is obviously the case of small children, the sick and the injured, the elderly who have lost their fi nancial independence, and the disabled. Furthermore, women face social discrimination in most cultures: this vulnerability is social rather than cultural, because discrimination against women is usually a feature of human society, whatever the culture. Cultural vulnerability can however be an aggravating factor, depending on the region and lifestyle.

Cultural vulnerability

In cultural vulnerability, inadequacy in responding to phenomena results from economic, educational, legal or political practices inherent in the culture in question, that is, the acquired behaviour specifi c to a society or community. It is, for example, the absence of norms regarding the exploitation of given secondary resources, which can nonetheless become vital in case of diffi culty; behaviour types transmitted through education which can arrest development and creativity, or weaken the attention given to dependants (e.g. harmful weaning practices); the lack or inadequacy of community solidarity mechanisms, obscurantist traditional beliefs; institutions, practices or individuals, the respect for which can prove harmful when it is time to confront aggression; ostracism against individuals with specifi c defects (physical or psychological), or who have deliberately or unwittingly breached codes of conduct. But cultural vulnerability is also an expression of difference which can generate unease or envy, and can become a pretext for abuse and discrimination, even extermination.

Physiological vulnerability

Physiological vulnerability has been discussed above. With respect to nutrition, it concerns higher than average food needs, and susceptibility to illness, particularly infectious diseases. It is aggravated by inadequate access to healthcare, be it due to lack of resources (economic vulnerability at household level), or because the latter are inappropriate (political vulnerability at society level). The combination of malnutrition and infection increases physiological vulnerability, precipitating crisis towards disaster. It should be noted that, in every society, some individuals are particularly vulnerable from a physiological perspective; they constitute the customer base of any health structure, and are particularly prone to developing complex pathologies, combining malnutrition and infection.

Such persons thus face individual nutritional crises, which must not be confused with a signal of emerging crisis potentially affecting the entire community. Moreover, physiological nutritional vulnerability among infants refers to different nutritional needs than for adults.

Indeed, the energy requirements per kilogramme of body weight are higher for children than for adults. Children's protein needs are lower per consumed energy unit, while the requirements in essential amino acids are greater, owing to the greater speed of protein turnover. It is therefore necessary to specify in what way the nutritional requirement of small children is greater than that of adults and aggravates their relative vulnerability. This avoids prejudices, such as are used to justify in part selective supplementary feeding programmes.

Psychological vulnerability

Psychological vulnerability refers to the quality of the socio-cultural environment and the amount and magnitude of stress. The socio-cultural environment largely determines a group's resilience and self-confi dence. Stress also plays a major part in determining reactive capacity. At the inception of a stressful event, this capacity can be undermined by the refusal to face reality, just as much as it can be stimulated. On the other hand, if stress is too severe or protracted, post-traumatic disorders can follow, undermining or destroying the reactive capacity. This can infl uence the entire feeding process directly or indirectly, particularly for those who rely on psychologically affected persons, for example children in war.

IMPACT

In view of the large variety of phenomena and types of vulnerability from which they can arise, impacts are relatively easy to understand. Indeed, they manifest themselves very materially with respect to the feeding process.

Diffi culties in obtaining food

- Low food availability within the society, which often results in a rise in the price of essential commodities (additional impact).
- Insuffi cient economic production at household level, indicating an inadequate economic performance.
- Losses before and after the harvest.
- Loss of reserves through excessive sale, consumption or looting.
- Impoverishment resulting from the use of reserves to cover essential needs (due to an inadequate economic performance).
- A negative change in the management of time – particularly if more time is required to produce the same result.
- Market disturbances due to shortages, infrastructural damage and transport malfunctions alike.

Problems in food consumption

Insuffi cient food consumption, owing to shortfalls in the obtaining of food, discussed above.

Disturbed eating habits, owing to changes in the availability of food products, the available time for the preparation and sharing of food, and weaning practices. Lack of means and knowledge regarding the care of dependants, because changing circumstances impose unfamiliar or inapplicable measures. Exposure to infectious disease and the lack of healthcare due to modifi ed living conditions. Health problems affecting food consumption.

Problems in the biological utilization of food

- Ineffi cient biological utilization of food, owing to reduced and inadequate food consumption.
- Disturbed biological utilization of food, owing to insuffi cient intake and damage to the system.

IMPORTANT ASPECTS OF NUTRITIONAL CRISES

In the humanitarian world, referring to victims in numbers is signifi cant in defi ning the crisis itself, because it serves to justify intervention. Indeed, when a crisis affects only a limited number of households or individuals, it is likely that the resources required to address it will be found locally. This is no longer the case where crisis strikes large segments of the population. But the use of numbers is also contingent upon the parameters of the crisis, and is subjective in nature as it depends on the intervening agency, its mandate and the political environment.

Nutritional crises and malnutrition

To conclude, the effect of aggression on the food process is sometimes analysed according to the nutritional status of individuals or selected groups, giving an idea of the overall performance of the process. From this angle, nutritional crisis refers to malnutrition - being the last stage before death experienced by victims of dysfunctions in the food process. This approach to nutritional crises through malnutrition ignores the fact that some event has preceded malnutrition, and that it has caused problems that might have been resolved in a more timely fashion. It also ignores the fact that intervention, if it is to justify its humanitarian label, must not only alleviate suffering, but also pre-empt it. In practical terms, it is therefore unacceptable to restrict analysis to the performance of the food process *via* its result. One must, at the very least, consider the performance at each step of the process, and that of the crucial activities of each of these steps.

NUTRITIONAL CRISIS ILLUSTRATED

The following example illustrates the application of the formulation of the mechanism of a crisis.

For farmers relying on subsistence agriculture in an area where production alternatives are limited, where agriculture is essentially restricted to a monoculture vulnerable to water shortage, the impact of a major drought will be negative by signifi cantly depleting production. The most probable response will be to resort to resources intended to face the situation which, however, is probably not yet abnormal. If it is followed shortly by other dry spells, reserves are depleted and the abnormal frequency of drought becomes a phenomenon. Vulnerability to the phenomenon is illustrated by the plant's poor resilience to the lack of water, and impact is a production shortage. The latter translates into damage, being a net loss of resources. This loss constitutes a problem precipitating the crisis for those who can no longer compensate, that is, those lacking:

Such individuals face destitution. They show the second level of vulnerability (vulnerability to the impact), which is an economic vulnerability characterized by an excessive reliance on a climate-sensitive crop. They therefore face a crisis situation.

Their destitution increases their vulnerability, on the economic, social (they face isolation due to their misfortune or social status), and physiological (lack of resources restricts their access to healthcare) fronts.

Moreover, impact (production shortage) is observed to turn into a new phenomenon in combining with economic vulnerability. It then manifests itself in a new impact, being destitution. In turn, the latter acts as a phenomenon in encountering economic vulnerability, and its impact leads to a utilization of the reserves of the organism, ultimately causing malnutrition, with an increase of physiological vulnerability. This spiral can persist until the exhaustion of the reserves of the system, or until a contagious disease (new phenomenon) combines with physiological vulnerability to cause death of the system, this being the fi nal impact of the evolution of the crisis process.

This example shows that, owing to the multitude of cause and effect phenomena, crisis is characterized by increasingly numerous and accumulating problems, resulting in an increasingly signifi cant deterioration of the situation, which can end in disaster. Moreover, the crisis itself can go through different stages of seriousness (for example, by involving a growing number of individuals); one may also observe periods of respite depending on the time between the emergence of new phenomena, new types of vulnerability, and the resulting impacts. It will also be noticed that the crisis develops according to the process described above. The preliminary phase begins when a second dry spell follows shortly behind the fi rst drought, and so on, until relying on existing reserves can no longer deal with such an event. If nevertheless this then occurs, acute crisis - the crisis as such - begins; in the above example, the crisis does not develop into the recovery phase, but towards disaster. Whether acute crisis develops into recovery or disaster depends directly on external intervention. If external assistance is extended during the preliminary phase, it would prevent the exhaustion of reserves and provide safety in facing another abnormal drought episode; it would thereby limit damage. If assistance is delayed until the acute phase of the crisis, it encounters already highly impoverished individuals, possibly already facing problems related to the consumption or biological utilization of food. This is where the gamble - or the dilemma - arises with respect to intervention: is it preferable to intervene early during the preliminary phase, thus risking waste of resources if the drought is not repeated (this is however not the case for the recipients, who will be able to replenish their assets faster)? Or should the next drought episode be awaited to ensure that measures decided on are absolutely indispensable, at the cost, however, of greater damage to the victims?

10

The Pathology of Nutritional Crisis

The previous Chapter discussed the preconditions for nutritional crisis, in addition to providing a defi nition; it showed that crisis can affect groups or individuals in different ways, depending on the type of phenomenon affecting the nutritional need or the feeding process. This Chapter discusses the pathology resulting from nutritional crisis.

Disorders that appear within the food securing phase indicate damage to the household or group economy. Problems that arise during the food consumption phase may suggest earlier disorder – e.g. in the food securing phase – which can alter eating habits and reduce the availability of food; but it may also result from illness or family cell dysfunctions because of lack of means, time, motivation, or ignorance.

Ignorance is understood here in its broadest sense: a lack of knowledge regarding dietary balance or the specifi c care required by vulnerable groups, or compliance with deleterious rules, taboos, or methods that lead to imbalance and defi ciency. Problems associated with the biological utilization of food imply earlier disorders, either during the food securing or consumption phases, but also in the individual health status.

Crisis that emerges during the food securing phase can cause scarcity and famine. It rarely affects single households, but usually entire socio-economic groups and regions. If it occurs during this phase, it logically also affects the following two phases of the feeding process (i.e. the consumption and biological utilization of food), and may prove fatal.

Whatever its cause, crisis occurring primarily in the food consumption phase or in the biological utilization phase sooner or later causes nutritional disorder.

The review of famine and nutritional disorder refl ects the full spectrum of nutritional pathologies, which can take on epidemic proportions; it is this pathology that humanitarian agencies are usually expected to address, both in prevention and cure.

FAMINE

Famine is the most classical type of nutritional crisis. The defi nition of "famine" nevertheless remains hazy. This is no doubt because, although all famines result from a serious and protracted defi ciency in the securing of food, the process resulting in this situation, as well as its severity and prognosis vary considerably. The process is determined by aggressive phenomena and vulnerabilities, resilience and the timeframe set by economic performance. Its severity is determined by the magnitude of the food access defi ciency, its duration, and aggravating factors such as displacement, defi cient water and habitat hygiene, inadequate access to healthcare, exposure to contagious diseases, frayed social ties, and emotional trauma (particularly affecting the mother and child bond). The severity of the problem clearly shapes the prognosis. As a result, some famines cause millions of victims, while others are closer to scarcity or chronic malnutrition. One question is the subject of much debate: does the epidemic mortality that is characteristic of some famines result mainly from malnutrition, or rather from transmissible diseases that are exacerbated by deteriorated living conditions and social disintegration? This question is important to humanitarian operations that cannot view famine only as a food shortage to be addressed through food distributions, especially where risks of epidemics exist (this is not always the case). Whatever the circumstances, relevant humanitarian intervention cannot restrict itself to addressing the most obvious symptoms; it must attempt to address all the disorders that threaten the survival of victims, and as early as possible in order to limit suffering and avoid having to remedy it at a later stage. This concept assumes the availability (allowing for possible constraints) of all the means necessary for a global approach to problems and their prevention.

DEFINITIONS

As mentioned earlier, the defi nition of famine remains hazy. The commonest defi nitions are:

- *"Extreme and protracted shortage of food, causing widespread and persistent hunger, emaciation of the affected population, and a substantial increase in the death rate"*. (Encyclopaedia Britannica, 2006).
- *"Extreme scarcity of food"*. (Oxford Dictionary, 2000).
- *"Extreme food scarcity: a severe shortage of food resulting in widespread hunger"*. (Encarta, 2005).
- *"A regional failure of production or distribution systems, leading to a sharp increase in mortality due to starvation and associated disease"*. (Cox, 1981).
- *"A series of increasingly desperate actions by people to obtain food"*. (Seaman and Holt, 1980; Sen, 1981; quoted in D'Souza, 1988).
- *"A reduction in normally available food supply such that individuals, families, and eventually whole communities are forced to take up abnormal social and economic activities in order to ensure food. If these activities are unsuccessful, then starvation will follow"*. (D'Souza, 1988).
- *"Alongside the obvious manifestations of hunger, a more insidious form exists, which is usually termed misery but is, in fact, a state of chronic famine affecting entire populations of the third world and various groups in the industrial world, whose members face permanent dietary shortage, both in quality and in quantity. This chronic famine is associated with repartition that is dictated by economic and fi nancial concerns only, leaving the response to excessive distress to public charity"*. (Encarta Encyclopaedia 97, 1993–1996).

These defi nitions invite a number of comments.

Food shortage

Food shortage is an ambiguous concept: is food lacking in the absolute sense, or rather is it inaccessible to the affected population (because it is unaffordable or for any other reason such as crops are growing in a confl ict/ mined area) ? In fact, both are possible, and one does not exclude the other. It is therefore preferable to refer to an insuffi cient access to food, without attempting a more accurate defi nition.

Victims suffer from hunger (famine comes from the Latin *fames*, hunger)

That the victims of famine suffer from hunger seems self-evident. However, an insuffi cient access to food can confer different meanings on hunger, depending on the magnitude of the shortage and the prospects for improvement. In scarcity situations, people suffer from hunger without necessarily fearing for their economic and physiological security.

In the course of normal seasonal variations, it may be usual to go hungry for a given period – it is even sometimes a deliberate choice intended to preserve the household economy without serious penalty. In famines, suffering from hunger takes on a different meaning. This suffering results in abnormal and desperate behaviours that go well beyond the daily struggle for survival, even in conditions of extreme poverty or scarcity. These behaviours themselves contribute to the deterioration of the famine situation if its causes persist. Moreover, this suffering refl ects a degree of widespread malnutrition to be found only in such situations, when all age categories show the symptoms of serious energy defi ciencies, i.e. of Type II nutrients, sometimes combined with specific defi ciencies.

Widespread mortality

Widespread mortality may indeed be a major characteristic of famine, distinguishing it from scarcity. But this mortality, however frightful it may be, varies signifi cantly according to the cause of the famine, its duration, its severity, the associated risk of infectious disease, and the resilience of the affected population.

Famine affects specifi c geographic areas

Famine is a regional phenomenon. On the other hand, nutritional crisis that affects individuals or households can be explained by inadequate access to food, suffering resulting from hunger, and one or several deaths. As long as the phenomenon is restricted to single individuals or households, it is not famine, even if the affected individuals may consider it to be so. The expression famine refers strictly to the fact that a significant proportion of the population living in a given area suffers from serious hunger (whatever the size of the area under consideration) - corroborating the fact that famine is a collective phenomenon.

Duration

The process resulting in famine is undoubtedly lengthy. The concept of duration is questionable however, because it is not a precondition for famine. When a famine is said to be protracted, reference is being made to the period during which its victims have been suffering from hunger.

Famine may in fact develop rapidly, depending on the severity of the lack of food access. For example, a general strike in the transport sector of a capital city could cause famine within weeks, and result just as quickly in massive mortality if supplies do not resume. In the 1980s, population groups of the Angolan Planal to were displaced abruptly (in less than one day) and were cut off from their resource base accordingly; it was impossible to assist them, and severe malnutrition became general within six weeks.

Collective dimension

Widespread mortality and the regional dimension both suggest that famine affects a signifi cant proportion of the population of a given region. If these two concepts are accepted, then it follows that famine is a collective phenomenon.

Cause and effect

Famine results from a chain of causes; but the expression famine suggests the inevitable, and thus encourages fatalism when it would in fact be possible to address its causes.

Causes of mortality

The mortality associated with famine is much discussed: does it really result from malnutrition, or rather from disease? The mortality caused by disease is clearly worse than usual in famines. Similarly, the chaos surrounding many famine situations promotes the spread of infectious diseases such as typhus fever, cholera, tuberculosis, and measles. Generally, the fi rst to die are the more severely malnourished; in many famines, in fact, mortality is associated primarily with malnutrition. Mortality reaches its peak during the night or rainy spells, that is, in cold conditions. But it would be erroneous to conclude that cold is the killer in famine, and not malnutrition. Ultimately, death is caused by cardiac arrest. Whatever the immediate cause for mortality in famine, malnutrition is the underlying cause.

Regional disruption of food production and distribution mechanisms

The disruption of regional systems suggests a macro-economic approach to famine. But such systems may be of little importance, particularly in terms of distribution. The problem arises at a more individual level, through lack of the means to purchase food, for example because of speculation or infl ation. This underscores the fact that famine results from an insuffi cient access to food.

Increasingly desperate behaviour

Famine has two fundamental characteristics in this respect: it is the culmination of a process (as suggested by "*increasingly*"), and the economic disorder is eclipsed by the biological problem, which usually aggravates the economic disorder.

Desperate behaviour replaces a conduct intended to preserve economic self-sustainability with biological survival refl exes, induced by the suffering related to acute and protracted hunger, and by the absence of alternatives. If famine is indeed associated with increasingly desperate conducts, then it follows that famine is a process and not a situation.

Abnormal economic and social behaviour

The previous Chapter has shown that an unusually strong (in duration or magnitude) aggression provokes an insuffi cient or abnormal response. This is no doubt the crux of the famine problem. Abnormal economic and social behaviour suggests the existence of a famine process; urgent action is thus required in order to prevent the otherwise inevitable economic, social, physiological and psychological consequences. Assessment must highlight such abnormal behaviour or, better still for prevention purposes, the phenomena whose impact may lead to abnormal behaviour. Abnormal behaviour is discussed under Section 1.4 below.

The chronic and usually unnoticed misery of a signifi cant proportion of mankind

Authors generally agree that famine is different from abject poverty and scarcity (Rivers, 1976; D'Souza, 1988); according to them, the difference lies in the social disintegration typical of famine that arises from the inability of cultural equilibrium mechanisms to cope with the situation. They claim that chronic poverty can be addressed through considerable social, psychological and physiological adaptation, enabling its victims to cope in spite of all. The use of the word famine in relation to such situations, however tragic they may be, is therefore inaccurate because their consequences are different, and humanitarian operations as such cannot address them appropriately. Scarcity on the other hand amounts to a more or less serious food shortage, but does not itself jeopardize the functioning of society; it can however lead to famine if the crisis is protracted or deepens.

These remarks give a clear idea of famine, which must now be defi ned as a process or a specifi c situation resulting from a process. The word itself gives rise to a problem – which refers not to a process but to its result. Moreover, the word famine, like kwashiorkor, is common and – as noted by Sen – refers to an easily recognized condition, even in the absence of an accurate defi nition (Sen, 1981). This Manual takes the view that famine is the result of a process, and not the process itself. The following description can be derived from the aforementioned considerations.

Famine is the disaster stage of an evolving process. It affects a signifi cant proportion of the population of one or several regions. Access to food for the affected population is grossly insuffi cient. As a result, the population suffers from hunger to the point of widespread mortality caused by starvation, often combined with infectious disease. Economic and social disintegration result from abnormal and desperate behaviour.

THE CAUSES OF FAMINE

Famine always results from insuffi cient access to food; its direct cause is therefore an insuffi cient performance in the securing of food. This direct cause itself has two underlying causes that may combine:

- households cannot afford available commodities;

- the availability of food is limited.

These underlying causes have their own causes (i.e. secondary causes):

- household food production is insuffi cient or non-existent;
- the hunting, gathering and fi shing activities of households are insuffi cient or non-existent;
- household food reserves are insuffi cient or exhausted;
- the household purchasing power cannot secure locally available food:
- either because prices are high owing to actual shortage or speculation, inverting the terms of trade between food and production or possessions;
- or because the population no longer has enough resources, whatever the market price of commodities;
- food is unavailable on local markets owing to isolation, structural damage or insecurity, whatever the purchasing power:
- local food is unavailable, and the distribution network is sub-standard; the price of available food rises according to shortage, exposing the poor to famine; the problem then affects better-off households, depending on the duration and magnitude of the shortage – this is common in confl ict situations, when markets cannot be supplied because transport systems are the target of attacks and the necessary infrastructure is damaged or destroyed;
- food is absent from local markets because the overall purchasing power is insuffi cient to generate a suffi cient demand to encourage distribution networks – assuming that food is available elsewhere and could be transported to the region affected by famine, and that distribution networks could perform if demand were attractive:
- this is particularly common in rural subsistence zones, following harvest failure caused by drought, for example – production losses lead to an abnormally high dependency on local markets, while the absence of income, savings and reserves restricts demand and discourages the transfer of stocks from elsewhere;

- local social obligation and mutual assistance networks have collapsed or are non-existent;
- national famine prevention systems are inadequate, neglected or non-existent;
- international solidarity has not yet translated into humanitarian action.

Famine therefore results from cause and effect relations, and its possible causes are manifold. On the other hand, confi rmed famine indicates that prevention efforts (if any) have proven ineffi cient; this cause is constant. In view of man's right to acceptable living conditions, famine nowadays is a bitter failure. It refl ects the ambiguous side of human nature, which prompts man to lament such situations, while promoting them and fi nding excuses for inertia. However, in view of the world's current resources, there is simply no excuse for famine. It always results from deliberate action and/ or lack of goodwill, and the denial of fundamental rights. Real famine is rare, and the cost of its prevention is negligible in comparison to the expenditure of wealthy economies in other sectors. As an illustration, the belated rescue operations prompted by media reports of advanced tragedy are usually more costly than the preventive means that could have arrested the process. Nevertheless it is not always possible in practice to act in time, even if the means are available.

THE FAMINE PROCESS

Some famine processes are obvious, because their causes have rapid and clear consequences. Examples include the sudden displacement of populations who have lost all their belongings and depend entirely on outside assistance, and complete isolation such as that produced by a siege or a suspension of supplies, where food is no longer available, whatever the means to purchase it. In such extreme cases, the cause and effect relation is clear enough, and does not require further discussion. However, the commonest famine processes do deserve discussion; they pertain to a protracted economic counter-performance of production activities, which depletes both resources and alternatives. Such processes have brought about most of the major known famines of the 20th century, and can go unnoticed until resource exhaustion is considerably advanced. These processes must be identifi ed in order to be arrested. The famine process as defi ned here at once raises questions of predictability: the process is initiated whenever a phenomenon impairs the household economic performance, but it may not be irreversible because it stops as soon as improved conditions enable the affected households to recover. As a result, famine is rare in comparison to the frequency of aborted famine processes. For famine to culminate, a phenomenon must either destroy the household economy entirely and abruptly (these are extreme cases that do not warrant further discussion), or the duration and magnitude of a negative phenomenon (or of connected phenomena) combine with the existing and successive vulnerabilities of the economy resulting in an erosion of usable material resources to the point where only physiological reserves can cover the nutritional need. As mentioned above, efforts to stop the process must also have proven fruitless. Usually, when actual famine is close, the utilization of physiological reserves has already begun to compensate for the erosion of material reserves.

The famine process can be halted, provided that a spontaneous positive reversal of fortune or appropriate assistance can bridge the gap. Likewise, the process can develop in several stages, with stops, starts, and passing remission. Both reversibility and erratic development thus complicate the diagnosis and relevant action.

Households can and must decide the use and allocation of their resources according to their constraints and priorities. On the other hand, they have no infl uence on the external forces that determine their economic performance and local food availability. The famine process thus arises from the uneven confrontation between households and such forces when they become detrimental, that is, when the basic household needs exceed the capacity of available means to satisfy these needs. Because the evolution of the famine process is usually diffi cult to anticipate, households must allocate their economic resources carefully. In other words, their objective is to survive as long as possible, and remain economically sustainable as long as possible in order to maximize their chances of recovery when conditions improve.

The famine process is thus typifi ed by specifi c behaviour with respect to the use of economic resources when production activities can no longer cover all the basic needs. Such behaviour refl ects individual priorities that may not match those of humanitarian agencies. A common example is provided by the opening of therapeutic feeding centres intended to save infants whose malnutrition contributed to the triggering of humanitarian action, in spite of possibly diverging priorities on the part of their parents (such as preparing the fi elds ahead of the next planting season, the guarantee for longer-term survival), making the parent's obligatory presence with the child impossible.

No two famine situations are identical, and the same comment applies to their lead-up. However, in spite of such variations, similar household behaviour patterns will be found: in their absence, thought must be devoted to whether the situation qualifi es as a famine, or whether a specifi c element has escaped the analysis. Either way, the affected population is the soundest source of information, and can explain what may otherwise seem inconsistent to outsiders.

The famine process amounts to a crisis process, and the same type of illustration is thus applied to both; the illustration of the famine process however uses a terminology that corresponds to the use of economic and physiological resources, instead of the wording similar to the development of illness used in the crisis process. The following stages have been defi ned.

1. Adaptation is the stage in which households modify the relative importances of their normal production activities, in order to maximize the overall economic yield when the normal main activities suffer a fall in yield. At this stage, reserves set aside in anticipation of production and market fl uctuations are also used, and households avoid unnecessary expenses. The objective is to preserve a normal standard of living as much as possible. This stage does not warrant particular alarm, because adaptation takes place within the limits of what the culture considers to be normal variations of the factors that infl uence living standards. In rural areas, adaptation occurs almost every dry season, but is more acute when the previous harvest was less productive than expected.
2. Impoverishment begins when the factors that normally infl uence living standards change beyond what is culturally accepted as normal. It causes an increasing reliance on production activities that are considered to be minor or less appealing, the erosion of reserves intended to cope

with usual production and market fl uctuations, and the use of non-productive commodities that would otherwise be kept but must be disposed of for survival. Expenses are limited to the bare essentials. A controlled food restriction is usually normal and is often cultural, that is, it belongs to the habitual coping mechanisms of the society under consideration. Such a restriction may nevertheless begin to promote nutritional disorders, especially specifi c defi ciencies. At this stage, community social obligation networks are invoked to their maximum because reciprocity is fully guaranteed. Households resort to credit in order to preserve their means of production. The utilization of resources is also subjected to the preservation of the means of production, with a view to economic recovery when circumstances improve.

3. Capital loss is the stage where households are forced to use all available means of production for survival, to sell or barter all remaining non-productive assets and, more importantiy, the basic assets that enable them to lead a normal life and are thus converted into survival reserves. Such assets are those that contribute to economic production (means of production) in order to achieve suffi cient renewable economic performance, such as land, tractors, herds, savings, and means of transport. But they also include utilitarian domestic assets such as clothing, bedding, furniture, cooking utensils, and housing. The loss of assets that are essential to survival leads to destitution.

This change in the function of commodities that are required to lead a normal life is highly detrimental to the household economy. The sale of assets required for the conduct of renewable productive activities is an economically aberrant behaviour that fi nally dooms the normal economic household system: the exchange may produce some resources, but at the cost of independent production. The disposal of infrastructural household assets leads to precariousness, even vagrancy.

In both cases, such behaviour refl ects the urgent need to meet elementary requirements. It is the last economic resort to prolong life for a short time, but at exorbitant cost.

Capital loss forcibly restricts food consumption, which becomes increasingly uncontrollable; this implies an erosion of the physiological reserves inducing nutritional disorder, and a functional inability to ensure both production activities and the defence of the organism. During this stage, social obligation networks are also severely tried and weakened, and are eclipsed by the survival of the household within its increasingly hostile environment in which reciprocity is no longer common practice. Likewise, social regulations lose meaning; social life formerly provided survival guarantees and thus encouraged compliance, but it no longer does. Social disintegration therefore follows economic collapse. Both are catalysts for famine. As from the capital loss stage, the famine process fuels itself from the desperate economic and social behaviour of those who are obliged to submit to it. Capital loss is the stage where survival is the overarching objective, at any cost.

4. The starvation stage amounts to famine strictly speaking. Victims exhaust their last physiological reserves, fully develop nutritional disorders and abandon their homes in search of hypothetical outside assistance. This situation leads to the all too frequent tragic images of endless lines of destitute people, the desperation and death camps in the Sahel, Cambodia, Ethiopia, Rwanda, Somalia and Sudan, to name only the most familiar. At this stage, family social obligations and the strength of family ties weaken (but not always), and the mortality associated with malnutrition and infectious disease becomes epidemic. It is unfortunately usually only at this late stage that the international community reacts, whatever the previous warning signals may have been.

The four stages of the famine process are in fact not as clearly distinguished in the use of resources. Overlaps exist, as mentioned above: food intake may be restricted in a controlled manner during impoverishment - this implies the utilization of physiological resources up until weight loss with only limited functional capacity loss (if at all). Assets such as food may also be set aside in anticipation of yet harsher times (amounting to speculation, and probably inducing a price increase). This saving howerer involves debt in order to face unavoidable expenses. The most important aspect of this process is no doubt the fact that its victims look ahead, beyond the immediate needs of their stomachs, and what worries them more than hunger is the complete loss of their livelihoods, which is leading them to destitution and seriously affects their chances of recovery.

In short, the famine process is characterized by the shrinking of alternatives (or choices); this may be abrupt (owing to the confi nement or displacement of populations) or gradual (drought extending over several successive years). This reduction in alternatives is caused by phenomena that aggravate vulnerability and whose impact in a chain reaction impairs economic production, specifi c reserves, survival reserves, and physiological reserves in the following sequence:

- normal adaptation mechanisms fail, thus ending the adaptation phase;
- resilience intended to preserve livelihoods in compliance with culture also fails, thus ending the impoverishment phase;
- resilience intended to allow individual survival in compliance with physiological needs fails, thus ending the capital loss phase;
- physiological reserves are the last resort, driving people to migrate in search of assistance; in the absence of such assistance, the starvation phase - frequently aggravated by infectious disease - results in death.

Poverty grows as the famine process develops. A critical threshold is crossed when people lose the means that normally ensure their self-suffi ciency, precipitating them into destitution.

Furthermore, the famine process - marked by impoverishment and capital loss - creates dependency, and not only for food because their entire economy collapses. During the recovery phase, their usual basic economic needs, their assets lost in the course of the process, and their accumulated debt must all be compensated. Humanitarian operations, in order to achieve their goal, must therefore address all these parameters.

Bibliography

Bailey, Ronald: *Liberation Biology: The Scientific and Moral Case for the Biotech Revolution*, Amherst, Prometheus Books, 2005.

Barlow K: *Ecology of Food and Nutrition*, Oceania, New Guinea, 1984.

Barnum, R.: *Biotechnology: An Introduction*, Belmont, Thomson/ Brooks/Cole, 2005.

Bindon JR: *Food and Foodways*, Oceania, Samoa, 1988.

Carper J. : *Food Your Miracle Medicine*, Pocket Books, 2000.

Chaitow L. : *Stone Age Diet*, Macdonald Optima, 1987.

Chrispeels, Maarten : *Plants, Genes and Crop Biotechnology*, Sudbury MA, Jones and Barlett Publishers, 2003.

Conton L: *Social, Economic and Ecological Parameters of Infant Feeding in Usino*, Oceania, New Guinea, 1985.

Culton S. : *The Psychology of Stress and Nutrition*, National Book Company, 1991.

Daubenmire, R. F.: *Plants and Environment*, New York, Wiley, 1947.

Davies S., Stewart A. : *Nutritional Medicine*, Pan Books, 1987.

Dixon J: *The Changing Chicken: Chooks, Cooks and Culinary Culture*, University of New South Wales Press, Australia, 2002.

Doyle W. : *Teach Yourself Healthy Eating*, Hodder and Stoughton, 1994.

Feingold B. : *Why Your Child is Hyperactive*, Random House, New York, 1975.

Ferro-Luzzi G: *Food Patterns and Nutrition in French Polynesia*, Oceania, Polynesia, 1962.

James W.P.T. : *Healthy Nutrition: Preventing Nutrition Related Diseases in Europe*, WHO Regional Publications, 1988.

Jenkins, C; : *Diet and Survival among the Hagahai of Papua New Guinea*, Papua New Guinea, Hagahai, 1993.

Junsji C., Collin-Campbell T., Junyao C., Peto R. : *Diet, Lifestyle and Mortality in China*, Oxford University Press, 1993.

Kruvant, W.J.: *People, Energy, and Pollution*, Cambridge, Ballinger Publishing, 1975.

Leverkus C. : *The Great British Diet*, The British Dietetic Association, 1985.

Mason, Jim : *Animal Factories*. New York: Crown Publishers, 1980.

Murton B: *The Cambridge World History of Food*, Cambridge University Press, Maori, 2000.

Nancy M. Brown: *Mendel in the Kitchen: A Scientist's View of Genetically Modified Foods*, Washington, Joseph Henry Press, 2004.

Norcross, JC, : *Changing for Good*. Avon Books, NewYork, 1994.

Pollock NJ: *The Concept of Food in Pacific Society: A Fijian Example*, Oceania, Fiji, 1985.

Powdermaker H: *Feast in New Ireland: The Social Function of Eating*, Oceania, New Ireland, 1932.

Prochaska, JO, : *Changing for Good*. Avon Books, NewYork, 1994.

Regan, Tom : *Empty Cages: Facing the Challenge of Animal Rights*, Maryland: Rowman & Littlefield Publishers, Inc., 2004.

Rody N: *Journal of Nutrition Education*, Oceania, Micronesia, 1978.

Singer, Peter : *Animal Liberation*. New York: New York Review/ Random House, 1975.

Stewart-Truswell A. : *ABC of Nutrition*, British Medical Journal Books, 1993.

Suchman, M.: *Envisioning Life on the Nano-Frontier*, Dordrecht, Kluwer, 2001.

Walden, Richard: *Genetic Transformation in Plants*, England, Open University Press, 1988.

Werbach M.R. : *Nutrition Influences on Mental Illness*, Third Line Press, 1999.

Wurtman J.J. : *The Serotonin Solution*, Fawcett Columbine, New York, 1997.

Index

□□□